To the Memory of Lisa Ann

Cotton Crisis

The Fred W. Morrison Series
in Southern Studies

Cotton Crisis
Robert E. Snyder

The University of North Carolina Press

Chapel Hill and London

© 1984 The University of North Carolina Press

Manufactured in the United States of America

Library of Congress Cataloging in Publication Data

Snyder, Robert E., 1943–
  Cotton crisis.

  (The Fred W. Morrison series in Southern studies)
  Bibliography: p.
  Includes index.
    1. Cotton trade—Southern States—History—20th
century. I. Title. II. Series.
HD9077.A13S66 1984   338.1'7351'0975 83-14747
ISBN 0-8078-1584-5

Contents

Acknowledgments

This book began while I was at Syracuse University. Professor David H. Bennett encouraged me to pursue the topic, worked hard to pry loose funds for travel and research expenses, and counseled me at different stages along the way. Syracuse University was always generous in its support. Senate Research Grants enabled me to spend the summers of 1974 and 1977 in manuscript collections around the country, and University Fellowships facilitated my studies. At one time or another, Michael A. Flusche, Norman W. Haight, and Ralph Ketcham provided me with timely advice and letters of support.

Along the research path several archivists provided cordial and valuable assistance. For the many courtesies extended to me I would like to thank M. Stone Miller of Louisiana State University in Baton Rouge, Louisiana; Henry L. Simmons of the University of Southern Mississippi in Hattiesburg, Mississippi; and Helen F. Ulibarri of the National Archives in Washington, D.C.

I tried out some of my thoughts in the annual southern history writing competition sponsored by the Kemper and Leila Williams Foundation of New Orleans. My thanks to the anonymous referees for awarding my essay the General L. Kemper Williams Prize for the Best Article Length Manuscript on Louisiana History for 1974. A small amount of the material that appears here was introduced in articles in the Spring 1977 issue of *Louisiana History* and the February 1978 issue of the *Journal of Mississippi History*. The Mississippi Historical Society was most gracious in awarding my article the Willie D. Halsell Prize for 1978. The Louisiana Historical Society and the Mississippi Historical Society were considerate in granting me permission to use some of the material that originally appeared in their journals.

Putting the manuscript into final form was made possible by the University of South Florida, Tampa. A grant from the President's Research Council underwrote the concluding research and the Arts & Letters Typing Service typed the final draft.

My heaviest indebtedness in completing this work is to my entire family, especially my wife, Joan, and children, Kristin and Dylan. They showed patience and endured sacrifices over the years that this study entailed. Without them this book would never have been finished.

Introduction

"Cotton Crisis." The words alone were enough to strike fear into almost every Southerner, and with good reason. More people in the South owed their daily existence to cotton than to any other enterprise. A break in the cotton market could paralyze the commercial life of an entire region and send financial tremors around the world. Over the years Southerners had come to fear the financial and psychological damage that disruption of the cotton market could cause as much as they did a hurricane battering inland or the Mississippi River cascading over its banks. Peter Molyneaux, the long-time editor of the *Texas Weekly*, went so far as to characterize a cotton crisis as an "experience worse than going into battle, and . . . quite as frightful."[1]

Beginning in late July in the southern reaches of Texas and ending in late November in scattered northern sections of the South, the cotton crop was harvested. The harvest was always the most feverish season of the crop year. Cotton farmers raised the crop on credit, and they were heavily obligated to a long list of retainers. Throughout the South furnishing merchants provided farmers on credit, and at high interest rates, all the commodities necessary to make the crop. Over the years farmers ran up substantial bills for food, clothing, fertilizer, feed, tools, and other living and operating necessities. These merchants and bankers protected their loans by securing from farmers either personal notes, liens against the crop, or even chattel and land mortgages.[2]

Cotton farmers and local furnishing merchants were simply the extremities of a credit structure that extended from Wall Street and operated according to policies set down largely in Washington. Viewing the various credit agencies that served the cotton industry, an adviser to President Herbert C. Hoover once defined this hierarchy along the following lines:

> Federal Reserve Board
> Great Banking Institutions
> Federal Farm Board
> Federal Farm Loan Board
> National Banks
> Cotton Cooperatives
> Federal Intermediate Credit Banks

     Agricultural Credit Corporations
     Large State Banks
       Local City Banks
       Commission Merchants
       Country Banks
       County Merchants
         Planters
         Farmers[3]

As money began to flow during the harvest from cotton gins, seed mills, and marketing agents to the farmer, creditors stretching literally from Main Street to Wall Street lined up for the repayment of debts.

There were, however, several volatile ingredients that could seriously influence the price farmers received. At any time, the weather, insects, and diseases could conspire to change the size of the crop and alter its condition. Problems with workers in the fields could dramatically handicap the progress of the staple to market. The federal government could exacerbate matters by wrongly forecasting crop size and conditions months before the final figures were in. And international depressions or diplomatic hostilities could jeopardize foreign markets and disrupt commodity exchanges.[4]

Since the slightest tampering with market forces could severely damage the ability of farmers not only to repay obligations but also to survive, people associated with the production of cotton were usually in a highly excited state during the weeks of harvest. "It is the time of year when men will believe anything, for whatever has been the price of cotton or what may be the price of cotton, it is the price at picking time that counts to the farmer," the *Country Gentleman* reported. "Anything will start a panic. . . . Each grower, merchant, broker, and banker is during part of every day in a state of high exhilaration or in the depths of a more or less private panic."[5]

Economically hard-pressed farmers watched the latest in crop information with intense interest and responded vociferously to the least unfavorable information. Reports indicating small acreage and poor conditions were translated to mean small supply, which had a bullish effect on the market, while large acreage and good condition were interpreted to mean large supply, producing bearish results. "They kill every crop several times before it matures," a crop statistician from Dallas, Texas, once complained. "They seem to think there is only one side to the market (the bull side) and that anyone who cannot see the failure of the plant to fruit, the insects destroying the squares and bolls, the storms breaking it into the ground, despite the fact that the cotton plant is going along about its business in a normal way, is a vicious heretic."[6]

All the anxieties involved in the cotton industry reached a fever pitch on crop-reporting day. It was not uncommon for a federal report indicating a large crop to cause a severe break of 100 points or more in cotton prices and start the South on the way to a cotton crisis. Of the various reports that the Department of Agriculture issued, the August statement always provoked the highest passions, for it was the first of the monthly reports in which the federal government tried to forecast what farmers might produce for the entire year, and by the time it was issued the crop had already begun its move to market.[7] "I pity the poor old farmer. At every turn of the road, he seems to be the goat," a resident of Kankakee, Illinois, lamented. "The Department of Agriculture makes crop estimates and the Board of Trade makes use of them to murder prices. Between them the poor old farmer is squeezed good and hard. And then, while the referee (Wall Street) is counting him out, the fellow holding the mortgage comes along with foreclosure proceedings. With all of his burdens, the farmer, when once down, is not a Gene Tunney."[8]

King Cotton's Dilemma

The literature on cotton is considerable. Federal and state governments, trade sources, and individual experts have devoted a great deal of attention to the financing, producing, marketing, and, above all, trying to live off the proceeds of the staple. In all that literature, however, there is no comprehensive study of a cotton crisis. The disruption of the cotton trade caused by World War I has received some scholarly attention.[9] But the traditional cotton crisis, in which such cross-currents as crop size, government forecasts, carry-overs, and labor unrest broke the price on commodity exchanges and threw the South into a financial and psychological tailspin, has been neglected.[10]

Of the many cotton crises that have ravaged the South, the cotton crisis of 1931 offers a case eminently worthy of consideration. Those who had suffered through some of the most traumatic disruptions and dislocations of the past—the hurricane year of 1906, the war year of 1914, the boll weevil year of 1921, and the record crop year of 1926—considered the cotton crisis of 1931 the most devastating ever.

Cotton farmers did not share in the general prosperity of the 1920s, as large crops, rising costs, and increased foreign expansion made international competition particularly keen. During the 1920s, cotton production rose from a post–World War I production low of 7,954,000 bales in 1921 to the record high of 17,977,000 bales in 1926.

The most serious attempt to control this perilous climb in production, and carry-over of surplus crop from year to year, came after the crisis of

1926. Governor Henry L. Whitfield of Mississippi called for a South-wide cotton conference. At the Memphis gathering various officials from the southern states agreed that cotton pools should be established in all the principal states to withhold some of the price-depressing surplus from market; no cotton should be accepted in the pools unless producers agreed to reduce acreage 25 percent; and banks should refuse loans until satisfied that the borrower would devote more land to other crops. Although the Memphis cotton conference was the most concerted campaign up to that time to bring the cotton situation under control, the failure to make the recommendations legally binding through legislation continued to plague cotton.[11]

Throughout this period of expansion the boll weevil disorganized and demoralized the cotton industry at home. The Department of Agriculture estimated that the weevil did an annual average damage to cotton lint and seed of $200 million. In the worst year, 1921, the weevil completely wiped out the long staple Sea Island cotton of South Carolina and damaged $610,341,000 worth of the cotton crop.[12] As the weevil drove the cost of production up, the yield and quality of cotton down, and labor off the land, foreign nations undercut American cotton on overseas markets. Foreign countries increased their consumption of cotton produced outside the United States from 7,484,000 bales in 1921 to 11,554,000 bales in 1929.[13] "The present price of cotton is 10¢ per pound below production costs. The owners of land have not made any money on cotton in the past five or six years, because everything the farmer has got to buy costs 500% more than it did before the great World War, and he is not getting adequate prices for what he raises," the part owner of six thousand acres of cotton land in Alabama and Mississippi wrote President Calvin Coolidge. "I fear, Mr. President, if quick action is not taken by the government, we will have the most destructive panic the Nation ever had."[14]

With the stock market crash in October 1929, the condition of southern agriculture became even more deplorable. In the first year of the Great Depression, income from cotton lint and seed fell from $1.5 billion to $826 million, and the South was well on its way to becoming what Franklin D. Roosevelt would later call "the nation's number one economic problem." "We don't need to go to China to find want, poverty, squalor, disease, and death because of lack of food and clothes," a resident of Greenville, Texas, observed. "It is here among us as never before since the South was left bleeding after the Civil War."[15]

Southerners customarily responded to cotton crises with a lot of desperate remedies. To relieve the pressure of a large crop, the expedient frequently advanced was to either buy-a-bale or burn-a-bale of cotton to simply get it off the market. To curtail debilitating pests and diseases, the prescription commonly issued was the establishment of one-hundred-mile-wide buffer zones of no cotton at all. To stop the federal government from meddling in cotton markets with projections of crop size and condition, the reaction usually was a demand to abolish the Crop Reporting Service and deport the secretary of agriculture. Because of the disastrous situation that existed by 1931 there was a desire for action more drastic and extreme than anything previously contemplated. "If we were justified in taking heroic measures to conduct the World War," a farmer who introduced cotton into New Mexico under the Carlsbad Reclamation Project argued, "similar measures are surely justified now and for the same reason; self-preservation for the individual and the nation."[16]

No matter how bizarre the remedies of the past, nothing seemed to surpass in insanity the recommendation that Governor Huey P. Long of Louisiana made in 1931. Long proposed that the South should observe a *Cotton Holiday*—one entire year off from producing the staple. Long told the whole region, not just a single city or county, to completely stop, not just gradually cut back or reduce, the production of its most important staple. The implications of a sabbatical year for an entire industry staggered the imagination back then just as they do today.[17]

As the governor of a Deep South state, Long was in a position to do something about the deplorable condition of southern agriculture, and he rose to the challenge. In a few short weeks, he transformed the holiday from a rough idea into a South-wide movement, and he took the region further down the road to agricultural reform than anyone ever expected. "This is not a trifling matter," a resident of Montgomery, Alabama, observed. "It is bigger right now than all other matters before the people of Alabama put together."[18] Indeed, the possibility of ameliorating the crippling influences of cotton through a holiday occupied the southern mind so thoroughly during the summer and fall of 1931 that it took its place alongside other great issues in the region's past. In many ways, the cotton crisis of 1931 would prove to be not simply a capstone to the agricultural protest of preceding decades but a foreshadowing of certain future national policies as well.

Cotton Crisis

1   The Market Crisis of 1931

Cotton farmers awaited the government's report on 8 August 1931 with more optimism than they had allowed themselves in the past. In light of a recommended voluntary reduction of 10 percent in cotton acreage and a suggested cutback of at least 30 percent in crop fertilizer from 1930 levels, the cotton industry was confident it had finally reversed the recent trend toward perilous production increases and disastrous price declines. Henry G. Hester, secretary of the New Orleans Cotton Exchange, estimated the 1931 commercial crop would yield 13,893,000 bales, a decrease of 620,500 bales from 1930, and 1,892,000 bales less than 1929. An average of ten private surveying groups placed the eventual yield at 13,813,000 bales.[1]

As usual the size of the crop would be the critical factor in determining the price farmers might expect to receive for the staple.[2] Although experts never envisioned, not even in their fondest dreams, a crop for 1931 as small as 10 million bales, leaders of the cotton trade provided a projected price scale based on crop sizes ranging from this imaginary level on upward. A yield of 10 million bales would result in the lofty price of 16½ cents a pound, while a crop approaching the frightful figure of 15 million bales would bring the disastrously low price of 7½ cents a pound. The emotional excitement of a great crop beginning its move toward market quickened as commodity exchanges reported marketing the first bales from the 1931 crop.[3]

When the Crop Reporting Board finally announced a forecast for the 1931 crop year of 15,584,000 bales, it struck the cotton industry like a death knell in the night.[4] Not only was the government's projection 1.5–2 million bales above private estimates, but only twice before had the United States actually produced more five-hundred-pound equivalent weight bales of cotton, some 16,103,000 bales of lint in 1925 and 17,977,000 bales in 1926, the all-time American production record. Producing the third largest crop in cotton history was even more catastrophic given the on-hand supply of 6,369,000 bales of cotton, as compared to 4,530,000 bales in 1930 and 2,311,000 bales in 1929.[5] According to the forecast of the Crop Reporting Service, the 1930 carry-over would eventually climb to a disastrous 8,700,000 bales. With worldwide consumption of American-produced cotton hovering around 12 million bales, the combined production and carry-over for 1931 would total more than 24 million bales, or a two-year supply.[6]

The cotton exchanges of New Orleans, New York, and Chicago halted trading on Saturday morning to receive the Agriculture Department's eleven o'clock announcement. Describing the scene at the New Orleans Cotton Exchange, the *Times-Picayune* reported: "An audible hush spread over the ring and the exchange floor as traders, clerks, and members waited patiently, and most of them confidently, for the government figure. The first figures of the crop estimate indicating a crop of over 15,000,-000 bales brought gasps of surprise and as the figures in the thousands were added the expectancy developed into exclamations of excitement." A sense of astonishment swept over traders everywhere. Reporting on the reaction in Memphis, a noted cotton columnist said: "When the figures were first posted, there was a somewhat general feeling that an error had been made in transmission; as time went on and no correction came, doubt that the crop board had issued such a figure gave way to amazement."[7]

The only cotton market in the world remaining open after the Crop Reporting Board's forecast was the Chicago Board of Trade. In a frenetic forty-five minutes of trading, futures in an estimated sixty thousand bales of cotton changed hands. The volume was reportedly five times the normally active pace. As orders poured in from all over the world, brokers deserted the hectic grain pits to participate in the even more furious cotton market. Gesticulating wildly in a language of shouts, grimaces, and other mannerisms only commodity gamblers seem to understand, floor men executed orders plunging cotton prices down an average of 150 points or $7.50 per five-hundred-pound bale. Applying the day's average decline of 1½ cents a pound to the Crop Reporting Board's forecast, traders estimated the price drop meant a $121,555,000 loss in the value of the 1931 crop.[8]

The dark cloud of economic uncertainty enveloping cotton cast a shadow over other agricultural commodities. Wheat, cocoa, coffee, and hides exhibited a weakness in sympathy with cotton. Rubber and copper were also reported to have suffered large losses. "Corn tumbled late today to the lowest prices reached since 1902," the Associated Press observed from the floor of the Chicago exchange. "The collapse resulted from a general rush of selling that took place after a big break in the cotton market owing to bearish aspects of the government's crop report. December corn, representing the 1931 crop, plunged down to 39¼¢, with other corn deliveries as well as wheat, oats, and rye suffering sharp setbacks."[9]

Over the weekend of 8–9 August people associated with the cotton industry worried about whether or not the decline manifested first in

Copyright *Dallas Morning News*, 13 August 1931. Reprinted by permission.

Chicago would continue elsewhere, plunging cotton prices completely through the 7-cents-a-pound-level. Trade sources feared that once cotton prices penetrated this psychological barrier, there was no telling how far cotton prices might fall. Listening to the hastily made observations of Washington officials only heightened the anxiety. "When the trade is faced with the increase indicated in the report, it is natural it would become panicky," Carl Williams, cotton member of the Federal Farm Board, commented. "But it will recover, and the Board sees no sound reason why prices should go lower. While it is true on the basis of this report the cotton crop is larger than expected, also it is true that consumption is going to be much larger than generally anticipated." Exactly how a nation and a western world already suffering from the ravages of the Depression were going to generate the purchasing power necessary to increase cotton consumption by the 2–3 million bales envisioned by Williams disturbed farmers nearly as much as the government's report.[10]

When trading reconvened on Monday, 10 August, attention focused on the early-opening European exchanges of Liverpool, Manchester, and Bremen. In Liverpool, Frederick Mills, president of the Federation of Master Cotton Spinners, issued his gloomy prediction: "The prospect of a crop of 15,500,000 will knock the bottom out of the market." Soon foreign correspondents began reporting frenzied trading in a collapsing commodity, market prices breaking toward the full extent permitted by exchange rules and overcrowded galleries witnessing the spectacular decline.[11]

The Bremen Exchange opened 150 points lower than its previous close, as European exchanges bore the brunt of a world liquidation of cotton. "The Liverpool market opened 90 points—or nearly 1 pence a pound—below Saturday's price. This is the heaviest fall in a generation bringing cotton down 3½ pence a pound, meaning a decline of $150,000,000 in the capital value," read the Liverpool dispatch. "Crowds came not to see fortunes made, but to watch what threatened to be the collapse of the world's greatest cotton market." News of tumbling Liverpool prices brought business to a standstill on the Manchester Royal Exchange, where all textile stocks shared in the price beating cotton received. The market downturn in Europe resulted in huge national losses. Japan was reported to have incurred exceptionally heavy reverses on its willingness to purchase American cotton more readily in advance of the government forecast than other nations had.[12]

The precipitous decline reported in Europe continued in America's financial centers later that same morning. At the opening of the New York Cotton Exchange, the largest futures market in the world, cotton options plunged from 122 to 142 points, depending on the delivery date, and brokers expressed fears the decline might reach 2 cents a pound, the largest daily decline permitted under the New York Cotton Exchange's rules. The selling out by those individuals who had purchased futures in anticipation of a smaller crop, and the liquidation of stale long accounts, kept the market under pressure from the start. At one time, the October delivery declined to 6.7 cents a pound, the lowest price recorded for any cotton option since January 1905. In New Orleans cotton prices closed down 104 to 111 points, or from $5.29 to $5.55 a bale less.[13]

The devastating blow inflicted on cotton farmers sent shock waves through the South's entire financial structure. Every dollar denied hard-pressed cotton growers affected many other enterprises throughout the region. "The reduction in value of the South's principal agricultural product by some $150,000,000 must be absorbed," the *Houston Post-Dispatch* observed, "by business, by industry, and by the millions of persons who make their living through the handling or processing of cotton after it leaves the fields." Trade sources figured the potential loss to correlated enterprises in the South might reach a staggering $100 million.[14]

The August Forecast Comes Under Attack

The South responded to the market crisis the Crop Reporting Board's forecast had precipitated in financial centers around the world by vigorously contesting the credibility of the projection. It seemed only appropriate that Senator Ellison D. ("Cotton Ed") Smith should be the first southern politician to protest. A member of the Senate since 1908, the South Carolinian identified his political career closely with cotton.[15] In fact, "Cotton Ed" had begun voicing his doubts about the projection even before its appearance, when he asked Secretary of Agriculture Arthur M. Hyde to defer issuing the August crop report. Smith felt that the unusual crop conditions he had observed during his travels through the South demanded at least a delay and more likely a revision in thinking. "Condition of the present crop is unlike any in my knowledge," the South Carolina senator cabled Washington officials. "The crop on the average is three weeks later, fertilizer is more than 30% less and of inferior quality. The present condition on account of lateness is what it ought to have been in June. Any August 1 estimate is at best a mere guess."[16]

But the Department of Agriculture refused to defer the forecast. Hyde's administrative team said the Department of Agriculture had absolutely no latitude in the matter, since federal legislation made the August report mandatory. Legal authority to postpone a report was neither needed nor desired, the Department indicated, because "methods have been evolved for making allowances" for the very kind of conditions people had recently expressed apprehension about.[17]

As they had for other large projections, cotton analysts across the South were quick to produce evidence that the August forecast should be considered premature and inconclusive, if not downright misleading and deceptive. "Reports during the week from the experiment stations in South Carolina, Mississippi, Oklahoma, and Texas indicate that weevil and other insect activity continues to increase and complaints of rank growth, poor fruiting, and shedding are becoming more general," the weekly syndicated letter of the Orvis Brothers advised subscribers. "It seems more than likely, therefore, that the first estimate may be more than ordinarily deceptive and subject to subsequent decided downward revision."[18]

Even if all the conditions necessary for producing one of the largest cotton crops in history did coalesce, analysts continued, it was very doubtful farmers would pick the full crop. Trade leaders expected price considerations to induce considerable abandonment. "It would cost more to pick, gin, bale, and sell the low grades than can be obtained for them," the firm of Fenner and Bean pointed out. "A strong holding movement is apt to develop while hedging operations are likely to be reduced to very moderate proportions owing to the low price." When the many uncertainties confronting the successful development of the crop were taken into consideration, all concluded, the government's forecast had to be considered too early for reliability.[19]

Cotton farmers immediately petitioned their southern representatives to request that Washington reconsider the forecast. "It is a habit of the United States Department of Agriculture to overestimate the cotton crop, in the interest of the crop-shooters, who are worse, morally and economically, than the crap-shooters," a resident of Anderson County, Texas, perceptively commented. Senator Tom Connally wholeheartedly embraced the evaluation given by his fellow Texan. "Deterioration has clearly set in," Connally agreed, "and this year's crop will be at least a million bales under the guess."[20] From around the South politicians demanded that the Department of Agriculture revise the estimate downward.[21]

Southern newspapers held the Department of Agriculture up to public ridicule and kept the demands for a downward revision of the estimate constantly before the general public. "That the estimate will be whittled down by the department's cotton experts is not to be doubted," the *Memphis Commercial Appeal* confidently offered. "Year after year the government's first report is a gross exaggeration and its subsequent reports give much satisfaction to those individual estimators whose original estimates must be gradually approached by the government as the season wears

Copyright *Memphis Commercial Appeal*, 11 August 1931. Reprinted by permission.

on." And as the editor of the *Greenwood Commonwealth* protested, "It is time for the government to stop guessing about cotton crops. A large measure of relief to the cotton farmers would come from the abolition of the bureau's reports, which have become classic for their errors."[22]

The department insisted, however, all figures had already been reviewed, and by experts from the South itself. There was absolutely no reason for altering the judgment. "The Crop Reporting Board, which handled this report, is made up of men familiar with cotton conditions, in fact, the majority of them were called in from other cotton states to prepare the report," a federal official reported to Senator Connally. "Since the report was issued, the data from crop correspondents and field statisticians have been again reviewed, with the result that there would seem to be no reason for changing this report at this time."[23] Anyone doubting the government's forecast of a large and high-quality crop need only look at the Shafter, California, farm in which President Herbert Hoover had a financial interest, where excellent-quality long staple cotton was produced three weeks ahead of the 1930 pace.[24]

Southern Politicians Threaten Investigation

Since the speculative August forecasts had over the years adversely affected southern agricultural concerns, and since the Department of Agriculture refused to redress forecast-related grievances, some of the South's most influential spokesmen demanded that the federal government be prohibited by legislation from engaging in crop forecasting. Southern politicians were asked and encouraged to back up their intemperate accusations with equally intemperate actions against Washington. "The record of the Crop Reporting Service has been one of conspicuous failure since its start to issue approximate correct estimates of the growing and harvesting crop," the highly regarded *Atlanta Constitution* declared. "By a clear reading of the record of the Crop Reporting Service, Southern congressmen should be convinced that the service has more often hurt than helped the cotton farmers, kept their markets in uncertain balance, and caused enormous losses to the agriculture and commerce of the South."[25] Confronted with this call for radical action, however, most southern politicians revealed a preference for revision rather than revolutionary change.

Writing from Lexington, Kentucky, Ron L. McKellar told of the emotional shock and fiscal damage done by the government's forecast. In a letter to his relative Senator Kenneth D. McKellar of Tennessee, he stated that the 8 August cotton projection had resulted in an immediate trading drop of $7.10 per bale in some places and a paper loss of something like $100 million to the cotton producers of the South. "I believe that it is generally understood that the Government's Agriculture Department is operated primarily in the interest of the farmer and, if so, it looks at this time that the cotton forecasting plan is an uncertain benefit," he continued. "It is my suggestion that you give consideration to an investigation of this particular forecasting feature." He advised that before launching an all-out official inquiry of the recent forecast, a statement should be prepared for each forecast beginning with the year 1900 and brought up to the present time to determine how well the system performed over time.[26]

Kenneth McKellar concurred completely. From his political base in Memphis, he had already written to Arthur M. Hyde asking the secretary of agriculture to send him several pieces of information: all the cotton estimates issued from the beginning of the crop-estimating service down to the present time, a copy of the law authorizing such activity, and the actual crop results for every year since the board began making estimates. The Department of Agriculture complied with McKellar's request by sending the senator a mimeographed overview of the board's work, which federal officials had hastily compiled to meet the unexpectedly large number of questions flooding in.[27]

McKellar was deeply distressed by what he learned. "The records for the last fifteen years, since the Government started guessing at the crops, show that the Government has been wrong quite as often as it has been right, and its guess is no better than anybody elses who is familiar with the situation," the Tennessee senator stated. "Yet the guess of the Government is taken by the trade as being substantially true. The Government ought not to guess on the number of bales of cotton." And he contemplated some steps for redressing the situation. "I am going to offer a bill at least cutting out the August and September estimates, and I am inclined to think nothing but actual ginning reports should be published by the Government," he said.[28]

During the 1920s, McKellar had worked diligently for the extension of federal programs and spending for the South and agriculture. He had expressed his progressive tendencies by being the first southern senator publicly to endorse the price parity legislation proposed by Senator Charles L. McNary of Oregon and Congressman Gilbert N. Haugen of Iowa, and he had been one of the few southern senators to vote for the McNary-Haugen bill when it failed in the Senate in 1926.[29] Knowing that McKellar had always fancied himself a conscientious protector of the general welfare of his section, cotton interests challenged him to prove he still deserved that reputation by taking action against the federal government.

McKellar was urged by many cotton concerns, like R. T. Fant and Company of Clayton, Mississippi, to introduce a bill preventing the federal government from issuing any more cotton forecasts during the growing season. Fant outlined for McKellar some of the more inaccurate forecasts, which he candidly described as not even "within shouting distance of the true crop," to justify that recommendation. "It may turn out that we are right and the government wrong, but we will not find this out until the cotton has passed from the growers hands. But what an injustice will have been done if the crop should turn out to be two or three million bales under the government estimate," Fant persuasively argued. "If the government could make any claim to accuracy in its reports there would be that justification for them, but this it cannot do. Its record for accuracy is terrible. The fact is that there is nothing more unreliable, nothing more misleading than these reports, especially those issued during the growing season." Fant insisted he could get all the statistics he needed for marketing his crop advantageously from cotton exchanges and private sources.[30]

McKellar indicated he was working earnestly on the problem. Besides contacting federal officials, McKellar revealed, he had sought out George Fossick, a noted private cotton statistician, for his professional advice. "I am going to offer a bill at least to cut out the August, September, October, and November estimates, or guesses, and I think we ought to simply substitute ginning reports," McKellar advised Fant. "The government's guesses, in advance of the maturity of the crop, are no better than the guess of an individual, and yet the whole country assumes that they are correct because the government makes them. I think it is time to stop it." McKellar further disclosed he intended to use the letters of cotton interests in pressing the case in Congress because the correspondence covered the proposition so absolutely.[31]

Although southern representatives promised to alter existing arrangements, cotton farmers wondered if this was just another case of the region's politicians talking a better game than they would ever play. The farmers wanted to know exactly where the truth ended and the duplicity began. For more than a decade southern representatives had found the cotton reports a convenient whipping post. At one time or another in the 1920s senators John Craft and J. Thomas Heflin of Alabama, Nathanial B. Dial and Ellison D. Smith of South Carolina, Pat Harrison of Mississippi, Walter George of Georgia, and Thaddeus Caraway of Arkansas joined congressmen John E. Rankin of Mississippi, Eugene Black and Earle B. Mayfield of Texas, and James B. Aswell of Louisiana, among others, in threatening to investigate and to regulate more closely or to cut off funds for crop-reporting activities.[32]

Of the many vituperative critics of the Crop Reporting Service, Senator

J. Thomas Heflin and Congressman John E. Rankin stood out as the most caustic. Both Heflin and Rankin used the most abusive language and scurrilous charges imaginable in vilifying federal officials and condemning reports. "This is the first time Senator Heflin has attacked the crop reporting work for some time. Formerly he was constantly breaking into print, severely criticizing our cotton estimates, and always insisting our figures were too high, and giving his own estimates of the crop," a surprised William F. Callander, the head of the Crop and Livestock Reporting Service of the United States since 1923, commented to a colleague. "We gave up trying to answer all of his outbursts and have heard nothing from him for two or three years. I do not believe that it would be wise to make an answer to Senator Heflin's criticism, because from past experience it would probably lead to endless controversy. I suggest that the matter be dropped."[33]

As members of Congress from cotton-growing states, both Heflin and Rankin considered themselves not simply representatives of cotton interests on Capitol Hill but experts on all things relating to cotton. Federal officials failing to show Heflin and Rankin the kind of deference they felt their positions deserved usually provoked the volatile southern politicians into lodging another even more acrimonious complaint with the next highest authority. Rankin commonly carried his grievances right up to the president. The Mississippi congressman repeatedly tried to impress on various presidents that inaccurate reports represented a kind of misconduct. "I appealed to the Secretary of Agriculture and received an offensive reply," Rankin protested to President Coolidge. "Instead of removing those responsible for the great loss to the cotton farmers last year he promoted some of them to positions which they were either unqualified to fill or unworthy to hold."[34]

For southern representatives these emotional outbursts were probably intended to show the folks back home that they were alert and active in Washington. Although publicly southern politicians condemned the reports, most recognized the timely marketing assistance the government hoped to provide producers and consumers alike and had no intention of actually attempting to reform the system. James B. Aswell was among the most frequent and vocal critics; yet even he accepted the need for federal reports, and privately communicated his feelings to the appropriate officials. "He says there is a very strong sentiment, in Congress and out, for abolishing the reports, and he considers this sentiment misguided," a federal official reported on a personal conference initiated by Aswell. "His purpose is, therefore, to sidetrack plans for abolishment of the reports, on the one hand, and to meet the psychological situation in the South, on the other, which seems to demand that 'something be done.'"[35]

In the crisis year of 1931, Senator Tom Connally of Texas made some of the loudest and most foreboding complaints of any southern politician protesting against the government's forecast. Connally demanded of Secretary Hyde that he take every precaution in preserving all records pertaining to the forecast "for a thorough investigation of not only the accuracy and good faith of this report, but of the propriety of such reports in the future." The Democratic senator from Texas warned that Congress would be asked at its upcoming session to legislate on crop reporting.[36]

Newspapers in Texas declared that Connally's call for a probe of the government's crop-reporting services should win the hearty approval of the entire South. "When a government forecast, whose value is questionable, causes such a dizzy decline in commodity value, an investigation is in order," the *Houston Post-Dispatch* editorialized. "Senator Connally, in assuming the leadership in the movement for a complete congressional probe, is performing a worthwhile service for the entire South and for the cotton industry as a whole." The newspaper went on to encourage others to join in the movement for a complete inquiry into the usefulness of government forecasts.[37]

Connally's outburst gave expression to the substantial number in the South who felt that government bear raids over the years had robbed cotton farmers of millions of hard-earned dollars. His threatened investigation earned him praise for being a vigorous watchman of southern economic interests. "We need men of courage to defend the South against such statements as was given out and its dire consequences," an admirer wrote. "If nothing is done, the Department of Agriculture will continue to issue bear reports and ruin the South. . . . If the Agriculture Department is correct, then we are sorely in need of some drastic form of legislation to curb cotton production. But if they are wrong, as I believe they are, we have been imposed upon by an agency of government and the farmer robbed of countless millions by bear raids on the market."[38]

The West Texas Chamber of Commerce heartily applauded Connally for his initiative in calling for a probe of the government's cotton estimate. Representing the expansive territory running westward from Fort Worth and Waco across the entire state, which it called the "Raw Materials Capital of the World," the chamber offered to seek out any information Connally considered vital for fighting the Crop Reporting Service. If Connally could secure from federal authorities the cotton estimates for individual counties, the Chamber of Commerce proposed to run a check on the reports for those counties within its jurisdiction. "I am sure," the chamber's manager asserted, "we could give you information that would forcefully refute those estimates." The chamber pushed too hard and fast for Connally's liking, however, so he backed off from the proposition. "Beg to say that an investigation cannot be authorized until Congress meets and passes a resolution to that effect," he privately informed his West Texas backers.[39]

Connally's call for an investigation of the cotton report prompted a newspaper editor from Granger, Texas, to ask him why southern representatives had failed to enact legislation in Washington stopping speculation on boards of trade and the issuance of production reports in advance of harvest. Back home the people were "cussing the Congress" for inaction on these vital issues. Connally offered a spirited defense. "I have had pending for some time a bill to curb futures trading. I have voted for legislation preventing speculation and manipulation on the exchanges, and have favored such legislation for years," he replied. "However, the representatives from the cotton states represent only one-fourth of the membership of the houses of Congress. It is difficult to get through Congress legislation in which we are alone primarily interested."[40]

Indeed, displeasure with the cotton reports had caused Connally to harass the Department of Agriculture on and off for the past several years. He commonly baited officials with requests for a statement comparing monthly forecasts with actual year-end results. Sometimes he teamed up with his fellow Texan Senator Morris Sheppard to make his protests more impressive and threatening. Usually, Connally timed his request for just before the opening of Congress, and traditionally he made some forewarning. "As you no doubt are aware, there is at this time great interest in the subject of crop reporting by the Department," Connally would always say. "The matter will probably receive considerable attention at the session of Congress which convenes next Monday." Over the years the department was not the least bit intimidated. It had come to accept Connally's chronic protests as more a matter of paying lip service to his constituents' anxieties than a sincere commitment to overhauling agricultural affairs. The department recognized Connally's complaining as part of keeping up a good front for the public.[41]

Democratic party strategists operating out of the National Press Building in Washington wanted Connally to exploit the situation for all the political capital it was worth. Party hacks kept encouraging him to ride roughshod over the Republicans. "Say, what's the matter with you getting me up a statement for future release on the short-sighted policies of the Federal Farm Board whose repeated failures are typical of the other Hoover boards and commissions," Robert M. Gates of the Democratic National Committee asked. "Both the Coolidge and Hoover administrations rejected the equalization fee and next the debenture—Hoover demanding the creation of the Federal Farm Board, which after buying cotton outright then bought futures to increase the value of its holdings—sustaining double losses. . . . You know the line of attack."[42]

Connally agreed the time was propitious for raking the opposition.

But like so many other southern politicians, he declined to do the man-handling. He claimed the Republicans would in time do themselves in through their own ineptness. So acting as hatchetman would only expose one to unnecessary risk. Connally concluded, "Political prospects are so bright that I am afraid we are being fooled by them. If we don't act the fool, we ought to win hands down." While southern politicians waited for political events to play themselves out, cotton farmers were left once again to fend for themselves. As luck would have it, the federal government precipitated another volatile agricultural controversy that temporarily relieved the pressure on southern politicians to carry out their threats against crop forecasting.[43]

Crop Reporting Officials Tour South

In an attempt to explain the work of the Crop Reporting Board and defend its August estimate, William Callander embarked on a hastily arranged tour of the South. As head of the agency, Callander was directly accountable for its overall performance, and figured to occupy a prominent place in the investigation that several politicians threatened would follow. On his personal survey of southern agriculture he took along Joseph A. Becker, a senior statistician in the Bureau of Agricultural Estimates, to provide a careful and authoritative check on crop conditions. The crop-reporting chief kept his beleaguered Washington colleagues apprised of his whereabouts as he made his way through Georgia, Alabama, and Mississippi in case his immediate attention was required on some matter.[44] From select cities in the Deep South, Callander defended the estimate, as well as his own precarious position, by assuring skeptics that "our estimate will be found to be reasonably accurate." Not to be intimidated, Callander informed those critics headed by Senator Connally that all the bureau's records were "open to those authorized to inspect them."[45]

Callander was attempting to placate a very surly South when the Farm Board unexpectedly fueled more agricultural discontent by announcing a decision on cotton which virtually every farmer below the Mason-Dixon Line considered as ill conceived as the Crop Reporting Board's forecast. "Nothing of a spectacular nature has come up since you left," a member of the Division of Crop and Livestock Estimates informed the weary Callander. "We have not heard or seen very many statements on our August forecast, the recent move of the Farm Board having apparently focused all attention in that direction."[46]

2   The Federal Farm Board

 A crowd of more than sixty thousand people gathered in the football stadium of Stanford University on the afternoon of 11 August 1928 to hear Herbert Hoover formally accept the nomination of the Republican party for president of the United States. Standing before a battery of microphones which carried the ceremonies to a national audience, Hoover praised the security, comfort, and opportunities Warren G. Harding and Calvin Coolidge had brought the average American family. "We in America today are nearer to the final triumph over poverty than ever before in the history of any land. The poorhouse is vanishing from among us. We have not yet reached the goal, but, given a chance to go forward with the policies of the last eight years, we shall soon with the help of God be in sight of the day when poverty will be banished from this nation." After Hoover had made sure the American voter recognized the progress and prosperity of recent Republican administrations, he acknowledged that agriculture had not kept pace with industry, and he singled out agriculture as "the most important obligation of the next administration."

During the presidential campaign of 1928, Hoover told audiences that those in agriculture had not kept up with the rises in the standard of living of those in other industries because of disorderly and wasteful methods of marketing, deflated prices, rising transportation rates, increased costs of mechanization, marginal lands, and competition for the domestic market. To bring prosperity and contentment to the agricultural sector, Hoover proposed a protective tariff, a modernization of the inland waterways, and a federal farm board. The purpose of the board would be to reorganize the marketing system on more stable and efficient lines through farmer-owned and farmer-controlled agencies. The farm board would be granted federal funds to assist farmer cooperatives and stabilization corporations in acquiring warehouses, providing capital advances against commodities lodged in storage, and purchasing market surpluses created by seasonal gluts. Besides improving the marketing system, the board would be authorized to investigate every field of economic betterment for the farmer; to devise methods of eliminating marginal lands or adapting them to other uses; to develop industrial by-products; and to secure assistance from other allied fields.[1]

Hoover also carefully and deliberately underscored that at no time should the federal government get into the business of subsidizing farm prices or underwriting agricultural losses. "No governmental agency should engage in the buying and selling and price fixing of products, for such courses can lead to bureaucracy and domination. No activities should be set in motion that will result in increasing the surplus production, as such will defeat any plans of relief." In creating a federal farm board, Hoover concluded, the government would be simply doing for agriculture what it had already done for banking and transportation in the form of the Interstate Commerce Commission and Federal Reserve Board.[2]

Throughout the 1920s farmers agitated for relief largely in support of what came to be known as McNary-Haugenism. During the early 1920s several bills were introduced in Congress by senators George W. Norris of Nebraska, E. F. Ladd of North Dakota, and Frank R. Gooding of Idaho and representatives Charles A. Christopherson of South Dakota, J. H. Sinclair of North Dakota, and Edward C. Little of Kansas proposing, in one way or another, government purchases of farm products and price fixing. None of these measures could, however, muster the kind of bipartisan and intersectional backing necessary for passage.

Outside Congress, George N. Peek and General Hugh S. Johnson, both executives with the Moline Plow Company of Moline, Illinois, formulated a far more popular plan called "Equality for Agriculture," which involved a fluctuating tariff and a two-price system. The American farmer, according to Peek and Johnson, would receive a fair exchange for his product by selling it in a domestic market protected by a high tariff and at a price on a parity with prewar value. After selling whatever he could at the higher domestic price, the farmer would go through a government corporation to dump his surplus abroad at the lower foreign price. Any losses sustained by overseas dumping would be covered by a tax or equalization fee paid by the farmer. During the mid-1920s, Senator Charles L. McNary of Oregon and Congressman Gilbert N. Haugen of Iowa gave their names to various bills promoting these principles.[3]

The South was never as enthusiastic about McNary-Haugenism as other agricultural regions. Since most of the American cotton crop was sold overseas, cotton farmers were more concerned with world price than domestic price and tried to obtain the best price in world markets through a steady and orderly marketing of their product. Short crops and reasonably good demand in the early 1920s permitted cotton farmers to remain aloof from overtures from the Midwest to support the McNary-Haugen legislation, and cotton was actually dropped from the list of staples in early versions of the bill.

Southern politicians took advantage of the congressional debates to impress on the public some of their most cherished biases and fears regarding government involvement in the marketplace. Congressman James B. Aswell of Louisiana called price parity legislation "unsound, unworkable, full of Bolshevism, purely socialistic, indefensibly communistic." But low cotton prices, and pressure from rice interests, brought southern politicians increasingly behind McNary-Haugen legislation until by the late 1920s senators and congressmen from below the Mason-Dixon Line spelled the difference between victory and defeat for the measure.[4]

Twice McNary-Haugen bills passed Congress only to have President Calvin Coolidge veto them. As secretary of commerce under the Harding and Coolidge administrations, Hoover was at the forefront of the opposition to McNary-Haugenism. He was unalterably opposed to McNary-Haugenism because he feared it would create uncontrolled inflation in food prices and wages; allow various vested interests to take advantage of government subsidies and generate the same kind of overproduction that the world war had; encourage other beleaguered industries to ask for similar treatment; and foster international trade wars involving acts of retaliation and causing diplomatic complications.[5]

Once Hoover defeated Al Smith in the 1928 election, and had been inaugurated president, he called the Seventy-first Congress into special session to redeem his campaign pledge of farm relief. Congress responded to Hoover's request by passing on 14 June 1929 the Agricultural Marketing Act. The act provided for the creation of the Federal Farm Board, comprising eight members appointed by the president, with due consideration given to having the major agricultural products produced in the United States fairly represented. The Farm Board was to invite cooperative associations to establish a commodity advisory committee to represent the commodity in matters before the board. Upon the recommendation of the advisory committee, the Farm Board could recognize a stabilization corporation to act as a marketing agency in preparing, handling, storing, processing, and merchandising a commodity. Congress appropriated $500 million for the board to use as a revolving fund in carrying out its operations.[6] Signing the Agricultural Marketing Act into law, Hoover observed, "After many years of contention we have at least made a constructive start at agricultural relief with the most important measure ever passed in aid of a single industry." Others were less impressed. Republican Senator William E. Borah of Idaho thought it "only postponed the day of execution."[7]

The president immediately took steps toward implementing the Agricultural Marketing Act by instructing his secretary of agriculture, Arthur M. Hyde, to canvass farm organizations and agricultural colleges for advice on who should sit on the board. Although Hoover asked for recommendations, he had no intention of nominating anyone whose philosophy of agriculture did not comport with his. He requested assistants to check all nominees "on loyalty and on the equalization fee." The name Hoover and his associates came up with for cotton representative on the Farm Board was Carl Williams of Oklahoma City.[8]

Carl Williams Irritates the South

Carl Williams had been a wheat, corn, and livestock rancher in Colorado, managing editor of the *Oklahoma Farmer Stockman*, founder of the Oklahoma Cotton Growers Cooperative, and a tireless organizer of agricultural associations designed to improve the financing and marketing position of farmers. Recognizing his experience in marketing and cooperative associations, the agricultural establishment of farm organizations, agricultural colleges, and agricultural journals gave Williams a substantial recommendation for membership on the Farm Board. Williams clearly met Hoover's qualifications; he did not, however, meet those of the average cotton farmer of the South.[9]

To represent cotton interests, cotton farmers desired a person actively involved in the production end of the staple; Hoover, though, looked at marketing and financial experience in considering candidates. Of equal importance, cotton farmers wanted their staple to be represented by a nominee from the Deep South; the Hoover administration professed a desire to avoid political and regional obligations in considering the board's membership. In insisting on nominating Williams, Hoover showed an insensitivity to some of the South's deepest anxieties.

The dramatic increase in cotton production within the United States during the 1920s was due largely to the increased cultivation of cotton west of the Mississippi River, in states commonly referred to as the western section of the cotton belt. In the period from 1921 to 1926, cotton acreage in the United States increased by an astronomical 16,578,000 acres, from 30,509,000 to 47,087,000 acres. Texas and Oklahoma together accounted for better than 60 percent of the expansion. Texas jumped its cotton acreage from 10,745,000 acres in 1921 to 18,374,000 acres in 1926. Oklahoma likewise went from 2,206,000 acres in 1921 to 4,676,000 acres in 1926.[10]

The expansion of cotton in the Southwest placed the older states of the East at a tremendous disadvantage. While many cotton farmers in the East were confined to fields that were depleted, wet, hilly, and irregularly shaped, the expansion to the west took place in many cases on fresher, dryer, flatter, and larger fields. These more favorable physiographic features provided farmers to the west greater yields and permitted the application of machine rather than hand labor. Cotton farmers in the West were able not only to cultivate more cotton more efficiently but also to harvest more cotton more rapidly as well.[11]

With western states cutting into the world cotton market as forcefully as several foreign countries, the Deep South saw in Williams as much of a threat to its interests as any overseas competitor. When Farm Board nominations were sent to the White House in 1929, southern politicians made their feelings known. Alabama's influential and emotional Senator Heflin articulated his region's desires by suggesting qualified residents from Georgia and Alabama, none of whom Hoover considered.[12] Soon several southern dailies criticized Hoover for discriminating against the South in selecting Farm Board members, even though two other Farm Board nominees, James C. Stone and C. B. Denman, were from Kentucky and Missouri, respectively. From the *Norfolk Virginian-Pilot*, *Houston Post-Dispatch*, and *Asheville Citizen* came complaints echoing the words of the *Montgomery Advertiser*: "Mr. Hoover has kept Southerners out of his Cabinet; he has kept them off the Farm Board, where it was of the utmost importance that a Southerner should sit."[13]

Politicians from below the Mason-Dixon Line simply waited for, first, the confirmation hearings held before the Committee on Agriculture and Forestry and, later, the debates on the Senate floor itself to unleash the full force of their displeasure. Senators Heflin of Alabama, McKellar of Tennessee, and Smith and Coleman L. Blease of South Carolina took turns in verbally assaulting the Williams nomination.

Senator Smith provoked the critical controversy of the hearings on Williams by getting the nominee to say under vigorous and sometimes confusing questioning that he thought 18½ cents—some 1 to 1½ cents above the current selling price but about 4 cents less than the average price for cotton over the past ten years—was a fair return under existing conditions.[14] When Williams subsequently sought to clarify his position through a letter submitted to the committee, and also inserted into the *Congressional Record* by his sponsor, Senator Elmer Thomas of Oklahoma, Senator McKellar skillfully ridiculed his efforts. "If he did not have sense enough to know what he was testifying to when he was brought before the committee, and had to explain afterwards why he thus testified against cotton when he ought to have supported it, he ought not to be on this Board," the Democratic senator from Tennessee concluded.[15]

Just how staunchly southern politicians opposed Williams as cotton representative on the Federal Farm Board was revealed by the Senate confirmation vote. McKellar of Tennessee and Furnifold Simmons of North

Carolina joined the two senators each from Alabama, Georgia, South Carolina, and Texas in voting against him. Edwin S. Broussard of Louisiana, Thaddeus Caraway of Arkansas, and Pat Harrison of Mississippi abstained from voting. From the major cotton producing states of the South only Ransdell of Louisiana, Robinson of Arkansas, and Stephens of Mississippi dared vote in favor of Williams. Although a coalition of senators from the South and Midwest failed to override the nomination of Williams, filling the position on the Federal Farm Board had engendered considerable animosity.[16]

Farm Board Policy Shifts

After assembling at the White House on 15 July 1929 for its first meeting, the Federal Farm Board set out to create permanent business institutions for serving agriculture and to adjust production to demand. Relying on an extensive network of local and regional cooperatives as a springboard, the Farm Board tried to forge national cooperatives for each of the major agricultural commodities. Its initial loan policy to these cooperatives offered sufficient money to bring total advances from all credit sources to 90 percent of the market price of cotton fixed for sale.[17]

The Farm Board had been in operation only a couple of months when the stock market crash precipitated panic conditions in the markets for agricultural products and forced the board to change its original strategy. Commodity markets were in a particularly vulnerable position because the American farmer had produced his crop largely on credit and, at the time of the market crash, was still trying to liquidate loans through the natural marketing of his product. A drop in commodity prices, and a rise in the calling in of loans, threatened to cause the widespread dumping of farm products, defaults on loans and mortgages, forced sales of property, and further collapse.

During the summer and fall of 1929, the rapid harvesting of cotton, and developing weaknesses in the stock market, pushed the price of cotton down and called for special efforts by the board. On 24 October 1929 the board announced it would advance to qualified cooperatives such amounts as would enable them to borrow from all credit sources up to 16 cents a pound on 7/8 middling cotton. In response to deteriorating economic conditions, the Farm Board was forced to shift its approach from market reorganization to price support and to attempt to place a floor underneath farm prices, rather than reorganize the marketplace.[18]

The board was gratified by the early response of markets to the attempt at price cushioning. For several weeks cotton prices remained in the 16½-to-17-cents range. Unfortunately, cotton prices could not sustain themselves. Once cotton broke through the sixteen-cent level, cooperatives could not dispose of the staple at a price sufficient to pay loans, transportation expenses, and carrying charges. On 13 January 1930 the American Cotton Cooperative Association (ACCA) was incorporated to handle the cotton of member associations and to protect their financial position. The board estimated that more than 150,000 growers were affiliated with the nine statewide associations and two regional associations that went into making ACCA and that between 2.5 and 3 million bales of the 1930 crop would be delivered to member cooperatives for marketing.[19]

President Hoover once again affirmed that the price support activities of the Farm Board were of a temporary nature. "The Board should in this emergency exert every power at its disposal not to fix prices, but to maintain and restore to the farmer a free market based upon the realities of supply and demand," Hoover told Alexander Legge in a letter on 15 March 1930. "I am concerned with the necessity of drawing for the future a complete defined separation of the government from stabilization activities and the building of a sound system of independent farmer-marketing institutions through other powers of the Board."[20]

The continued deterioration in the price of cotton caused the Farm Board to call the Cotton Advisory Committee into attendance in May 1930 to evaluate the whole situation. The committee recognized that any forced liquidation of cotton by cooperatives would depress the market still further and generate heavy losses on loans, and it decided these serious consequences could be avoided only by withdrawing from the market cotton held by the cooperatives. Thus, the committee reported to the Farm Board that an emergency in the American cotton market existed sufficient to require a stabilization operation. On 5 June 1930 the Cotton Stabilization Corporation was formed, and on 30 June 1930 the Farm Board extended the corporation a loan of $15 million for stabilization operations in cotton.[21]

The Cotton Stabilization Corporation proceeded on 30 June 1930 to purchase a total of 1,318,000 bales of cotton. As the 1930 crop came to market, it became evident that demand continued to be somewhat restricted and supplies would exceed all consumption requirements. It was decided to hold stabilization cotton off the market for the remainder of the crop year rather than depress prices still further by dumping it. On 25 September 1930, E. F. Creekmore, president and general manager of the Cotton Stabilization Corporation, announced that present holdings would be retained until 31 July 1931 unless in the meantime the price advanced to above the purchase price. The cotton market had become so depressed by this time, however, that Creekmore's announcement had no discernible influence upon the decline in cotton prices.[22]

In response to criticism that it was plunging millions of dollars into a bottomless pit, the Farm Board argued that cotton prices had been kept above the levels they would have fallen to had farmers been forced to dump their cotton on an unwilling market. By holding more than 1.3 million bales of cotton off the market in the 1929–30 season, and over 2 million additional bales in the 1930–31 season, the board reasoned it had added millions of dollars to the income of producers and saved many southern banks, merchants, and other businesses from insolvency.[23]

Nonetheless, the board recognized that it had failed to adjust cotton production and stabilize cotton prices, and present loan, purchasing, and withholding policies regarding the staple could not continue. "Many groups want stabilization corporations always to buy and never to sell. That is asking the impossible," the board declared in its *Second Annual Report*. "Stabilization operations cannot maintain prices continuously. So long as surpluses continue to pile up, artificial means can only temporarily offset their effects." The Farm Board was still seeking some way to make cotton farmers reduce production, sell its own stocks of stabilization cotton, and get back to Hoover's original intention of reorganizing the marketplace when the Crop Reporting Board issued the infamous forecast that plunged the South into the cotton crisis of 1931. The Farm Board had to take some action to stop plunging prices and soaring production, but the question remained what to do.[24]

Destroy Every Third Row

One of the first public officials to respond to the crisis the Crop Reporting Board's forecast precipitated in 1931 was Mississippi's irrepressible governor, Theodore G. Bilbo. With the South facing the specter of bankruptcy because of the possibility of 5-cent cotton, Bilbo proposed that the cotton-producing states attempt to alleviate their production and price dislocations by picking only two-thirds of the crop. On 10 August he cabled the governors of the cotton states asking them to prevail upon farmers, merchants, bankers, and other interested parties to sign an agreement to leave every third row unpicked in the field. "This will cut the present crop to less than ten million bales, which will sell for fifteen to twenty cents per pound, instead of five with the full crop gathered. Leaving every third row in the field will add fertilizer to already impoverished cotton lands besides saving one-third of the expense and labor necessary to pick and gin the present crop." The Mississippi governor concluded his proposition by offering to coordinate a public announcement from all public officials so that the whole South could move forward together.[25]

As public officials in the cotton-growing states gathered and forwarded to Mississippi opinions proffered from influential agriculturalists, the scheme to leave every third row standing in the field quickly fell apart. Describing Bilbo's idea as "nonsense," Harry D. Wilson, Louisiana's commissioner of agriculture, asked, "What farmer, after plowing, fertilizing, and cultivating would abandon one-third of his crop, when it is waiting to be taken off the ground?"[26] Knowledgeable parties from Alabama to Arizona underscored the point that loan arrangements with banks, contacts with manufacturers, and other legal entanglements committed producers to seeing the crop through to harvest.[27]

Two days after Bilbo had articulated his proposal, yet before public criticism had a chance to lay bare all its defects, the Farm Board suddenly proposed a program in many respects identical to that of the Mississippi governor. On 12 August, James C. Stone, chairman of the Federal Farm Board, wired the governors of fourteen cotton-producing states.[28] The governors were informed that over the last two years of a severe and deepening national depression the board had attempted to protect cotton growers from market vagaries by purchasing from cooperatives and withholding from market 1.3 million bales of cotton for stabilization purposes; making loans on seasonal pool cotton sufficient to enable cooperatives to support 16 cents per pound on middling ⅞-inch staple cotton; and even permitting cooperatives to loan up to 90 percent of the current market value of the new crop. These measures might have been sufficient to prevent a further deterioration in the cotton situation, but growers obstinately persisted in producing at excessive rates. To allow the present price and production crisis to continue and deepen, Chairman Stone observed, would "bring direct disaster to cotton producing states and indirect distress to the nation."

A crisis of the magnitude and all-pervasiveness of that confronting the cotton industry called for, in Stone's words, a "drastic remedy" and a "major operation . . . rather than attempts at lesser measures." Under the provisions of the Agricultural Marketing Act, the Farm Board was invested with the power to investigate and formulate plans for preventing and controlling agricultural production fluctuations. "In line with the above mandate from Congress and in view of the existing situation the Farm Board suggests that you immediately mobilize every interested and available agency in your state, including farmers, bankers, merchants, landowners, and all agricultural educational forces to induce immediate plowing under of every third row of cotton now growing." By destroying every third row of cotton in an organized and orderly fashion, the Farm Board estimated, farmers could eliminate 4 million bales of cotton from the 1931 crop.[29]

Although the Farm Board formulated this plan, it absolved itself from administering and enforcing the scheme. "It is up to the people of the South if they want to accept a drastic remedy for this situation," Williams, cotton member of the board, stated. Chairman Stone himself proclaimed, "The Board believes that the time has now come when cotton producers themselves must be called upon for immediate and drastic action."[30] In the opinion of the board, it was the obligation of the governors of the cotton states to induce producers to comply with the board's request for destruction—a scheme which should commence not later than 1 September and be completed not later than 15 September. "If the ten largest cotton producing states accept and carry out this program this Board will pledge itself," Chairman Stone promised, "to permit no sales by the Cotton Stabilization Corporation of its holdings before July 31, 1932, and will urge upon the cotton cooperatives financed by the Board the desirability of similar action by them of their stocks of 1932 cotton now held." Through destruction and withholding, the Farm Board believed, 7 million bales could be kept off the 1931–32 market.[31]

Hoover Discriminates against the South

If the August forecast of the Crop Reporting Board surprised, stunned, and even stupefied those in the cotton industry, then the solution proposed by the Federal Farm Board for dissipating the crisis infuriated and incensed them. "The Governor of Mississippi has in recent years pulled so many asinine stunts that this suggestion will hardly occasion any surprise, much less will any serious weight be given to it," a drug company official in Montgomery, Alabama, wrote to his governor. "However, the stupidity of the Farm Board clearly indicates imbecility and incompetence, and I am hoping . . . you will say a few things that will express the chagrin and indignation of sensible people."[32] Viewing the board's plan as a futile grasping at straws, the people of the South angrily struck back. Within days virtually every governor addressed by Chairman Stone, hundreds of state and local officials, and thousands of citizens rejected the board's proposal as "unsound," "unwise," or "impractical." Reaction was swift and overwhelmingly negative for a variety of reasons.[33]

Cotton farmers felt that the Farm Board was asking the South to make sacrifices and concessions not imposed on other regions and staples.[34] Since loan regulations required that the net proceeds from the sale of the cotton crop be applied first to federal loans, cotton farmers considered it only fair that they be released from one-third of their indebtedness. But regional loan offices answered that they had no authority to release farmers from any liability, even though the federal government was asking them to destroy part of their crop. When growers asked the federal government at least to extend the terms of their seed loans, the secretary of agriculture refused to make any commitment, saying only, after more than a month's delay, that each case would have to be considered on an individual basis.[35] "It's a fine kettle of fish," the *Abilene Morning News* indignantly declared. "First, the government loans money to raise crops, taking an ironclad mortgage to insure repayment of the loan. Then the Farm Board advises the mortgagor to go out and destroy a portion of that crop. If the farmer does what one branch of the government tells him to do, he may be prosecuted by a second branch of the government on an agreement with a third branch."[36]

For plowing up one-third of the cotton crop, the federal government promised to withhold from market for another year the cotton it had acquired during stabilization operations. But cotton farmers considered full compensation the only reasonable settlement. If the government could reimburse Florida fruit growers and truck farmers for losses sustained in the campaign to eradicate the Mediterranean fruit fly, cotton farmers reasoned, then federal officials should develop a similar proposition toward the boll weevil that would allow compensation.[37]

Furthermore, cotton farmers wanted to know why the Farm Board hadn't at least explored the possibility of commodity swaps with other nations before asking them to make such financial sacrifices. After all, the board had already agreed with Brazil to exchange wheat for coffee. Through monthly installments beginning in September, some 25 million bushels of wheat were to be swapped for 1,050,000 bags of coffee. In this gigantic transaction even the expense of grading, handling, and storage was to be met by barter. The Bush Terminal of New York had agreed to perform the necessary services for 225,000 bags of coffee. Looking at what the Farm Board had already done for fruit growers and wheat farmers, but not for cotton interests, southern agriculturalists felt discriminated against.[38]

Resentment over the economic sacrifices and enforcement obligations the board expected the South to make was only part of the overall indignation. The South was angered still further by other imperfections and defects in the plan. Some of the strongest, best reasoned, and most logical criticism of the board's plan came from none other than Bilbo himself. The Mississippi governor carefully cataloged the reasons why plowing under every third row, instead of simply leaving it in the field as he had originally suggested, would be a distinct waste. "In the first place it would cost the South a million dollars in time and labor to do the plowing. Second the stalks plowed up thrown against the remaining rows with their dead leaves and limbs would be a serious handicap in gathering the other rows. Third not to permit every third row to mature would destroy a wonderful fertilizer crop in the mature seed." The proposal to destroy every third row was so unworkable that the only logical conclusion a reasonable person could reach was that the board hoped implementation would result in an even greater crop destruction.[39]

After cotton farmers had spent years instructing work animals to walk between the rows so as not to damage the crop, the federal government was now asking growers to force their beasts of burden into helping them do what training had taught was wrong. "Can you imagine how a cotton field would look if you went into it with a pair of mules and a big middle buster and plowed up every third row?" Harry D. Wilson asked. "The United States has been noted for production and construction. It seems now that we want to change to destruction. Please, farm leaders, endeavor to think of some practical common sense methods in this time of world-wide depression and readjustment." The program was considered so impractical that prominent southern officials and cotton farmers accused the Farm Board of simply trying to place itself in a position whereby it could once again claim its corrective measures and advice had been scorned.[40]

The idea of raising the price received by the producer by reducing supply was a suggestion agricultural movements had been making for some time, and farmers were coming to recognize restraint in production as an inescapable fate. But the suggestion of achieving a fair price by destroying a crop, after time, money, and labor had already been committed to raising it, ran counter to the American sense of decency.[41] Just as many Americans would in the near future protest against the New Deal's slaughtering of livestock at a time when people were hungry and could not afford to purchase meat, so people also revolted against the wasteful implications of destroying cotton, particularly at a time when one-third of the nation was supposedly ill-clothed. "No one but a nit-wit would destroy every third row of cotton any more than he would kill every third pig or chicken if he had to reduce his herd or flock. Instead he'd select the unfit for destruction and save the best," a resident of Ponchatoula, Louisiana, observed with remarkable foresight. "Funny that so many so-called big men would advocate a policy or a plan that the average 10-year old could and would see at a glance was idiotic."[42]

To carry the destitute through the winter of 1931, farmers recommended that the Farm Board should release cotton and wheat supplies from stabilization holdings to appropriate charities for the production of clothing and food. "A large part of our population is hungry and starving, half clad and almost naked. Instead of destroying our cotton, why not give it to these unfortunate people?" A. C. Wright, congressman from Georgia's Fourth District, asked. "The stupidity and selfishness of the Republican administration has caused it to overlook fundamentals and resort to expedients and nostrums."[43]

Copyright *Dallas Morning News*, 22 August 1931. Reprinted by permission.

The Farm Board agreed it was "an anomalous situation" for the federal government to withhold vast stocks of direly needed supplies through one agency and appeal to charities through another to care for distressed individuals. But the board insisted it had no legal right under the Agricultural Marketing Act to dispose of stabilization stockpiles for charitable purposes. The only concession the board would make was an offer on 3 October 1931 to sell stabilization cotton to charities under a deferred payment schedule.[44]

Not until 5 July 1932 would Hoover approve an appropriation of five hundred thousand bales of cotton from Farm Board holdings to the Red Cross. The president described the allotment in his memoirs as providing "over a dozen yards of cotton cloth to every family on relief."[45] Although Hoover thought the five hundred thousand bales to be a sizable contribution, it was actually an inexcusably small and tardy response. James L. Fieser, a Red Cross administrator, announced that local chapters indicated there were 15 million men, women, and children in need of clothing, 8 million of whom were actually destitute. From the Farm Board appropriation, the Red Cross calculated, it would be able to provide less than one dollar's worth of cotton per individual, and cotton had to be considered just one of several clothing necessities.[46]

From beginning to end the Farm Board adamantly opposed all moves to appropriate cotton without return compensation. The board complained about being undercut and farmers shortchanged. "The Board is in full sympathy with the humanitarian spirit which prompted gifts from governmental holding of wheat and cotton for the use of needy and distressed individuals. It does not consider it fair, however, for the United States Government to make a gift to one group of its citizens by requiring that gift to be paid out of funds previously charged up to agriculture and set aside for the benefit of farmers who have been in distress for more than a decade." The board calculated that the transfer of five hundred thousand bales of cotton reduced the revolving fund by $43 million, or nearly 10 percent of the amount appropriated by Congress. The Farm Board's protests made it appear that members were more concerned about trying to perpetuate a fund already destined for liquidation than providing food and clothing to the living.[47]

Plow Under the Farm Board

Disenchantment with the Farm Board's recommendation automatically rekindled the South's disdain for Carl Williams and revitalized calls for placing a Southerner on the board. The *Atlanta Constitution* demanded "justice for the South" in a hard-hitting editorial by that title. "While the

Federal Farm Board is trying to devise some means of helping the cotton industry it should, in all reason, have the benefit of the best available expert assistance. In other words, there should be on the board some member who knows the cotton industry of the South inside and out," the *Constitution* declared. "Yet the singular fact is that no such man is on the board."[48]

Pressing the case for a representative from below the Mason-Dixon Line, politicians joined newspapers to form a powerful lobbying coalition. Governor Benjamin M. Miller and his commissioner of agriculture, Seth P. Storrs, actively urged Agriculture Secretary Hyde to prevail upon President Hoover to nominate an outstanding southern leader. Alabama's agricultural and political leaders insisted the South needed someone "around whom we may rally and thus steady and stabilize the destressing situation confronting our people." Without someone from the region representing cotton, Southerners would never support the Farm Board nor develop any confidence in its proposals. "This is the supreme opportunity for the President to serve the Southern people," Secretary Hyde was informed. Alabama's agricultural forces pursued the proposition right through to the president himself. "The desperate condition of agriculture demands the best leadership of the nation be placed on the Farm Board," Miller and Storrs told Hoover.[49]

Williams contributed to making a bad situation even worse through his own disregard for diplomacy and discretion. He defended the highly unpopular Farm Board proposal in an inflexible manner. If cotton farmers want more favorable prices, he said, "there is no substitute, in our opinion, for destruction of a part of the crop." He took the same hard line in insisting that the South acknowledge its culpability in the present agricultural dislocations, remarking indelicately, "The Board is concerned that the South shall for once in its life recognize its own responsibility for its own situation." It was this kind of attitude on the part of federal officials that seemed to confirm what a resident of Newport, Tennessee, once told Senator McKellar: "You can't go wrong to oppose anything Hoover wants. You know he hates the south and wouldn't let us Southern people breathe air if he could help it."[50]

Southern farmers replied to Washington that the Farm Board should be destroyed rather than any cotton. Instead of plowing under cotton to relieve the crisis, Representative J. E. Mundy of Clayton County, Georgia, angrily recommended, the South should "destroy every third member of the Farm Board." Over the next several weeks demands that the Farm Board be scrapped continued to build. In a regional radio address, Governor Harvey Parnell of Arkansas called on southern senators and representatives to get together in Congress to abolish the board. "To be perfectly frank," Parnell charged, "the Farm Board has done more to destroy the market price of cotton than overproduction or increase in foreign acreage." Across the South newspapers agreed that the board would be one of the heaviest burdens that the Republicans would shoulder in the 1932 elections and suggested that several politicians would fall by the wayside because of their association with it.[51]

As criticism against the Farm Board steadily mounted and took on more ominous and threatening tones, Hoover attempted to keep the White House as far as possible from the controversy. A Washington dispatch hastened to explain on Friday, 14 August, that the plan to destroy every third row was "done wholly on the initiative of the Farm Board and not at the instigation of President Hoover."[52]

The Hoover administration attempted to gauge the amount of damage done by the Farm Board proposal through a survey of newspaper editorials from around the country. White House staffers set about analyzing editorial opinion for the period from 13 August through 16 August. They completed their summary based on 158 newspapers with a total circulation of nearly 12 million readers on 17 August and sent it to President Hoover marked in bold letters CONFIDENTIAL. The results demonstrated widespread and intense dissatisfaction—46 newspapers attacked the destruction proposal as one of desperation, wanton waste, and futility; 72 declared the plan impracticable, impossible of fulfillment, and of no assurance to the farmer; 15 considered the scheme a grave reflection on United States regulation and consumption; and 5 felt it would be better to give surplus cotton and wheat to the needy, rather than destroy such staples. Only 8 newspapers believed the proposal was the only step left to bring any measure of help, and another 12 assailed farmers for lack of cooperation.[53]

With this evidence of overwhelming rejection of its policies in hand, the White House fell strangely silent. In a country where civics books had always taught that rocky periods and thorny issues were opportunities for testing the national fiber, the political stage now seemed to be devoid of leadership and direction. The South viewed Hoover's stoic withdrawal as typical of the bankrupt leadership that Republican administrations had been providing the country with, and a sad commentary on the depths to which a nation noted for its stewardship had fallen. "The people, all powerful, but wholly impotent without leaders, feverishly plead and pray for a way out," a resident of Texas's Gulf Coast noted in his diary. "Oh, shades of Jefferson, Jackson, and Roosevelt how restless, sad, and angered must be your state beyond the Stix as you contemplate your beloved country's dilemma." As the South lamented the decline in leadership and the lack of direction, cotton farmers searched around for some way out of their dilemma. The time was ripe for reform and leadership. The only questions were who would do the leading and what the path would be.[54]

3   A Holiday for Cotton

With the Federal Farm Board blaming cotton producers for their own plight, and with nearly all of the cotton-growing states contemptuously rejecting the board's proposed solution, the South faced a catastrophic cotton crisis. As people in the cotton industry turned away from the federal government toward their state governments for leadership, the public officials of many cotton-growing states attempted to shirk responsibility for trying to resolve a controversial and explosive problem. "This is poverty speaking in this land where money talks," a resident of Corpus Christi, Texas, reminded Governor Ross S. Sterling of Texas. "While Hoover, you, and our Mayor suck your thumbs, we unemployed wander. Rip Van Winkle where do we go from here?"[1]

In response to rapidly deteriorating social, economic, and political conditions in the cotton-growing states, Governor Huey P. Long of Louisiana assumed the leadership so many others were avoiding. On Sunday, 16 August, Long announced he was sending a telegram to the governors, senators, congressmen, and lieutenant governors of all the cotton-producing states requesting their attendance at a conference to be held in New Orleans on Friday, 21 August, to consider dissipating the effects of the cotton crisis through a mandatory cotton holiday.[2]

The present cotton situation, Long observed, was the fault of all persons associated with the industry. "The Lord told us to lay off raising these crops one year out of every seven to let the people have time to consume them," he reminded his colleagues. As the cotton industry had failed to observe the Lord's advice, the responsibility for devising solutions rested with the duly elected representatives of every cotton-producing state, and the only plan for immediately ameliorating the crisis was a mandatory cotton holiday. "We can restore the prosperity of the South and materially the balance of the world within less than two weeks time if the cotton producing states have governors and officials who have the courage to act now and decisively," the Louisiana Kingfish declared. "The only way this can be done is to prohibit by law at once the raising of a single bale of cotton in all cotton growing states during the year 1932. . . . If such action be taken by all the states immediately the farmer will get more for this year's crop alone than they will get for this and next two cotton crops they raise."

Since New Orleans was the official home of the American Cotton Cooperative Association, and the industry's leading shipping, marketing, and financial center, Long reasoned the Crescent City would be the most appropriate place to hold such a conference. Although formal invitations would be extended only to public officials, the conference should be considered a "people's meeting" with the public informally invited to attend and participate. "We want the people to meet and get behind the officials. Let 'em light a fire under them," Long enthusiastically declared. "It will be a meeting for anybody to come and discuss my plan or any plan he might want to suggest."

Louisiana would make the holiday plan a state law, Governor Long further announced, if other cotton-producing states would promise to join the Pelican State in such action. "Come here and let's get to work on something that actually settles the cotton trouble," Long wrote to his colleagues in public office. "Please issue notice to your farmers to gather their cotton and sell none of it until the result of this meeting is accomplished, because we want the benefit to go to the farmer. When that is accomplished all business prospers."[3]

Many of the big-city dailies that had been critical of Long's politics in the past jumped at the opportunity the call for a holiday offered for gouging him again. The *Dallas Morning News* mocked the holiday by calling it the "'Hooey' Long Plan."[4] Indeed, on the face of it the cotton holiday seemed an example of the wild and impractical posturing so many southern demagogues were noted for. Yet Long had a record of constructive reform that made one wonder whether this would prove to be some of the cold, hard realism he was capable of coming up with in emergency situations and bringing others around to.[5]

During the 1920s, Long worked diligently on Louisiana's Railroad-Public Service Commission to roll back and rebate increases by the Cumberland Telephone and Telegraph Company, reduce the fares on Shreveport streetcars, lower the rates of the Southwest Gas and Electric Company, define more strictly the common-carrier status of large oil company pipelines, increase severance taxes, and introduce proceedings to bring other corporations more completely under the commission's jurisdiction, among many other reforms.[6]

Running on his record as a champion of the common man, Long was elected governor in 1928. Through a dynamic social service welfare program he subsequently gave Louisiana many badly needed reforms: new schools and free textbooks, charity hospitals and mental institutions, paved roads and toll-free bridges, a modern state capital and an updated state university system, and many more expanded and inexpensive public services. In the minds of the ill-housed, ill-fed, and ill-clothed, Huey Long was the liberator of the downtrodden.

Copyright *Memphis Commercial Appeal*, 30 August 1931. Reprinted by permission.

Thousands upon thousands of Louisianians supported Long, and a workingman from New Orleans offered one important reason why. "I am a man of fifty years of age and wish to express that I have seen in one year more of what he has undertaken accomplished than I have seen accomplished in the past fifty years by those who have promised and have never been able to see any castles left behind them."[7] Long relied on his gubernatorial performance to get elected to the United States Senate in 1930, a post he refused to assume until he could see his slate of candidates through the state elections in 1932.

Origins of the Holiday Idea

Although Governor Long articulated the holiday proposal and planned the New Orleans cotton conference, he credited others with originating the idea of a sabbatical year. Long identified Congressman John Sandlin as the person who brought to him in rough form the idea he polished and refined into the holiday concept. A group of north Louisiana farmers had talked with Sandlin about the possibility of a one-year layoff from planting cotton, and the congressman from Louisiana's Fourth District had gone out to drum up support. Governor Long studied the proposition— for twenty-four hours, he claimed—and then declared himself wholeheartedly in favor of it.[8]

At the same time that farmers and politicians were pursuing the holiday action in Louisiana, disgruntled individuals elsewhere in the South were also advocating that cotton land be left fallow for one year. "If the cotton growing states will cut out planting cotton for one year, the surplus will be completely wiped out," a cotton and gin seed dealer from Orangeburg, South Carolina, wrote Long a couple of days before the holiday plan was formally announced. "It seems to me that when a surplus of any product is a menace to the country, it could be cut out by law. Any one can see this surplus is ruining business for the whole country."[9]

Former United States senator John L. McLaurin used the pages of the region's leading newspapers to recommend that legislatures of several states pass stringent laws forbidding the planting of a single acre of cotton in 1932. "As soon as it was apparent that no cotton was to be planted," the Bennettsville, South Carolina, resident reasoned, "the value of the two crops would be imparted to the crop on hand and mills all over the world would begin to bid for it." For the cotton industry to be saved, McLaurin further insisted, the South would have to take drastic action, and probably act by itself. "We must depend on ourselves and our state governments for relief. Mr. Hoover and his board have demonstrated their utter incompetency to do anything but blunder and then create more boards to correct the aforesaid blunders."[10]

When Long announced the holiday proposal, he tapped an idea that was already on the minds of many and the tongues of a few. Other politicians had had the opportunity to act on suggested cotton bans before he did, yet none had come forth. "I was in Austin last Wednesday and called at your office about 11:00 o'clock. I desired to call your attention to the very idea that Long has now suggested. Several callers were in your business office waiting to see you and I decided to defer my call until some more convenient time," a friend from Ganado, Texas, told Governor Sterling. "However, I did call on Attorney [General] Allred and suggested the cotton idea . . . but of course he would not press on it without some study and did not urge any definite expression."[11]

Southern politicians were not the only public officials given the chance to act on the holiday before Long introduced it. Federal officials knew there was sentiment for a one-year cotton interdiction on a national scale. "We earnestly suggest that you call an extra session of Congress at once, while the producers have the cotton in the field," some Arkansas farmers wrote President Hoover, "to enact a law that would give the producer a legal contract with the Farm Board that would bind tenants and landlords not to plant a cotton crop until 1933."[12]

Long realized that a large and committed showing at the New Orleans conference would be crucial to getting the holiday idea off the ground. To mobilize the people, and get their politicians behind the holiday would require a massive public relations effort. With less than a week existing between the holiday announcement and the New Orleans conference, Long turned to the radio and newspaper for assistance and secured the support of Will K. Henderson and James M. Thompson.

Media Contacts Henderson and Thompson

Will K. Henderson was as innovative and controversial in the field of radio as Long was in politics. Sometimes referred to as the "Bolshevik of radio," Henderson was a highly aggressive and flamboyant broadcaster based in Shreveport. He constantly warred with federal authorities over the dial location and broadcasting power of what he called in 1929 the "Hello World Broadcasting Corporation." When the federal government in 1930 authorized Henderson to operate at 1100 kilocycles and 10,000 watts of power, KWKH became the largest privately owned, clear-channel radio station in America. Commenting on the range of Henderson's reach, Harold McGugin of Kansas once told the House of Representatives that KWKH was heard "in every Southern state, every state in the Mississippi Valley from Canada to the Gulf, and, in short, every state with the possible exception of two or three states on the Pacific and some Northwestern states."[13]

As the owner of KWKH, Henderson did not have to depend on other broadcasters to sell him radio time. He enjoyed the enviable tactical position of being able to disseminate whatever ideas and sell whatever products he chose to. Whether promoting Old Man Henderson's 100 Proof Whiskey and Hello World Coffee, discoursing on patent medicines, life insurance, and real estate, organizing the Merchant Minute Men to combat the proliferation of chain stores, campaigning on behalf of Al Smith, or championing the cause of the laboring man and cotton farmers, Henderson used radio as a forum for the presentation of matters of public concern, and he was always near the heart of developing controversies.

To many scattered around the South, the greeting "Hello World! Doggone your buttons. Don't go way. This is KWKH in Shreveport, Lou-ee-siana, and Old Man Henderson talkin' to you . . ." marked the beginning of an evening spent with the entire family gathered around the radio. After a hard day's work, his listeners settled down for the time in an otherwise barren life for absorbing information and experiencing entertainment. "Whenever we took an automobile trip, north, east or west," Cecil Morgan, a member of the Louisiana legislature from Caddo parish, has said, "people seeing our Louisiana automobile license, in filling stations and elsewhere, would approach us and ask about KWKH, W. K. Henderson, and Huey Long."[14] For many forsaken souls in isolated, out-of-the-way places, KWKH broadcasts were their only contact with the outside world. In Henderson, Long secured not simply an influential media contact but a person who thought very much as he did. Long knew Henderson could be called upon to carry on the cause whenever and wherever needed.[15]

Complementing Henderson's radio influence was the newspaper support of Colonel James M. Thompson of New Orleans. Colonel Thompson often marshaled the news, editorial, and advertising facilities of his *New Orleans Item* behind various issues and candidates. The *Item* had attacked Long vigorously and persistently as an enemy of good government, and Colonel Thompson was among the powerful figures who had maneuvered to impeach the governor. With the introduction of the cotton holiday plan, though, Thompson saw Long in an entirely different light. He placed the holiday suggestion alongside Long's support of various flood-control measures as a progressive reform that attempted to come to grips with the natural forces that generated crises in the South. By securing the support of Thompson and other previously antagonistic publishers, like Colonel Robert Ewing, who had newspapers in Shreveport and

Monroe, Long could count on front-page editorials, full-page coverage of activities involving the holiday movement, personal appeals to powerful individuals throughout the region, and speeches in several states on behalf of a sabbatical year. In return the papers stood to gain substantial increases in subscriptions and advertisements from the state administration.[16]

Following up on his pledge to Long, Colonel Thompson contacted important parties across the South regarding their attendance at the New Orleans cotton conference. He apprised influential private citizens of the endorsement accorded the holiday idea by the *New Orleans Item* and *Tribune* and appealed to them for regional cooperation in the matter. "Long's proposition has a right to be considered by your state in the interest of the entire South," Thompson wired Arkansas Governor Harvey Parnell. "In doing this we subordinate past and possible future political differences with the governor because of vital character of the emergency and need for immediate action." The following day, Thompson received an assurance from Parnell that either the governor or a personal representative would be in attendance at New Orleans.[17]

Not all southern politicians were as easy to communicate with as the governor of Arkansas. Some of the more inflexible politicians in the South repudiated the holiday idea. "It is impractical and un-American to tell the farmer what he cannot grow," Governor Henry Horton of Tennessee protested. "He ought to be allowed to raise whatever he pleases so long as it is of benefit to the community." Henderson and Thompson nevertheless put in many long hours trying to convince these individuals of the virtues of their attending the New Orleans conference.[18]

Henderson told Benjamin M. Miller of Alabama that the conference would offer him the opportunity to argue for or against many propositions. He urged Miller to be present so that all practical plans could be discussed by the South's most influential politicians, and perhaps some definite course of action actually adopted. "It means everything to our Southland," Henderson pleaded. Thompson chimed in with an equally persuasive appeal to Miller. "It would amount to almost a tragedy from the standpoint of the cotton situation in the South if you and other governors fail at least to attend this conference or send delegates."[19]

Recognizing the paramount position Texas occupied in the cotton industry and the prominent role Texas would play in any action affecting the commodity, holiday forces went out of their way to accommodate politicians from the Lone Star State. Upon hearing that Texas Lieutenant Governor Edgar E. Witt might not be able to attend unless he could be sure to return to Texas by 23 August, Long dispatched an airplane to Austin and placed it at Witt's disposal.[20]

Governor Sterling also came in for his share of preferential treatment.

"I believe Governor Long's plan the soundest that has been advanced on the cotton situation," Thompson wrote to Sterling. "I think the matter is of more importance to Texas, the South, and the country than anything that can possibly come up for consideration. I am earnestly supporting this absolutely aside from politics." Colonel Thompson even appealed to a fellow member of the publishing fraternity, W. P. Hobby, two-term governor of Texas (1917–21) and editor of the Sterling-owned *Houston Post-Dispatch*, to prevail upon the man he had politically endorsed and become professionally associated with.[21]

Sterling indicated that the implementation of martial law in the oil fields would prevent him from attending. He nonetheless took care to telegraph his best wishes to Long and to grant the Louisiana governor permission to tell the conference he was "willing to do everything I can toward helping the great cotton industry of the South." Sterling also dispatched J. E. McDonald, commissioner of agriculture, officially to represent Texas.[22] On his arrival in New Orleans on 20 August, McDonald asserted that Texas was ready "to go the limit." "Governor Sterling, whom I represent and who himself may arrive later in time to attend the conference, assures me that anything I agree to, he will back up—even complete prohibition of cotton for the period of one year."[23]

The New Orleans Cotton Conference

The city of New Orleans had been the scene of some great cotton conventions in the past. It was in New Orleans in 1905 that farmers, merchants, politicians, and other representatives of the cotton industry gathered to organize the Southern Cotton Association. The sense of history and emotional electricity that had permeated the air in 1905 was present as the representatives assembled for the holiday conference in 1931.[24]

When Governor Long finally called the holiday conference to order at 10 A.M. at the Roosevelt Hotel, all the major cotton-growing states had sent representatives. A couple of thousand people excitedly milled around the hotel and through the nearby street. Governors Ibra C. Blackwood of South Carolina and Harvey Parnell of Arkansas and senators Thaddeus Caraway of Arkansas and Edwin S. Broussard of Louisiana joined Long on a dais that expanded as other luminaries were called from the audience to speak to the conference. "United States senators and congressmen and federal and state judges were as thick as flies around a hash joint," Eugene Talmadge, Georgia's commissioner of agriculture, observed.[25]

Seated side by side in the audience were some of Louisiana's bitterest political foes. Reporters noted that State Senator N. C. Williamson, a leader in the movement to impeach Governor Long, was seated next to

Congressman John Overton of Alexandria, chief of the corps of attorneys who had defended the governor in his impeachment trial. Interspersed among hundreds of planters, merchants, lawyers, and other concerned individuals were up-and-coming politicians, like Congressman Wright Patman of Texas. In less than a week's time Long had assembled, with the help of Henderson and Thompson, a more representative audience than many people originally thought possible.

Governor Long introduced Congressman John Sandlin to the cotton conference as the "man who really started this thing." Sandlin expressed appreciation for the honor, but insisted the plaudits should go to north Louisiana farmers. "This plan was suggested to me by the farmers in my district, and I am in no way due the credit for its origin," Sandlin modestly remarked. "Those farmers knew what they were talking about, and if the rest of the Southern farmers understood the no-cotton movement, they will be its most enthusiastic supporters." Calling the prohibition idea the Long Plan, Sandlin concluded the proposal was sound because it went to the very heart of the question of production itself.

To the sound of tumultuous applause and cheering, Long rose to address the conference. "If we prevent the cotton crop of 1932 by suitable legislation, the government can far better aid the farmer if he knows there will be no crop," Governor Long informed the delegates. "So long as a surplus exists it is a sword over the head of the market, and if the market is glutted, it can get no relief." Plans calling for one-third to one-half reduction would fail because not only were they inadequate but also they could not be enforced. "There has not been enough detective agencies in the last twenty-five years big enough to enforce the law under such conditions. Not that the farmers are more dishonest than others, but everytime a farmer hears some other section is going to reduce acreage, he starts planting more for himself."

The only viable solution to the cotton crisis, Long concluded, would be total abstinence in 1932. Once again he promised that if the New Orleans conference took affirmative action on drop-a-crop—another term Long used in referring to the holiday—and if other states pledged themselves to follow the convention's judgment, Louisiana would be the first state to demonstrate its faith by making the cotton holiday state law. "It will not be an easy matter to put over this legislation. However, more people have endorsed this plan than have endorsed all the other plans put forward this year. The Louisiana legislature can meet tomorrow morning and pass the necessary bill by Monday," he said, slightly overstating his case. "I know some of you governors can't act that fast. However, unless something is done the South will be bankrupt; it is bankrupt now."

From the very opening of the conference it was evident the representatives were interested in discussing only two plans, either total abstinence or a 50 percent reduction. After delegates from the major cotton-growing states met in an executive committee meeting, McDonald, Texas's commissioner of agriculture, presented the case for a 50 percent reduction in 1932. Attempting to counter drop-a-crop's burgeoning popularity, Commissioner McDonald stressed the dangers of immobilizing the cotton industry for one entire year. "Approximately 10,000,000 persons are dependent on cotton. Not merely the farmers, but the employees of a number of vital Southern industries must be considered. Cotton mills, cottonseed oil industries, railroads, trucking, banking and other interests are directly affected by the annual crop. One year without a crop would mean complete disorganization," Commissioner McDonald warned the conference. "Something must be done immediately, and I shall lay before the [Texas] legislature the results of the conference here." The audience was not impressed by McDonald's impassioned plea, voting down the Texas 50 percent reduction plan by an overwhelming majority.

With defeat of the Texas plan, the New Orleans conference moved toward acting affirmatively on Governor Long's proposal. Governor Blackwood of South Carolina promised to call the South Carolina legislature into special session to make the cotton holiday state law, provided other cotton states followed suit. "This is not the first dark hour when Southern people have met to discuss some cause," Governor Blackwood said. "I feel safe in saying that this is one of the most important movements that has been launched in several decades. The necessity of the hour has ushered us into an atmosphere of possibility."

Claude Weaver, legal adviser to Governor William H. Murray of Oklahoma, told the conference that drop-a-crop was designed "to drive the specter of want, the wolf from the farmer's door." And Eugene Talmadge laid the groundwork for a positive response to drop-a-crop by outlining the distressed conditions confronting growers in his state, particularly the price of 5 cents a pound reported at some markets earlier in the week. "That price was not sufficient to pay for the bagging and ties, and if it stays at that price it will ultimately bankrupt every bank and financial business institution in the state," Commissioner Talmadge observed. "I believe this conference should adopt resolutions calling on the governors of the cotton growing states to call their legislatures together on fixed dates to pass this necessary remedial legislation." In conclusion, he called upon the delegates to provide the South with a legislative victory comparable to the military one Andrew Jackson had realized over a century earlier in the very same city.

Flushed by the success of overriding the Texas plan and caught up in the positive rhetoric of the speakers, the New Orleans conference overwhelmingly endorsed Huey P. Long's cotton holiday plan, adding the proviso that such a law would be binding only when states producing three-fourths of the total crop passed similar legislation. The inclusion of the three-fourths provision was clearly aimed at the state of Texas, since in the 1930–31 crop year the Lone Star State harvested 40 percent of all the acreage devoted to cotton in the United States and produced nearly 35 percent of the total crop.

Mandatory Regulation

Long's success at the conference caused his opponents to stiffen their attacks. The *Dallas Morning News* told readers not to laugh at the pundits who assembled in New Orleans, "for they were desperately in earnest and earnestly desperate. But they were and are ridiculous just the same." Reflecting on the decision to ban cotton cultivation in 1932, the *Montgomery Advertiser* declared: "If that is the only thing to do, nothing will be done." But the *Shreveport Times* cautioned against scoffing at any recommendation because it appeared unusual or extreme. "The remedy proposed for the American cotton situation is radical, but radical ills require radical cures."[26]

The federal government reacted evasively. Both James C. Stone and Carl Williams said they were in favor of "any sound, workable plan," but neither would comment directly on the Long Plan. Williams said the action taken by the conference "shows the South is thinking about the necessity for reducing production." Stone claimed the purpose of the plan to destroy every third row had been all along to get the South seriously to consider the problem. "The one thing we are trying to do," the chairman said, "is bring forcefully before the South the absolute need for cutting down on production until the existing surpluses have been done away with. That was what we had in mind when we advanced our plan."[27]

Long realized that to rely once again on voluntary cooperation would be to repeat the mistakes of the Farm Board and the Department of Agriculture. Even with compulsory compliance, he knew farmers would attempt to continue cultivating cotton partly to flout a plan they might disagree with and partly to meet the demand of economic necessity. "I want to say that when we have a King or Queen we will have to do as they say, but until then no governor, elect-senator, or nobody else can prevent me from planting what we want and can raise on our farms," a farmer from Atlanta, Georgia, protested. "We have to plant what we eat or go hungry, for we cannot sell what we have raised. We have to raise a little cotton to buy sugar, coffee, salt, pepper, and such things that we can't raise ourselves." Threats of refusal to comply only confirmed in Long's mind the necessity of legislation to make the holiday mandatory and the need to include strict enforcement provisions in any holiday law.[28]

Since Texas produced more than one-third of the domestic crop, Long reasoned, all legislation would be contingent on what Texas did, and it was, therefore, incumbent on Texas to take the next step. "The whole world has its eyes on Texas to see what Texas is going to do, and at the first sign of a rift in the skies from that state, I will call our legislature into session," Long promised. "So far as Louisiana is concerned, the necessary legislation is as good as passed already. The same is true of other states, and the whole world, consequently, has its eyes on Texas."[29]

The *New Orleans Item* credited Long with acting wisely in deferring to Texas. The paper felt Governor Sterling should be given the opportunity to act as strongly on behalf of cotton farmers as he had already for oil interests.[30] When overproduction in the oil fields drove down the price of crude oil, Sterling called a special session of the legislature, got proration laws passed, and dispatched the militia to the oil fields to enforce the edicts. The troops stationed in the East Texas fields assured that the stream of oil from eighteen hundred wells did not exceed 225 barrels per well per day. After a few weeks of proration limitations, the price of crude shot up from 15 cents per barrel to 98 cents.[31]

"If the governors of the states can shut down oil wells until one dollar per barrel is affirmed, why can they not shut down the market of cotton until a living price is obtained," a resident of Junction City, Louisiana, asked. And as a resident of Phoenix, Arizona, also asserted: "It does not appear to me to be any more radical to tell a farmer how much cotton he can sell from his farm in order to be prosperous than to tell the oil well owner how much oil he can sell from his wells. The proposition is exactly the same."[32]

Thompson made a personal appeal to the governor of Texas through the columns of Texas newspapers. He noted that a large and representative delegation of Texas state officials had attended the New Orleans cotton conference and affirmed the decision to seek South-wide action on the cotton holiday. He asked Texas politicians to set their factional differences aside just as he had done in endorsing drop-a-crop. "I think that practically every state in the South will follow with legislation when the disposition of Texas is known. The reason I urge immediate attention in this vital matter by cotton raisers and people of Texas is because speed is vital if anything is to be done for 1932. Likewise if this legislation is to be enacted it must be passed before the cotton crop of the South is picked and before the cotton has passed from the hands of small farmers and growers, for whose benefit the New Orleans conference was called." Thompson urged the press of Texas to give cotton events the widest possible coverage.[33]

Henderson traveled to Austin to confer with Governor Sterling and Commissioner McDonald. The Shreveport radio owner said he was prepared to "roll up my sleeves and go to work to obtain a living wage for the Southern cotton farmer." He invited McDonald to speak over KWKH for as long as he wanted to and free of charge. "Texas is the key to the entire cotton situation," Henderson remarked after meeting with state officials. "As Texas goes, so goes the cotton belt." McDonald announced he would embark on a week-long speaking tour of cotton areas in Texas to gauge public opinion on the cotton situation and would also deliver six addresses in three days over KWKH.[34]

The *Houston Chronicle*, owned and edited by Jesse H. Jones, demanded that Governor Sterling face the cotton problem squarely and urged him to give the cotton holiday serious consideration. Jones reminded Sterling that the interests of the South were also the interests of Texas. It was neither the time nor the issue to use the paramount position of Texas to toy with the well-being of an entire region. "Whether we wish it or not, we can not live for ourselves alone," Jones pointed out. "In facing the grave cotton problem which confronts the whole South now, if Texas says 'No' to any proposal which may be made for its solution, we can not escape the responsibility of saying 'No' for all the South."[35]

But Sterling discounted his obligation in the matter and threw the whole cotton holiday issue back in Long's lap. "It's Governor Long's baby," Sterling insisted. "Let him wash it first." Upon hearing of Sterling's derisive remark, Long issued an even more daring challenge. "Fine! Louisiana will wash this baby from head to foot, dress it up, and put it on Governor Sterling's desk where it can say 'da-da' to Texas."[36]

Power Politics in the Pelican State

Long had placed Louisiana's legislators on alert on Saturday morning, 22 August. The governor issued a public notice advising all legislators to hold themselves in readiness to be called to Baton Rouge for a special session upon a few hours' notice. "The members will not be called on to put in much time in Baton Rouge," Long assured Louisianians. "I will call the session to convene just before midnight so that we can introduce our legislation, wait for midnight, and then a few minutes later, handle it on the second days procedure. They will not be kept in Baton Rouge a moment longer than is necessary for the physical handling of the bills."[37]

On Monday evening, 24 August, Governor Long issued a call from Baton Rouge for the Louisiana legislature to convene for a special six-day session commencing 10 P.M. the following evening, 25 August, to consider legislation making drop-a-crop state law. Reports from the nation's leading cotton factors and brokers indicated, Long observed, that unless radical corrective action were taken, cotton futures would plummet to 4½ cents. The only conceivable plan for immediately raising prices and reducing supplies was 100 percent prohibition. "I urge every farmer, merchant, and banker of the cotton growing states to act at once. They must build a fire for their legislators and governors to read by. We are on the brink of prosperity on one hand and ready for total bankruptcy on the other," Long vigorously contended. "I urge again that the farmers hold their cotton in the seed until this plan has had a chance. It is being done for the farmer and if he sells either his cotton or his seed he defeats the whole purpose of the plan."[38]

Long was roundly praised for the daring and intrepid character he exhibited in calling the Louisiana legislature into special session. "It will show the world," the Shreveport brokerage firm of Sewall and Adger declared, "that Louisiana has the courage of its convictions and will strengthen the hand of every other governor."[39] For Long to get his holiday plan through the Louisiana legislature, however, he would need the support of a ruling oligarchy which had not simply controlled Louisiana politics from the Civil War up to his gubernatorial election in 1928 but had also opposed him passionately since his entry into state politics in 1918 and attempted his impeachment in 1929.

Virtually every southern state had at one time or another experienced the control—economically, politically, and socially—of some kind of elitist, upper-class group. The hierarchy that controlled Louisiana was in all probability the most powerful and sinister of all southern oligarchies. Louisiana contained powerful economic elements either not found elsewhere in the South or at least not present to the same degree.[40]

The tremendous commercial possibilities of the Mississippi River attracted a broader spectrum of mercantile interests to Louisiana than to most southern states. Shipping, financial, service, and utility interests were even more prominent in Louisiana because many were headquartered not simply in a single city but in the region's largest city, the sprawling metropolis of New Orleans. Towering above all these corporations was the Standard Oil Company, a financial titan in the state and in the South. Providing these economic interests with a degree of political power unparalleled in the South was a genuine big-city machine entrenched in New Orleans. The Regulars, or Ring, as it was called, cultivated alliances with courthouse groups in outlying parishes who represented cotton, sugar, rice, and lumber interests. Over the years Louisiana's oligarchic rule fostered a case of arrested political development and created the closest approximation to a closed society that has ever existed in the South.[41]

The first successful revolution to bring Louisiana's ruling oligarchy to task began in 1918 with the election of Huey P. Long to the Railroad–Public Service Commission and culminated in his elevation to the governorship in 1928. It was a latent social and political protest that dated back to the repeated failures of the lower classes to overthrow the ruling oligarchy during the Secession crisis of the 1860s, Populist disturbances of the 1890s, and Progressive and Socialist rumblings in the first third of the twentieth century.[42]

Long fought Louisiana's ruling elements so vigorously as a public service commissioner and governor that in 1929 his enemies combined in an attempt to impeach him. Although Long escaped the ambush, the impeachment attempt deeply scarred his personality. It hardened him as no other event ever had as he saw the lengths his opponents would go to destroy him.[43]

For Long to get the holiday approved by his enemies in the press, the corporations, and the legislature appeared to be an impossible task. Yet in one of the most unusual displays of harmony that Louisiana had ever witnessed, T. Semmes Walmsley, mayor of New Orleans, appealed to his Old Regular and Choctaw adherents temporarily to bury their political hatchet with Long. Since attending the cotton conference, Walmsley explained to his followers, he had consulted with knowledgeable people in the cotton industry, and was convinced that drop-a-crop was both practical and feasible.

"The city of New Orleans for years past depended upon the wealth of cotton to build upon. Today, if the city can help these farmers who contributed so much to make New Orleans, the cotton producers will not find her failing them," Walmsley said in pledging his support. "If Governor Long calls a special session to put over the conference plan," the mayor proclaimed on the eve of Long's announcement, "I will do all in my power to have the bill passed unanimously. I now call upon those who have opposed the governor in the past to unite in an effort to put over the conference plan and to set aside our political differences for the relief of the suffering cotton growers."[44]

Machine and planting interests may have opposed Long politically, but when it came to economics, particularly the economics of the cotton holiday, they supported him wholeheartedly. "At no time in your entire public career have you been nearer right than you are right now in your crusade for the cause of cotton," wrote W. D. Brown, a planter from Lake Providence. "With you 100% in Franklin Parish. Keep the good work up. Planters of 5,000 acres of cotton," the T. B. Gilbert Company of Wisner wired Long. From James Pullen of Plantation Thirty, a two-thousand-acre establishment in Benton, came a similar response. "I am actively in accord with your 'Cotton Plan' and am glad to see . . . Representatives and Sena-

tors . . . lay their political enmity aside and do the will of the people. . . .
Me and my tenants will make the grade without any cotton." As John O.
Roy, manager of Ramsey Plantation in New Roads, informed Long, "For
the sake of all the farmers, try to put over your plan. Not only will it save
us, but it will put you in a mighty strong position. I, for one am for you
100%, especially on your cotton plan, and everyone I speak to in Pointe
Coupee feels the same way, except cotton buyers, brokers, etc." And as
State Senator Norris C. Williamson, president of the Louisiana Cotton
Cooperative Association and himself a plantation owner in East Carroll
Parish, said, "I am for anything that will help cotton. I believe the country
could skip a year of raising cotton without any trouble, and such would
be a good idea."[45]

Louisiana Makes the Holiday State Law

When the Louisiana legislature convened on Tuesday evening, 25 August,
for a special six-day session, Governor Long addressed a joint meeting of
the House and Senate, accentuating the arguments he had been making in
favor of the cotton holiday since proposing the plan on 16 August. That
same evening the cotton holiday bill was introduced into the House of
Representatives and referred to committee by two politicians previously
antagonistic to Longism, Representative Horace Wilkinson of West Baton
Rouge and Representative Reuben T. Douglas of Caddo.

Both men came from families prominent in local politics. Wilkinson
operated a lucrative sugar plantation and refinery near Port Allen, and
Reuben T. Douglas owned a cotton farm near Gilliam. Both men were
among the oldest members of the Louisiana legislature and had signed the
impeachment resolution against Long in 1929. Douglas heartily com-
mended Long on calling the New Orleans cotton conference and right
from the beginning offered to support the holiday. "It is a drastic move,
but desperate diseases require desperate remedies, and I don't believe
anything else will be of any value."[46]

While the public realized that the avowed purpose of the Wilkinson-
Douglas bill was to prohibit cotton cultivation in 1932 in order to reduce
supplies and raise prices, Long, drawing on his legal expertise, couched
the measure in agricultural terms. Already he was thinking about potential legal challenges to crop control legislation and taking every precaution to assure the constitutionality of a cotton holiday. According to the
bill's preamble, drop-a-crop was designed to provide for the extermina-
tion of the Mexican boll weevil, "anthonomous grandis bohemian" as
Long called it, and eradication of "phymatatrichum omnivorum duggar,"
more commonly known as cotton root rot.[47]

Although the objective of the special session was to consider and get enacted one single piece of legislation, Louisiana's legislators exhibited a more aggressive and radical reforming zeal than even Huey P. Long might have hoped for, threatening on occasions to push drop-a-crop beyond its original conception. Several legislators looked ahead to contingencies that would have to be taken care of during a sabbatical year and revealed a willingness to break new ground in preparing for them. Resolutions were introduced calling for a moratorium on taxes, mortgages, and debts for the period cotton land would be withheld from production. Speaking about the holiday bill and the wellspring of supportive measures, Representative Douglas observed, "Regulation by law is coming more and more to the front every day, and the time is coming when there will be regulation of all products, including wheat. Louisiana today is faced with a crisis and we must make every effort to do the best we can. I am for this prohibition bill, and do not want to see it gummed up with amendments."[48]

In his concluding remarks to the legislature, Representative Douglas encouraged his colleagues to rise to the challenge of present conditions. He explained that the repeated failure of voluntary measures over the years had finally converted him into a believer in mandatory legislation and asked them to support the holiday until such time as experience showed something that was better. "We are blazing a way through a wilderness which we must cross some time or some where so that good may come," Douglas commented. "Our business today is to do this revolutionary act to meet a revolutionary situation. Let there not be a dissenting voice here today and let us bring order out of chaos."[49]

On Thursday, 27 August, Ernest O'Bannon of Claiborne Parish was the chief speaker on behalf of the holiday measure before the House. O'Bannon tried to place a sound legal footing under holiday legislation by defining the purpose of drop-a-crop to be the eradication of cotton diseases and pests. From his experience as a cotton farmer for thirty years near Homer, Louisiana, O'Bannon argued that the boll weevil was more responsible for the cotton farmers' plight than any other factor. The weevil had forced the cost of production up from 7 to 8 cents per pound to 15 to 20 cents and the quality of cotton down. "There has been continuous warfare between the Southern cotton growers and the boll weevil for a quarter century," O'Bannon observed. "Hundreds of methods for fighting the weevil have been proposed, tried, and abandoned."

For American cotton producers to regain the competitive edge in price and quality, the United States had to destroy the boll weevil, and a sabbatical year provided an opportunity for doing just that. By taking away from the weevil the plant that it fed off of and propagated on, the holiday promised to decimate the insect and return cotton farmers to a more competitive position. "This bill providing for no cotton production next year is the key to the situation," O'Bannon concluded. "It will unlock the doors of depression for the South."[50]

The Louisiana House of Representatives voted unanimously in favor of the Wilkinson-Douglas bill on Thursday, 27 August. Initially, Representative Stanley McDermott of the anti-Long citadel of New Orleans voted against the measure. Heeding Mayor Walmsley's call for unanimity, however, McDermott retracted his objections "so as to present a united front" to the other cotton-growing states. Upon hearing of the lower house's action, Governor Long proudly exclaimed: "The most conservative state in the Union has today seen its House of Representatives vote 77 to nothing to outlaw the planting of cotton in the State of Louisiana for the year 1932." Long considered the vote to be a complete affirmation of the New Orleans cotton conference. "It would be a crime," he observed, "for the legislatures of the cotton growing states to let pass this opportunity to restore prosperity to their people."[51]

The Louisiana Senate followed the lower house's example on Friday evening, 28 August, by unanimously ratifying, in less than ten minutes and without discussion, the holiday plan, 32–0. It was around 1:30 A.M. on Saturday morning when the bill was rushed from the Capitol to the State House and the governer awakened from a sound sleep for his signature. With a typical flare for the dramatic, Long signed the holiday bill into law in his bedroom while wearing a cotton nightshirt and sitting on a cotton mattress covered by cotton sheets and blankets. A fuzzy-eyed Long complimented Louisiana's legislators for the equanimity shown and held them up as an example worthy of emulation. "Here is the unanimous vote of two houses, some of whose members are among the bitterest political enemies of my life, and yet they realized the wisdom of this legislation and the necessity of its immediate adoption." The governor said he would accept personal responsibility for the assertion that there would be 20-cent cotton in the South in three weeks if other states followed suit. He cautioned the cotton states against pinning any hopes on help from Washington and urged them simply to concentrate on doing their share. "God helps those who help themselves. It is all right to call on Hercules, but they should put their own shoulders to the wheel . . . the way Louisiana did."

After photographers had completed their picture taking, the governor reportedly discarded the nightshirt and slipped back into his customary silk pajamas. The cotton plan that Long signed into law prohibited the planting, gathering, and ginning of cotton in Louisiana in 1932; authorized the governor to suspend such legislation if states producing 75 percent of the crop failed to enact similar legislation; fixed 15 January 1932

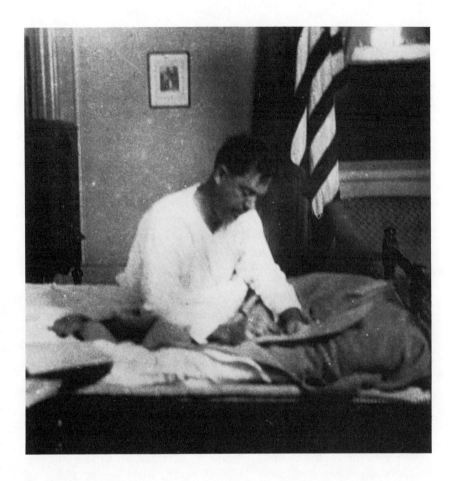

Huey P. Long in a cotton nightshirt.
Photograph in T. Harry Williams Papers, Louisiana State University, Baton Rouge.

as the deadline for contingent action by other states; empowered the commissioner of agriculture to destroy any cotton growing in 1932; provided for penalties ranging from $100 to $500 and 10 to 60 days in jail for violators; and memorialized President Hoover to prevail upon the cottongrowing states to enact prohibition legislation.[52]

Long Capitalizes on Public Acclaim

The response of the public to the cotton holiday was phenomenal. The governor's office was deluged with letters, telegrams, and telephone calls. A qualitative survey of the correspondence indicated that support for the holiday plan was not confined to a single sector of the cotton belt or any one handling or processing specialty. Long was complimented by farmers, buyers, merchants, ginners, suppliers, and other cotton interests in virtually every cotton-growing state.[53]

Among the correspondents were representatives from the legislatures of cotton-growing states requesting copies of the Louisiana law. Some of the legislators indicated a desire to spearhead the drop-a-crop plan in their states, while others simply wanted to be prepared in the event their legislatures were called into special session to consider Long's plan or similar proposals. "We shall have all kinds of plans offered, but I favor cutting cotton out entirely for the year 1932," wrote J. Scott Davis, a member of the Georgia House of Representatives from Floyd County for ten years. "I think it is the only plan that will be worth anything to the Southern cotton growers. They are the ones that need our help right now and I want to give them 100% strong."[54]

Requests for copies of the Louisiana holiday law also came in from southern representatives away in Washington. Members of Congress needed information on the cotton holiday to answer questions being posed by their constituents back home. These politicians also recognized that a thorough working knowledge of the statute would be helpful should the holiday movement become national in scope and reach the federal government.[55]

The sheer number of communications would have discouraged many politicians from answering, but Long seized the chance to provide each correspondent with a written reply. He had already adopted cotton stationery for official use in Louisiana's executive office. At a cost of $7.50 per one thousand letters, he had been ordering paper manufactured out of cotton from an out-of-state concern. "There is agitation down this way that we should enlarge our use of cotton goods," he explained to a national publication, "and some of we more or less super-cotton patriots, including fellows like myself who have picked cotton for 16 hours a day for 35¢, are having stationery printed on the cotton fabric. I think it is very neat and dignified looking stationery."[56]

Long composed a form message and had the Ramires-Jones Printing Company of Baton Rouge print it on the cotton stationery. The cotton letter revealed some of Long's best qualities—his tremendous flair for the dramatic and his keen eye for even the smallest detail. Printed in blue at the top of the cambriclike paper was the Louisiana state seal—a floppy mother pelican feeding a nest of young birds all encircled by the legend "Union, Justice & Confidence." There followed in black ink the three-paragraph cotton message and the flowing signature of the governor.

> I have received so many responses to my efforts to alleviate the condition of the Southern cotton farmer that it has been physically impossible to reply formally to all of them, and I take this method of thanking you for the interest manifested by you and your communication. A great many other plans were suggested to me, but after careful thought and study, I am convinced that the one and only plan for relief is that unanimously adopted by the Legislature of Louisiana, prohibiting the planting of cotton in the year 1932.

Long concluded his letter by thanking his adherents for their interest and support, "which has helped to bring the condition of the South to the minds of those from whom relief must come—the public officials of the cotton producing states."[57] Having guided the cotton holiday through the New Orleans cotton conference and the Louisiana legislature, Long set out to get it adopted South-wide.

4   Mass Meetings Spread the Word

 Getting the New Orleans cotton conference to pledge itself to drop-a-crop and then calling the Louisiana legislature into special session to enact the holiday into law had been formidable achievements on Long's part. But it was only the beginning of a much longer and broader struggle. States producing 75 percent of the crop had to make the holiday mandatory in order to assure compliance, reduce supplies, and raise prices. "You are aware of the fact that the Federal government has done everything it could to try and persuade the Southern farmers from a large acreage in cotton this season, to no avail. The bankers have withheld funds from them to hold the acreage down, to no avail," a resident of Waco, Texas, observed. "This ought to serve to each and every thinking and soundminded person the important fact that nothing short of statuary law can ever control cotton production in the South."[1]

Long knew that since the legislatures of the cotton states were either in recess or on biennial schedules, holiday legislation would require the calling of special sessions. He recommended that residents of the South hold mass meetings to voice their sentiments on the cotton holiday and to petition leading politicians to convene their legislatures in extraordinary session.[2]

The holiday proposal raised serious questions for the people of the South: the cost of special sessions, the legality of the measure, the impact of a layoff on employment, the effect of foreign competition on American markets, and the possibility of diversifying southern agriculture during a sabbatical year. Mass meetings seemed to be a democratic means for discussing these topics and marshaling public opinion either behind or against drop-a-crop. All those affected by a cotton holiday could get together on a specific date at the town square or county courthouse to debate the proposition and simply by a show of hands indicate whether they approved or disapproved of a special session on holiday legislation.

"I feel that wise action demands that the farmers, merchants, bankers, and others who are interested should get together in county-wide mass meetings," Lafayette L. Patterson, a member of the United States House of Representatives from Gadsden, Alabama, recommended, "and pass resolutions which will in turn elect delegates to a state convention which will in turn elect delegates to a national meeting." While Secretary of Agriculture Arthur M. Hyde withheld endorsement of any single plan, he approved of mass meetings as a medium for open discussion of the cotton crisis. "I have no criticism to offer," Hyde told the congressman, "and am hopeful that out of all this may come some valuable ideas leading toward the control of agricultural production."[3]

Shortly after returning home from the New Orleans conference, both governors Blackwood of South Carolina and Parnell of Arkansas provided just such a rallying point. They called upon the residents of their respective states to gather in countywide mass meetings on Saturday, 29 August, or as soon thereafter as could be arranged.[4] Several other governors were still reluctant to use mass meetings as a forum for discussing the cotton crisis and a prelude to legislative action. "Evidently you are not a judge who is willing to establish precedent," the owner of the Woodbank Plantation, Tuscaloosa, goaded the governor of Alabama. "You had an opportunity to act before Governor Long acted, but you allowed golden moments to slip away."[5]

Since the governors of several states were hesitant about surveying public opinion, it was once again up to Huey Long to provide direction and guidance to the holiday movement. Long could not, however, leave Louisiana to campaign South-wide on behalf of the holiday because he was embroiled in a bitter feud with his lieutenant governor. To educate the public on the holiday and direct the movement's course across the South, Long resorted to that increasingly important communications medium—the radio.

Long Takes to the Air Waves

Long continued his close association with Will K. Henderson and still relied most heavily on KWKH. But he also occasionally contracted for time over radio stations with network connections. Through Robert K. Ewing of radio station WDSU in New Orleans, Long secured broadcasting time over the Dixie Radio Network, an affiliate of the Columbia Broadcasting System. From WDSU's studio in New Orleans, Long's broadcasts were transmitted to such affiliated stations as WBRC, Birmingham, WDOD, Chattanooga, WGST, Atlanta, WLAC, Nashville, WREC, Memphis, KLRA, Little Rock, and KLRD, Dallas. By broadcasting over KWKH and WDSU, Long could blanket the region.[6]

The range of Long's broadcasts actually extended far beyond the South. The radio signal was carried deep into the Midwest and far into the Southwest. Any given night's broadcast might result in letters from enthralled listeners in locations as far apart as New Mexico and Indiana. "I think it would awaken the farmers of our country to action if there were more men like you broadcasting all over the United States," an admiring listener in Ashtabula, Ohio, wrote. "The wheat farmers, the dairy farmers, all need your kind of ideas." "Located up here in northern Iowa, I accidentally tuned in and heard your speech on the cotton situation last night," an attorney residing in Humbolt, Iowa, indicated. "In this corn growing section of the country, we too are having plenty of agricultural trouble, due to poor prices and drouth, and sympathize with you in your territory's afflictions. I hope your plan for a 100% 'layoff' next year goes through."[7]

After the Louisiana legislature passed drop-a-crop, Long used the radio almost nightly. He frequently invited various authorities to appear on the broadcasts to discuss the proposed holiday. For example, State Senator James Eastland elaborated on conditions in his home county of Scott and the progress of the holiday movement in Mississippi. In the opinion of Frank Russell, an NBC vice-president in Washington, programs like "Meet the Press" and "American Town Meeting of the Air" were outgrowths of the early public information programs Long held on a number of pressing issues.[8]

Members of the radio audience urged Long to print copies of his addresses. Some listeners reported that static prevented parts of his addresses from being heard. A few expressed concern that people might have missed a broadcast because "they haven't the price of these Yankee contraptions by which thought and ideas are literally picked out of the air." Long explained that no complete record of his radio performances existed because he spoke extemporaneously. He suggested any person who missed a speech for whatever reason consult reports in the daily press for the substance of his remarks. I. I. Femrite of the United Press in New Orleans commonly asked Long to dictate an overview of what he was going to say on an evening broadcast. This way Femrite could give Long's radio address easy movement on UPI's wire and inclusion in morning editions of out-of-state newspapers.[9]

In a single broadcast, Long could reach more people over a wider area than any newspaper. Since most of the big-city dailies normally gave him a bad press, the radio enabled Long to counter criticism the same day that editors rolled it off the presses and then move on to the points he really wanted to cover. Recognizing the antagonism of the press to him and appreciating his intentions, people tried to assure the continuation of his broadcasts by offering to underwrite the costs. "The attitude of this morning's *Dallas News* on the cotton problem is proof that instead of being Texas' oldest business institution that they are the biggest bunch of jackasses in the state," a resident of Dallas wrote. "I am mailing you a check for $100 to help pay the cost of broadcasting. You are a God send to the South."

Long returned these contributions in the most graceful manner possible. He thanked the contributors for their kind offers, but insisted he was unable to accept such help.[10] Actually, Long had all the free radio time that he needed. Besides the unrestricted use of radio station KWKH that Henderson provided, community interest in the holiday prompted radio stations to ask Long to speak over their facilities and to offer him air time as a public service.[11]

The number of people Long reached via the radio—and who personally responded to his call—was vast. Typical of the many who were impressed by his presentation was Congressman Wright Patman. "You made a very plausible and convincing speech over the radio last night. I presume the vote you took by radio was the first ever taken in America in that way," the Democratic congressman from Texarkana, Texas, wrote. "I have been following with interest your campaign, and I certainly do admire your aggressiveness and ability. I never heard a more interesting speech." Another of Long's many radio admirers was M. D. Massengill of Piney Flats, Tennessee, reportedly one of the biggest farmers in the Volunteer State. "The old man likes to listen in while you are broadcasting. He thinks you are the 'berries,'" a mutual friend reported, "and when he finds out you are going to make a speech over the radio he immediately starts 'phoning all his friends and neighbors to tune in on you. Says you are the only person he would sit up late to hear."[12]

By refusing to set aside a time and place for mass meetings, the public officials of several states hoped to choke off and contain the holiday movement, but this strategy proved an inconvenience rather than a death warrant for the proposal. The radio enabled Long to circumvent the opposition of various officials and intrude right into their jurisdictions to advise and inform his followers on when and where to meet and what issues to discuss. The mass meetings that were held all across the South exposed contingencies that would have to be met during a sabbatical year and enabled holiday adherents to flesh in and fill out the proposal as they went along.

The Constitutionality of Acreage Control

If the cotton-producing states legislated the drop-a-crop plan into law, it would raise a fundamental constitutional question. Across the South there were individuals who automatically opposed any and all attempts at acreage control. These people considered mandatory regulation, whether in total or just a percentage, an infringement of individual liberties. They feared that compulsory compliance would provide the government with a foothold for moving on to control other areas of American life.[13]

Senator Josiah W. Bailey was one of several southern statesmen who warned cotton farmers of the perils that acreage control posed. The primary objective of the Constitution, the North Carolina senator told a Raleigh audience, was to preserve liberty—"the unfettered right to sow, to plant, to work, to produce, and to enjoy the fruits of one's labors." Nothing should be done that would encroach upon the liberties guaranteed under the Constitution. Anyone promoting acreage control was threatening to take the country down the road to Moscow and Rome. "Those who are advocating government control of production in America would alter the historic character of our country," a worried Bailey cautioned. "I concede that the situation is bad, but it is not as bad as in Italy and Russia; even if it were worse, I would not be willing to surrender our liberties for the difference."[14]

The constitutionality of acreage control was defended just as vigorously by its proponents. Texas Commissioner of Agriculture J. E. McDonald contended that sections of the state constitution on the conservation of natural resources provided the authority for making acreage control laws legal. He classified the soil among the state's great natural resources and expressed confidence the courts would uphold this view. He buttressed his case by noting how the legislature had used the natural resource section of the state constitution in writing oil proration laws and justifying water conservation districts.[15]

Long was absolutely certain that the holiday was constitutional in Louisiana.[16] When State Senator Joseph R. Bryson of South Carolina asked the Louisiana governor about the plan's constitutionality after hearing him on the radio, Long mentioned how the Louisiana commissioner of agriculture, acting on authority granted in a 1910 statute, had quarantined certain parishes and prohibited the growing of cotton in order to eliminate the pink worm in 1920. Long also cited his most powerful evidence, Article 6, Section 14, of the 1921 Constitution of Louisiana that stated:

> The legislature is hereby directed to enact laws fostering agriculture and immigration, and preventing the spread of pests and diseases injurious to plants and domestic animals. It may enact laws limiting or prohibiting the cultivation of specified crops in definite zones or areas and providing the necessary funds to compensate for damages caused by such limitations or prohibitions.[17]

Long was confident drop-a-crop could be made constitutional elsewhere. Either state constitutions already had provisions that could be interpreted in favor of a holiday or state legislatures could draft legislation tailored specifically to justify drop-a-crop action. Legal experts kept feeding Long advice on how the proposal should be couched to make it legal in other states. Robert Arrington, a partner in a Montgomery, Alabama, law firm, indicated that if the holiday plan were designated a police regulation—a law designed either to control or to eliminate a menace—it would be acceptable throughout the South. "Every cotton producing state is infected with the boll weevil. It is a pest and a menace, seriously affecting the general welfare of the land, destroying millions of dollars worth of property each year," wrote Arrington in support of prohibition. "With cotton selling below six cents a pound the South is facing bankruptcy and if some drastic measures are not taken immediately our people will suffer great misery and their poverty will render them subject to disease, pestilence, and death."[18]

Many farmers originally endorsed drop-a-crop because they actually equated prohibition with the eradication of natural enemies. Through holiday legislation states would be facilitating the destruction of predatory pests and diseases and encouraging the regeneration of agricultural lands. "It would eradicate the boll weevil thus enabling us to plant less land to cotton hereafter to make quantity of cotton desired and give more acreage to food crops. Peanuts would be a cash crop," a resident of Comer, Alabama, optimistically observed.[19] The elimination of natural enemies would, moreover, save farmers considerable expense and thereby generate additional benefits. As T. N. Mauritz, president of a state bank in Ganado, Texas, observed: "If the principal cotton pests were eliminated, the farmer could grow his cotton from twenty-five to forty percent less than he now can; on a cheaper basis he would be more able to compete with foreign products."[20]

Threats Posed by Competing Products and Countries

Anxiety was expressed at the mass meetings that substitute products and cotton from foreign countries might make deep and irreversible inroads into American cotton markets. The potential of cottonseed oil and meal in the production of various foods and feeds was so great that trade sources speculated cotton might someday be grown for the seed rather than the lint. Cotton farmers were warned that producers of cottonseed substitutes were just waiting in the wings for the chance to step into this $200 million annual market.

"The corn belt farmers' hog lard, and imported oils and fats, would welcome an opportunity to take over the markets the cotton growers now enjoy for the billion and one-quarter pounds of cottonseed oil shortening," Earl S. Haines, executive secretary of the National Cottonseed Products Association, said in a warning that played on sectional animosity and distrust. "Wheat middlings, corn glutten meal, and other northern feedstuffs could immediately capture the markets abandoned by cottonseed meal. . . . It is doubtful if those who promise to represent the economic welfare of the cotton growers can justify the surrender of the Southern farmers' markets for the cottonseed meal and oil to the immediate advantage of their northern neighbors."[21]

There was no denying that substitute products would cause some displacement during a sabbatical year. But one objective of the holiday was to force the South to diversify. Farmers could intensively cultivate soybean, peanut, and sunflower crops among others, holiday forces insisted, to secure the same revenues that cottonseed oil had formerly furnished, and these replacement crops would over the long haul establish a more varied and remunerative southern agriculture. Many industries already had commenced preparations to cushion the impact of a holiday by relying on indigenously grown cotton substitutes. "The largest independent fertilizer manufacturers and oil mill operators are favoring the 'no cotton plan,'" Leeman Anderson, the personal secretary of Governor Richard Russell, reported on prospects in Georgia. "The mill owners plan to continue operations using peanuts which produce practically the same oil as cottonseed. The oil can be used for shortening and cooking fats, and peanuts are easily grown in Georgia."[22]

Holiday forces further maintained that imports from foreign countries could be taken care of through a protective tariff. Ever since his election in 1926 as commissioner of agriculture for Georgia, Eugene Talmadge had spent considerable time speaking before various groups throughout the South and at hearings in Washington arguing that tariff barriers should be erected around edible oils, long staple cotton, jute, hides, pecans, spanish moss, and palm fiber. "Vegetable oils that are imported into this country are produced by naked peon labor where 10 cents a day is high wages," Talmadge wrote in Georgia's *Market Bulletin*. "If there is no protection given on the vegetable oil situation in this country it will lower the standard of living of our farmers in the South to the level of the peon laborer in the Orient." Talmadge insisted that American consumers had to be encouraged to buy domestically produced products and American markets protected from becoming a dumping ground for foreign countries. During a holiday year, Talmadge and others contended, the domestic market for cottonseed oil, peanut oil, soybean oil, hog lard, and dairy products could be safeguarded through a protective tariff.[23]

A second anxiety that surfaced in the mass meetings was the fear that foreign competitors might completely capture American overseas markets during a holiday year. Furthermore, if foreign countries did move into the void left by the withdrawal of American products, the United States would have difficulty in recapturing these markets. "I have listened to your plan to save the growers of the South from ruin. The plan sounds practical save for one loophole," a radio listener all the way from Evansville, Indiana, informed Long, "and this is that our Southern states cannot dominate the cotton markets of the world simply because there are too many other producers of this crop. Australia, India, with its teeming millions, Egypt and other large sections of Africa, the West Indies, northern and eastern sections of South America, Mexico and the rest of Central America, the Pacific Islands."[24] No one tried harder to scuttle the holiday by boring in on the implications of the plan for international commerce than the Federal Farm Board. Cotton representative Carl Williams told Long that he had discussed with Chairman Stone the issue of foreign competition and neither of them could see any way through it.[25]

The question of how foreign countries might react was indeed a key issue. During the 1920s, the British government boasted that it intended to spend $40 million developing cotton production in Uganda, Kenya, Nigeria, and other countries in Africa. Travelers to these nations brought back disheartening news. "Wherever I went in the British possessions, from Africa and India to Australia and the West Indies, I was impressed by the attention given to cotton raising, and by the tremendous expenditures undertaken in order to increase the output of British-grown cotton," an American businessman reported on his return from a world tour. "The principal idea of the British Empire that I have in mind is that it is simply infested with cotton plantations which are increasing in number and size every year."[26]

From these sensational reports it appeared that cotton production overseas was virtually unlimited. The truth of the matter, however, was that several obstacles to production existed in every foreign country, and Americans either failed to perceive these, refused to acknowledge them, or simply took them for granted. The British Cotton Growing Association established four requirements for the successful cultivation of cotton—suitable soil, sufficient rainfall, ample and cheap labor, and adequate transportation—and privately admitted that it would have to learn by trial and error the limitations of each foreign country. The fact was that nowhere—not in Africa, South America, or Australia—could the credit, labor, transportation, and cultivation requirements of cotton be provided as easily or quickly as some Americans feared.[27] "I am not going to agree, as the Farm Board seems to think probable, that Bolshevik Russia and other foreign countries can cut us out of the cotton business any more than they can whip us in a war on land or sea," a resident of Lancaster,

Copyright *Dallas Morning News*, 10 September 1931. Reprinted by permission.

Texas, observed. "I was taught in a country school at Bedford, Tarrant County, that the United States could wup any nation on earth, and I have patriotism enough left to still believe it."[28]

To allay American fears of foreign countries capitalizing on the situation, Long proposed that the federal government encourage major foreign producers of cotton, such as Egypt, India, Russia, and Brazil, also to adopt restrictive regulations. The model that Long recommended for use in reaching international agreement on cotton was the recently consummated Chadbourne sugar agreement.[29] Long considered the Chadbourne agreement eminently applicable to cotton because the United States' place in the world's production of cotton was the same as Cuba's in the production of sugar. The agreement contained, moreover, the four ingredients Long recognized as essential for international operation: control of production through export quotas, the segregation and orderly release of surplus stocks, government sanction, and supervision by a permanent international council comprising representatives from the producing nations.[30]

Quite significantly, foreign countries began contacting American diplomats about an international cotton conference and cooperation. The minister of foreign affairs for Egypt, for example, informed our ambassador that cotton-producing nations of the world should "join together with a view to examining the most appropriate means for the regulation of cotton cultivation." Deeply concerned over Egypt's heavy dependence on cotton and the financial repercussions for his country of the staple's decline, the minister of foreign affairs committed Egypt "to participate in any commission of inquiry or conference having in view the examination of the question of the production of cotton."[31] President Herbert Hoover was informed by the State Department of Egypt's willingness to "place itself at the disposal of the American government for the working out of details."[32] The press reported that Egypt had extended its offer to India, Mexico, the Soviet Union, Brazil, and Peru, and the overture was interpreted as a sign that the entire world was ready to tackle the evil of overproduction. Residents of the South asked their senators to encourage the president to negotiate treaties on cotton with foreign countries.[33]

The Possibility of Diversification

A third question, and one which elicited considerable debate, was whether the South could turn to alternative crops during a holiday year. Holiday forces insisted that drop-a-crop would remedy the age-old problem of one-crop agriculture in the South by forcing cotton farmers to plant other crops to sustain themselves during a one-year layoff. The cultivation of fruits, vegetables, livestock, poultry, and various other field crops and animals would have the beneficial effect of steering the South down the road of diversification. No one promoted agricultural diversification more aggressively and embraced the cotton holiday more enthusiastically than Commissioner Talmadge.

Elected to three consecutive terms as Georgia's commissioner of agriculture, Talmadge used the columns of the state's *Market Bulletin* to promote better farming and marketing practices. "We import into Georgia every year millions of dollars worth of hay, grits, corn meal, flour, corn, oats, rye, and barley. We also import into Georgia most of all our mixed feeds for mules, horses, cattle, and hogs. We even import into Georgia a mixed dog food," Talmadge complained. In his "Brother Farmer" editorials, Talmadge preached to farmers about raising stock for both beef and milk production; cultivating wheat, oats, and fall vegetables for market and home consumption; using terraces, improved ditches, and kudzu to stop erosion; and introducing Austrian and vetch peas and compost to increase fertility. He had his Bureau of Markets actively explore and extend markets for Georgia's agricultural products from Cuba to Canada. Talmadge traveled extensively across the Georgia countryside speaking to enthusiastic audiences about the cotton holiday.[34]

Detractors went after the diversification features of the holiday with a scatter gun. Enemies insisted farmers had neither the expertise nor the capital for switching over to other commodities. Critics charged the holiday was threatening to pull the linchpin out of the southern economy and the whole structure would come tumbling down. "This plan of growing no cotton next year is too serious to even consider," a planter and merchant in Wynne, Arkansas, nervously observed, "as cotton pays our taxes, builds our roads, pays our school expenses, buys our food, buys our clothes, builds our churches, pays the pastor, and pays our living expenses of every kind."[35]

Holiday forces countered that during a sabbatical year farmers would not be giving up agriculture altogether, only replacing cotton with other crops. The type of crops farmers would first turn to—potatoes, corn, greens, hogs, chickens—would initially require no more money, knowledge, or equipment than cotton planting and home gardening already required or county agricultural agents could provide.

Opponents of the holiday feared that the shift to other products by thousands of farmers would cause dislocations of overproduction in the new commodities. Farmers would be left once again with low prices and the headache of other surpluses to contend with. "I have just returned to my office after having made a hurried trip across Texas studying in pass-

Copyright *Dallas Morning News*, 27 October 1931. Reprinted by permission.

ing the agricultural situation that is now alarming so many," Dabney White, a farm writer operating out of Tyler, Texas, reported. "I find other staple crops are in a deplorable condition for we have just gone through gathering a tomato crop that did not pay for picking, an Irish potato crop that did not pay for digging, and a wheat crop that did not pay for thrashing, and a large sweet potato crop now facing us that will not pay for planting."[36]

Rapid diversification might prove as disastrous to the southern farmer as one-crop agriculture had been. Farmers would be getting into highly perishable crops that had to be either consumed or marketed right as they reached maturity. "No market is as sensitive to glutting as the truck market," an attorney from Texarkana, Arkansas, insisted. "I've paid freight charges on cabbages; plowed under radishes, beets, carrots, and turnips; hogged off the prettiest melon, spinach, and bean patches you ever saw; and have let spuds rot for fertilizer."[37]

Holiday forces pointed out that plans for meeting the production and marketing contingencies that a switch from cotton to other products would entail were already underway. A. D. Jones, head of the Georgia Bureau of Markets, planned a conference of commissioners of agriculture to prevent any state or product from glutting and interrupting markets. Jones felt states could be persuaded to grow during the sabbatical year only those products that were indigenously advantageous and induced to provide for the orderly exchange of those products. "If we can get neighboring states not to make inroads on our watermelon business, we can well afford to agree not to increase our strawberry crop, for instance, which might prove costly for Alabama, where they can raise strawberries much more cheaply than we can," Jones said by way of illustration. "On the other hand, we have dominated the markets in Kentucky, Maryland, and Virginia with our cowpeas, and demand is a long way from being saturated. If we can build up our cowpea acreage without other states too greatly increasing their acreage of this crop we can well afford to forego increasing crops now grown largely in other states."[38]

Adversaries of the holiday charged it was easy for Huey Long to promote drop-a-crop because Louisiana had a more varied economy than most southern states. This economic diversity would cushion the impact of the holiday and simplify the transition to other means of support. "Louisiana is not a typical cotton raising Southern state," a cotton farmer from Black Hawk, Mississippi, contended. "It has other staple crops such as rice, sugarcane, citrus fruits, as well as extensive fisheries. Hence Governor Long is not the man to lead in the distressing exigency which has arisen."[39]

While it was true that certain states had more diverse economies than

others, the Depression had inspired extensive live-at-home and diversification campaigns in every southern state. Federal, state, and voluntary
organizations had tried educating Southerners on how to grow and preserve their own food supplies instead of living out of tin cans and paper
sacks from the store until their money ran out. North Carolina was held
up as a noteworthy example. According to Governor Gardner's calcula-
tions, there were in North Carolina four bushels of sweet potatoes, three
bushels of Irish potatoes, and two bushels of wheat for every man,
woman, and child—not to mention "enough molasses to mop up the
depression."[40]

In withholding the participation of several states in South-wide holiday
action, various politicians claimed that cotton acreage had already been
cut back and comprehensive programs instituted to increase food and
feed crops and to can, dry, and otherwise preserve these items for home
consumption. What none of them expected was that the public would
interpret these developments as a sign of preparedness for weathering a
sabbatical year. "We have plenty of food and feed to feed every person and
all livestock until after the production of such crops would begin in
1932," Robert Beeland of Greenville, Mississippi, told Governor Miller.
"From our own experience I can give you hundreds of examples of health,
happiness, and prosperity accruing to farmers who have grown their food
and feed and made cotton a secondary and unimportant crop."[41]

Many landlords had in the past frowned upon home gardens and actively discouraged tenant plots. They felt gardens took land away from
cash crops and diverted time and energy away from the principal staple.
Landlords were also embittered by tenants who refused either to share
their produce or to reimburse them for the use of garden land. Years of
drought, crop failure, and hunger marches had the cumulative effect of
breaking down the hostility of landlords to gardens. "I used to grow only
cotton. I demanded that my tenants do likewise. Cotton brings ready
money. The return on a sole crop of cotton was so great it justified us in
buying our food and feed instead of growing it. But the drought taught me
a lesson," a planter from England, Arkansas, the scene of a hunger march
and riot in January 1931 explained. "This year I am planting alfalfa for
my livestock, clover for my hogs, and sorghum for my tenants. I've reduced my cotton to 60% of my crop."[42]

The national Red Cross was singled out for the commendable job it
had done in implementing a preparedness program among impoverished
southern households. The organization had distributed through local
chapters free garden seeds to enable rural families to raise home produce.
Red Cross representatives estimated garden seeds were distributed to over
thirty-three thousand families in Tennessee alone. The group followed up

the seed distribution with home canning demonstrations. Every family receiving seeds was requested to send a member to a canning demonstration for instruction on the proper way to prepare and preserve garden products. The two-day canning seminars were conducted by home and county demonstration agents. The Red Cross capped the whole program off by furnishing the needy with more than 1 million cans and jars. In Texas rural families put up an estimated 20 million cans of fruit and vegetables. As a result of Red Cross efforts the South was supposed to be ready and well fixed with food supplies in case of another drought, crop failure, or holiday.[43]

Sustaining Employment and Promoting Cotton Consumption

A fourth major objection to the holiday plan was that cotton prohibition would generate unemployment in cotton-dependent industries, thus complicating the crisis. Cotton-dependent industries would be forced to close, adding their unemployed to an already depressed labor market. "We have in large cities at present thousands and thousands of unemployed. If the Long plan is adopted by the cotton states, millions of people will be out of work next year," a cotton planter and landlord from Knox, Texas, warned. "This plan, if adopted, will cause a shut down of gins, oil mills, compresses, cotton mills, etc. The taxes, interest, and insurance will still have to be paid, the owners will be receiving no return on their investments."[44]

There obviously would be work cutbacks, layoffs, and stoppages during a sabbatical year. But holiday forces insisted that unemployment conditions would not be anywhere near as drastic and severe as critics feared. The United States would accumulate by the end of the year a carry-over projected at 8.7 million bales, and this could keep the many people engaged in transporting, storing, processing, and selling cotton busy during the holiday. "Every bale of this cotton will have to be hauled, handled, stored, sampled, taken out of storage again, put on cars for domestic mills, or put in shape for destinations beyond the sea," the *New Orleans Item* contended. "All this must go on just as it ordinarily goes on in a normal year." Those individuals unable to secure employment involving the carry-over would simply have to look for work related to the products farmers would produce in place of cotton.[45]

In the past the South had resorted to buy-a-bale campaigns to help cotton-related industries over rough periods. Americans in general and Southerners in particular were encouraged to purchase bales of cotton for reasons of patriotism, compassion, and self-interest, and the staple was either stored, destroyed, or sold at a less critical time later on. Bales of cotton were exhibited in storefront windows and on the front porches of houses, just as certificates of donation were displayed for other causes.[46]

To keep as many Southerners employed in as many cotton-related jobs as possible in the present crisis, several national corporations initiated campaigns of earmarking the receipts received from the sale of their products in the South expressly for the purchase of cotton. The William Wrigley Company and the Cudahy Meat Packing Company of Chicago led the way in setting aside revenue received from southern patrons for reinvestment in the agricultural labors of those very same customers.[47]

While there were substantial remnants of buy-a-bale thinking in the cotton crisis of 1931, the South looked beyond these stopgap and time-worn expedients to the possibility of actually expanding old outlets and developing new ones. Southerners felt more jobs and cotton-related income could be generated from the staple because cotton exhibited certain qualities conducive to widespread application. Besides the low price of the staple, cotton was noted for its strength, elasticity, and affinity for dyes. For many years cottonseed had been considered a worthless part of cotton. Thousands of tons had been allowed to rot annually. But the development of profitable food and feed products from the seed completely altered that picture. "What was done with cottonseed yesterday must be done with cotton today and tomorrow," the *Houston Chronicle* declared. "The challenge of declining markets must be met at home."[48]

At the center of the campaign for the increased consumption of cotton was the Association for the Increased Use of Cotton. From its Columbia, South Carolina, headquarters the association lobbied to make Americans cotton conscious. "Our idea is to keep hammering into the people the importance to the welfare of the South of the use of these products," an official informed Long. "We believe cotton to be our chief money crop, and that it is impossible to disassociate this section from it." The association encouraged Americans to demonstrate their cotton mindedness by pledging to use only 100 percent cotton bagging for wrapping cotton; buy food and feed marketed only in cotton containers; and wear from head to toe only clothing manufactured from cotton.[49] Suggestions poured in from around the country on thousands of potential applications of cotton. At mass meetings throughout the South cotton containers, clothing, and paper became rallying cries.[50]

State officials of agriculture distributed literature informing residents how they were squandering millions of dollars on competing products. "We have the amazing spectacle of cotton farmers buying feeds for their workstock packed in jute bags, and marketing cotton wrapped in jute bagging and cottonseed meal in jute bags. All these are normal and expected uses for cotton," the Mississippi Department of Agriculture stated, "but this foreign competition, a product of human labor little better than slavery, has usurped American markets to the extent of 1 million bales annually."[51]

Some of the largest corporations in America responded to appeals for a more intensive application of cotton by promising to increase the use of cotton in the manufacturing and packaging of their products. The association received pledges from such industrial giants as R. J. Reynolds Tobacco Company, Winston-Salem, North Carolina; Sears, Roebuck and Company, Chicago, Illinois; B. F. Goodrich Company, Akron, Ohio; General Cigar Company, New York, New York; Kellogg's, Battle Creek, Michigan; and International Harvester Company, Chicago, Illinois.[52] "Flour in any other sacks can hardly be found in Mississippi now. The same is true of salt, flour, and other feeds," the Delta Cottonseed Cooperative Marketing Association of Greenwood, Mississippi, reported. "The fertilizer companies are going to sell their fertilizer in cotton sacks and practically every oil mill in the state has bought a supply of cotton sacks for their meal. Our people have gone into the consumption program in earnest."[53]

The campaign to increase cotton consumption attracted some colorful promoters. Colonel William E. Talbot of the Southland Life Insurance Company launched a nationwide drive to popularize the cotton suit. Advertisements pictured Talbot dressed in a double-breasted suit and flanked by two lovely southern belles outfitted in cotton attire. "The majority of the northern people today are wearing suits of which the basic fabric is produced in foreign countries," Talbot informed the White House on stationery made of cotton. "If everyone in the United States would use cotton suits in the Summer time, it would solve this problem of the South." While consumption occupied an important place in the Hoover administration's conception of the cotton crisis, the president refused to in any way endorse any form of cotton on the grounds "he cannot discriminate against other textiles."[54]

Governor "Alfalfa Bill" Murray of Oklahoma helped set the pace for southern politicians by attiring himself in cotton clothes from head to toe and purchasing cotton suits for gifts. Among the pieces of cotton clothing that could be purchased from southern manufacturers was a one-cent cotton cloth handkerchief with the inscription "With Huey Long we take our stand, / We'll plant no cotton on our land."[55]

The South made various appeals to the federal government for assistance in increasing cotton consumption. Trade groups suggested that National Cotton Week be repeated. The Department of Agriculture, however, refused to participate. Having been severely chastised for recognizing the project before, the department insisted it was impossible for a government agency to endorse one product at the expense of another. "Unhappily, most agricultural products are possible substitutes for other agricultural products and other products can be substituted for them," Secretary of Agriculture Hyde pointed out. "In this Department we are not at liberty to foster any 'Eat More Meat' campaigns because it would unhappily mean 'Eat Less Bread.'"[56]

In another move to increase the consumption of cotton, Southerners asked the Treasury Department to print the nation's currency on an all-cotton paper stock. The Treasury Department declined, however, claiming cotton cloth did not have the durability of linen stock. The use of currency printed on cotton stock during World War I had shown that it stretched and tore too easily.[57]

Southerners next asked Washington about the possibility of using paper manufactured from cotton rather than wood cellulose throughout the vast federal bureaucracy. Senator Morris Sheppard of Texas pointed out to President Hoover that the cotton stationery he regularly used had the virtue of absorbing inks so well it eliminated the need for a blotter. Manufacturers of cotton paper insisted that letters written on it received closer attention. But federal officials maintained that cost and quality factors militated against widespread introduction of cotton stationery.[58]

Rebuffed on several fronts, the South once more turned inward. During the summer and fall of 1931, the governors of virtually every southern state were confronted with similar suggestions. Chief executives were urged to start a movement, which would be backed by newspapers, chambers of commerce, and other influential organizations, to use cotton letterheads to reduce the surplus, increase employment in allied manufacturing and printing industries, and conserve other precious natural resources.[59] "I live a long ways from the cotton fields, but . . . it seems to be generally conceded that finding new uses for cotton is one of the best ways to restore the price of cotton to a more reasonable figure," a resident of Waterford, New York, observed. "It seems to me that it should be used in the making of paper, thus saving our northern trees which take a lifetime to grow."[60]

Being a remarkably introspective politician, Long had thought about the possibility of increasing cotton consumption by manufacturing paper out of cotton rather than wood pulp before mass meetings began promoting the idea. "It takes one bale of cotton to make 35,000 letterheads," the Bridges and West Company, cotton merchants and buyers of Norwood, Louisiana, had informed the governor in June. "If every department of Louisiana . . . would use this kind of stationery . . . just think what it would do to help reduce the cotton surplus, which is depressing the market so at this time. What Louisiana could do could be done by all cotton growing states."[61] There was an excellent chance that private industry would also want to join in such a promotional effort. Some of the leading national distributors of office supplies contacted Long about purchasing paper from Louisiana sources.[62] Many business firms and individuals around the nation actually adopted cotton paper for their daily stationery.[63]

Since one bale of cotton produced thousands of sheets, the cotton crisis was not going to be stabilized even if every man, woman, and child in the South swore off wood pulp paper. But what better public relations could a southern state engage in for its beleaguered industry than to conduct official business on cotton stationery and encourage all residents to do the same? Cotton stationery could stand as a spiritual symbol for the whole crusade.

George W. P. Hunt, of Arizona, was one of the few governors to acquire a supply of cotton stationery for use in his executive office. In his correspondence with Arizona department heads and with officials in states far more dependent on cotton than Arizona would ever be, he highly recommended the stationery and strongly urged its adoption. "This would be helpful by increasing the use of cotton at a time when the industry is suffering from over-production and low prices," the Arizona governor said. Talmadge was another southern politician who ardently promoted cotton stationery. Across the bottom of the cotton paper used by the Georgia Department of Agriculture, Talmadge had printed in red letters the inscription "By the Use of Cotton Stationery We Are Helping the Southern Farmer."[64] Ironically, those politicians with the most at stake were the least receptive, and the vision of making cotton paper the official stationery of the South expired as so many other exciting dreams would in this year of the cotton crisis.

The Promise of Immediate Price Relief

Despite all of the potential difficulties surrounding the cotton holiday, Long's proposal did offer to thousands upon thousands of cotton producers in the South the possibility of immediate price relief. Supporters of cotton prohibition argued that once the industrial customers of cotton knew a sabbatical year was forthcoming, company buyers would have to purchase from the crop presently coming to market sufficient cotton to cover the estimated needs of both the rest of 1931 and all of 1932. There was no telling how high cotton prices would go. Holiday forces confidently predicted cotton prices would at least double and, thereby, enable the producers to earn enough in 1931 to cover the holiday year of 1932 as well.

"If a cotton holiday is declared by law all over the South and no cotton planted in 1932, it will . . . make competition keen among the spinners for the purchase of cotton and in all probability the price of cotton will go to 25 or 30 cents in 1932," a native of Tyler, Texas, pointed out to Governor Ross S. Sterling. "The spinners and speculators realizing this, will immediately start buying the 1931 crop and in all probability will run the price of 6 cents up to 12 or 13 cents. This will enable the farmer to sell half of this year's crop for at least what the entire crop would bring at present prices." And as a cotton-buying firm from Taylorsville, Mississippi, predicted, "The very minute that every cotton state in the Union adopts this plan, you will see spinners buy up as much as they can use. You will also see the merchant fill his shelves with goods. You will see the price go from 6¢ to 12 or 15¢ right now."[65]

By selling cotton at a higher price in 1931, and by planting lands to other agricultural crops in 1932 for both home consumption and sale, large numbers of farmers believed that they could not simply weather a sabbatical year but actually improve the agricultural situation for years to come. "I am a farmer and have about 3,000 acres of land leased for farming purposes. On this farm, I have about 340 negroes. At the present price of cotton and seed my negroes cannot pay their debts, not to mention the purchasing of clothes which they are badly in need of. If your plan goes through, as I sincerely hope it does, it will mean a better price for this year's crops," a resident of Winnsboro, Louisiana, wrote. "If this place is stopped by law from raising cotton next year, every family on it will live better than they have before. All of them have hogs and cows and chickens. They can raise an acre of irish potatoes and five acres of sweet potatoes and five acres of peas and as much pumpkins and squash and other vegetables as they can put away."[66]

Holiday forces readily admitted that a sabbatical year was a speculative proposition and would require personal sacrifice. Holiday supporters asked the South to take the calculated gamble and accept the restraint necessary for benefits later on. Some New Orleans cotton merchants came up with the slogan "One Year of Sacrifice for a Lifetime of Plenty." "In our judgment it seems far better to sacrifice one little short year so that we and our children will live the balance of our lives in wealth and comfort, rather than to live the rest of our lives in poverty and want, if we do not sacrifice one little short year."[67]

Whether the South would make the sacrifice that the holiday called for depended on Texas. Mass meetings had taken the holiday as far as it could go without a definite decision by the South's leading producer. From Fort Valley, Georgia, Long received a letter which touched the heart of the matter. "Our governor, in Atlanta, is waiting for Texas to move," this grower of Georgia peaches wrote, "and what I am afraid of is that Texas is waiting for Georgia to move in the direction of which your state has so nobly advanced the cause of the cotton farmers."[68] Yet before Texas could provide an answer, there were serious labor problems in the fields that demanded immediate attention. As the holiday had moved across the South toward a legislative resolution, so the cotton crop had advanced to harvesting and marketing. While cotton farmers had been protesting against planting cotton next year, field hands were refusing to pick cotton right now.

5   Labor Unrest in the Fields

 Cotton was one of the most labor-intensive crops in American agriculture. Large amounts of manual labor were required to hoe, chop, thin, and pick the crop. In the period 1927–31, it took an average of 85 hours of labor to raise just one acre of cotton. By comparison corn required only 13.3 hours per acre and wheat 8.6 hours. The planting of 41,031,000 acres of land to cotton called for the awesome outlay of 3.493 billion man-hours of labor.[1]

Landowners in the South relied on the tenantry system to secure the field hands necessary for meeting cotton's labor requirements. At the top of the tenantry ladder was the cash renter, who paid the landlord a fixed rate in exchange for land, a house, and fuel and kept whatever he produced. A few rungs lower in status was the share renter, who furnished as much of his own labor, machinery, and other necessities as he had been able to acquire in life and paid a percentage of his crop to the landlord for whatever else he used. At the bottom was the sharecropper, who had only the sweat of his brow to offer and paid dearly for everything the landlord provided.[2] According to the census, of the 1,640,025 cotton farms in the United States in 1930, 27.3 percent were owner operated and 72.7 percent came under some form of tenantry. Nearly three-quarters of the cotton farms were operated under some form of contract labor.[3]

While landowners, managers, and tenants carried out the day-to-day operations of cotton farming, wage labor was the critical element in determining whether a crop would be planted on time, harvested in good condition, and marketed at the best possible price. During the rush periods of planting, cultivating, and picking, the tenantry system proved inadequate to meet the daily workload. Planters were forced to hire wage laborers to assist in farm maintenance and field production chores. Since weather, insects, and disease could dramatically affect the total production and value of the crop, it was essential that a large supply of wage labor be available when needed.

At the end of each crop year planters calculated their labor needs for the next season, retaining only as many tenants as they deemed necessary to carry out projected operations. By downgrading croppers into the wage labor category, planters avoided the heavy annual advances and indebtedness of tenantry, yet kept a floating supply of labor nearby. At peak labor periods growers recruited wage hands from rural families who had lost their tenant status, from casual workers in nearby towns and villages, and from the younger generation of southern labor. Schools even closed during cotton's most demanding times so that every man, woman, and child could be on call. Pinched between the stratified tenantry system on the one hand and the temperamental cotton market on the other, planters saw wage labor as an elastic element which could be adjusted as the situation warranted.[4]

Hired in response to the immediate demands of the grower, wage laborers suffered the harsh fate of being employed for only a week, month, or season. Moreover, wage hands received few of the farm perquisites and privileges normally granted even the lowest tenant. A comparative study of sharecropper and wage labor in Laurens and Florence counties, South Carolina, found that the average sharecropper family worked 707.8 days a year to earn a net income of $412.29, while the average wage-laboring family worked a total of 446.0 days for $256.55. In addition, the average sharecropper family received home use goods and other perquisites valued at 2½ times that provided wage labor, some $240.48 compared to only $92.39 for the wage family.[5]

In his classic study of the agricultural systems of two Georgia counties, Arthur F. Raper touched upon the crucial role played by wage labor. "It is a tradition in Black Belt counties that all Negro workers, including the casual laborers about the towns, be subject to the call of the cotton fields at chopping time and at picking time. Sometimes they voluntarily go out to help relatives who live on owned or rented farms, while at other times there is an element of coercion in it, as when federal relief is discontinued in order to assure plenty of cotton pickers, or when police on Saturday night release the participants of a 'crap game' on the promise that everyone of them will find work in the cotton fields on Monday morning."[6]

No Welfare and Charity for Unemployed Cotton Pickers

Public officials in the South looked forward to the 1931 harvesting season for the possibilities it afforded in reducing unemployment. Knowledgeable observers of the southern agricultural scene estimated that cotton farmers would hire over one hundred thousand unskilled laborers in south Texas alone to harvest the crop, and the wages paid there would amount over the picking season to more than $8 million for the workers.[7] Southern authorities figured that after having spent a winter wandering from one charity agency to another in search of food, clothing, and shelter, many laborers would be anxious to get off welfare rolls and back into the work force. "We may let the needy of Houston earn their living this Winter," the chairman of the Houston Unemployment Committee announced. "There is a lot of work to do for 25 or 30¢ an hour. They could work in the parks, beautify the bayou banks, eliminate eyesores. The unemployed then would feel that they were not on charity—that they were earning what they got."[8]

For picking the 1931 crop cotton farmers offered field hands from 35 to 50 cents per hundred pounds of cotton, a wage that varied according to geographical location, condition of the crop, and time of harvesting. In some of the more depleted areas of the South, the wage scale reportedly bottomed as low as 25 cents per hundredweight. Compared to the 75 cents received the previous year, and the $2.50 to $3.00 received a decade earlier, the 1931 wage scale represented a drastic decline in an already niggardly low standard of living.[9] "Why Mr. Governor, it would pay you to visit some cotton field in this terrible heat," a laborer from Hartman, Arkansas, wrote, "where the whole family is forced out to pick cotton at 35¢ and 40¢ per hundred pounds, even the mother has to go along so the family can live, and get over-hot and ill in bed the next day with a child."[10]

Cotton growers justified the lower picking rates on several grounds. Many plantation operators argued that the Depression had reduced the standard of living. If workers were receiving less money than the previous year, planters reasoned, they should also be spending less for food, clothing, shelter, and other necessities. Growers further considered the predictions of an unusually large crop and the promise of neat and abundant bolls to be to the workers' advantage. Pickers should be able to make up in weight for what had been lost in rate.[11] Finally, planters were quick to underscore the many so-called free services provided. "We don't consider that the cotton pickers have any grievance," one planter offered. "They are provided free transportation to and from their work. They are provided sacks, the work's easy, and the cotton is especially fine and easy to pick."[12]

Of course, pickers did not accept the story of the golden harvest filling their pockets with money. They knew from years of experience in the sweltering heat of the fields how much cotton they could expect to pick in a given area. "The average cotton picker won't get over a hundred pounds a day this year. This will not feed us, so we are appealing to you to see what we will do, for clothes and food," a dissenting voice from Lepanto, Arkansas, protested to Governor Harvey Parnell. "Please investigate the condition of the laborer and sharecropper. If you want further proof of this we can send you names of hundreds of men who are in this condition."[13]

The tightening of economic controls precipitated considerable labor agitation in scattered sections of Texas, Arkansas, Tennessee, Mississippi, and Georgia. On a plantation near Charleston, Mississippi, a Negro who physically prevented others from picking cotton was shot and killed. The triggerman was subsequently acquitted when the court held he fired in self-defense after the Negro drew a gun.[14] Rumors circulated in Texas that the state government had ordered all cotton fields shut down until the staple's price increased. Believing martial law had actually been declared in the cotton fields, Negroes refused to work in several localities.[15] Near Temple, Texas, some disgruntled Mexicans were being taken back to town when a disturbance broke out among them and a cotton picker in a nearby field was killed. The truck driver claimed he had tried to quell the argument by firing random shots into the field and accidentally killed the worker.[16]

The most vigorous labor agitation took place among the disgruntled in Arkansas. On hot September evenings, night riders commenced campaigns of terror in several scattered counties. "Now we are just straight and plain. If you be caught picking cotton for 35¢ you will be sorry. You chopped cotton for nothing, but you can't pick for nothing," a menacing warning posted throughout Pulaski County read. "If you want to die just go out in these fields and you surely will die. If the Lord tells you to pick you can do so, but we will stop you with a shotgun." Investigations into the night-riding activities revealed that additional grapevine warnings of arson and murder had been circulating.[17]

Most of the night-riding activity was simply the spontaneous response of a people ground between the upper millstone of the national depression and the nether millstone of the deteriorating conditions of the cotton industry. Their demand for a living wage was couched in the form of a simple threat: "No cotton picking for 35¢. There's hell at the end, boys."[18] Some of the night riding was perpetrated by adherents of the cotton holiday movement who hoped to use intimidation to force reluctant elements in the cotton industry into subscribing to the Long Plan. Night riders who asked through typewritten notes for the closing of gins in the Georgia counties of Jenkins, Burke, and Screven also professed a desire for the Long prohibition proposal. "We, the farmers of Jenkins, ask close down your gins. We pray God you will cooperate and help save women and children from hunger and cold until something is done to lift the present depression. We are in favor of Governor Long's proposition," the placard concluded.[19]

Night Riders and Communist Agitators

The appearance of warnings threatening arson and murder generated an atmosphere of fear and suspicion and immediately paralyzed the harvesting of cotton in the areas plagued by night riders. In township after township, workers congregated around local dispatching points refusing to be transported into the fields, pickers already in the fields stopped working, and gins closed down.[20] Growers discounted the mounting fears exhibited by Negro pickers as more a matter of pretense than actual alarm. "Most of them love excitement, perhaps this gives them a sense of importance and maybe they hope that this agitation will get them a better price," one planter remarked.[21]

But to those Negroes who had witnessed the outrages of the Ku Klux Klan during the twenties or whose families had experienced the wrath of either Whitecapping activities during the Populist protest or the Klan actions during the Reconstruction eras, the thought of another revival of vigilante activity was a very persuasive deterrent to entering the fields. Visions of retribution played on the minds of pickers. "I have 2,000 acres of cotton ready to be picked down there, and can't get any Negroes because they are afraid of the night riders," a planter from Dahomy, Mississippi, explained to the police chief of Memphis during a trip designed to hire one hundred wage laborers for back home.[22]

The disruption of cotton picking at such a crucial time in a particularly critical year aroused southern authorities to move toward determining who was responsible for the agitation, taking remedial and punitive action against the perpetrators, and getting the harvesting promptly back into high gear. Since much of the unrest occurred in scattered sections of Arkansas, officials of the Razorback State naturally took the lead in ascertaining the causes and providing other southern states with a punitive model to follow.[23]

On the basis of some personal inquiries conducted by public officials and private citizens, Arkansas authorities immediately ascribed the fomenting of labor unrest to Communists. When cotton growers were unable to secure workers at the prevailing 35-cent wage, individual operators pursued personal probes into the warnings. Frightened workers in North Little Rock reported that they had been threatened by a person who traveled around the city warning, "Any man who would offer 35¢ to pick cotton should be shot, and any man who picks cotton for 35¢ will be shot." From information provided by other Negroes in Pulaski County that they had been threatened with death by men in uniform, growers concluded the agitators were Communist agents in disguise.[24]

Further investigation by law enforcement officials turned up several pieces of revolutionary literature in the fields. The subversive tracts included "The Southern Cotton Mills and Labor," "The Youth and Russian Revolution," "Lenin, Liebknecht, and Luxemburg," "Story of the Appeal," and "War in the Far East." Arkansas officials dramatically speculated that the quantity of literature confiscated would make up a veritable library on subversion and conspiracy.[25]

The appearance of such menacing literature affirmed in official minds that professional radicals and outside agitators lurked behind the scenes ever ready to foment disorder. Soon wire services informed people across the South about the perilous danger the Razorbacks were valiantly grappling with through dispatches headlining: "Arkansas Irate As Communists Turn to 'Night-Rider' Tactics."[26] Other southern states quickly picked up on the theme. Negroes were cautioned to guard against cagey Communist agitators whose offerings of friendship and support in the present crisis were only a pretense for exploitation later on.[27]

Newspaper editors promptly invoked the authority of their self-appointed positions as the unofficial watchdogs of southern society to caution disgruntled laborers against becoming too surly about their plight. Radicals were warned about the severe consequences their appearance might evoke. "We can sympathize with the Negroes," the *Daily Clarion-Ledger* of Jackson, Mississippi, editorially declared, "but any agitator, white or black, who tries to make capital of this condition, to promote unrest and racial strife, should be promptly handled, legally but firmly, by county and state authorities."[28]

Confronted by the possibility of financial disaster if the crop were left in the fields, growers joined together in a vigilante committee to protect their interests. At a mass meeting held in Little Rock, farmers outlined their problems and courses of action. "The sharecropper, the tenant farmer, and the landowner have obligated themselves for more than this crop will bring at present prices. In other words, they owe more than they will be able to realize from this crop, so the only one who will receive any cash income from the crop will be the pickers," the preamble of the growers' resolution read. "We are informed that certain vicious persons are going about the country spreading Communist propaganda and advising and threatening against picking cotton. If this crop is not picked it means financial disaster to the community. Not alone does it threaten the farmers, but men in all walks of life."

Under these circumstances city and county law enforcement agencies were requested to be diligent not merely in protecting the growers and their employees but "in arresting vagrants, persons who deliberately refuse to work, and persons who interfere with or encourage others not to work." To assist local authorities in discouraging the activity known as

night riding, the meeting offered a hundred-dollar reward to anyone providing information leading to the arrest and conviction of any person
posting notices or in any way engaging in acts of intimidation. To assure
the successful protection of people and property, the meeting further re-
solved "that all farmers and their employees constitute themselves a vigi-
lance committee to take whatever action is necessary to protect their laborers, tenants, or employees who desire to work."[29]

Arkansas officials responded to the mandate accorded them by vigorously cracking down on anyone even remotely resembling an agitator.
Authorities moved quickly to arrest one laborer living near England for
failing to terminate previous radical activities. The worker had been arrested one year earlier on charges of encouraging cotton choppers to
strike for one dollar a day. In the present crisis Arkansas authorities decided to revoke the suspension of his nine-month sentence and three-
hundred-dollar fine. Officials also arrested a Negro deputy constable at
Wrightsville for inciting Negroes by reading and commenting on newspaper articles to them. In addition to incarcerating alleged radicals, law enforcement officials increased their patrols of stricken areas, offered rewards for information and arrests, and backed up planters standing shotgun in the fields over their workers.[30]

While public officials ascribed the labor unrest to such nebulous
sources as outside agitators and professional radicals, the investigation
of some sharecroppers arrested in the Pine Bluff area for alleged night-
riding activities indicated that the conflicts between wage hands and
planters were of a much more indigenous and spontaneous origin. Police
questioning of the sharecroppers revealed that, following a discussion of
the picking rate among the cotton workers, a group of about twenty
simply pledged among themselves not to accept less than 50 cents per
hundredweight. No attempt was made by the disgruntled laborers to in-
timidate others into joining this rebellion.[31]

Demands for Pickers Outdistance Supply

The harsh measures and swift action taken by planters and police to ex-
punge radicals and eradicate protest effectively dispelled the paralysis
of cotton picking within days of the initial night-riding outbursts and
promptly returned many workers to the fields. Even though southern
officials had stifled what might have turned into a major rebellion in the
cotton belt, growers were still unable to secure adequate supplies of workers. Growers experienced difficulty in recruiting the necessary field hands
not only because favorable weather had produced the largest crop in cot-

ton history but also because the maturation of cotton bolls in several communities simultaneously easily outstripped local labor supplies.[32]

The requests for additional pickers emanating from labor offices in the capitals of such cotton-producing states as Texas and Mississippi are illustrative of the overall problem. During the third week of August the Austin labor office reported a demand for 800 to 1,000 additional pickers. Out of 124 laborers interviewed in a single day, only 18 were willing to make the trek into the fields.[33] Likewise, an appeal by the Employment Bureau at Jackson during the first week of September in response to the calls of planters along the Yazoo-Mississippi delta for additional pickers turned up only 3 transient Negroes willing to be transported to cotton fields.[34]

As days passed into weeks, demands for pickers became more pronounced and urgent. By the first week of October the labor office at Jackson was asking Memphis labor officials for assistance in fulfilling a statewide demand that had swelled to 10,000 pickers. Situated in the southwestern corner of the Volunteer State, Memphis had traditionally been called upon to provide labor to the tri-state agricultural area of Tennessee, Arkansas, and Mississippi. "I can't supply them," the manager of the Memphis bureau replied. "Right now I have demands for 800 to 1,000 pickers. I haven't that many applicants."[35]

At the height of the harvesting season some 3,000 to 3,500 Negro wage hands were transported in and out of Memphis daily. Beginning at 3 A.M. every morning, trucks lined up along West Virginia Avenue and Arkansas Street on the Tennessee side of the Harahan Bridge. In the several hours before dawn, field bosses shouted out their propositions. "Come on, you neg-r-o-e-s, this truck am leaving for the cotton fields, 50¢ a hundred pounds and back home by dark." "Let's go to Bruins, let's go to Whitehall, boys—a sack of greens free to every picker." Even with the added inducements, however, planters experienced difficulty in securing full picking crews. "They forced us to pay 50¢ to get our cotton out of the fields," one planter complained. "Last week when we offered 35¢ some of the Negroes would yell out, 'Don't go, wait until they pay 50¢,' and most of them waited."[36]

With the demand for pickers outdistancing the local supply of wage laborers, cotton farmers appealed to the United States Employment Service in Washington for the assistance of specialists in rural employment. They were obliged to seek assistance from the federal government because the private employment agencies that specialized in placing farm labor had virtually gone out of existence. The secretary of the Federal Farm Labor Service reported that in the state of Texas alone the number of agencies specializing in farm labor declined from 217 in 1930 to only 11 by the summer of 1931.[37] The Farm Labor Division responded to the appeals of state directors of employment by sending federal agents trained in recruiting and distributing labor into the troubled delta areas.

Specialists from the federal Employment Service opened labor offices in the principal cities of the cotton-growing states. Field hands recruited at one point were transported by truck into labor-short areas both nearby and in distant parts of the state. The desperate nature of the search for pickers was underscored by appeals placed in newspapers which carefully mentioned that "families of all nationalities are wanted." Agents concluded their recruiting efforts by calling for truckers to transport laborers into the fields at two dollars per head. Southern railroads assisted in the drive by offering groups of twenty-five or more cotton pickers special transportation rates. By the middle of September, the Federal Farm Labor Service reportedly had placed more than two hundred thousand cotton pickers.[38]

The practice of trucking workers out of the cities into the fields and cotton out of the fields into the gins was a very simple, yet highly dangerous, system of operation. The state of Texas alone tabulated 135 deaths caused by cotton trucks during just one thirty-day period of the harvesting season. The fatalities occurred in a variety of circumstances: reckless driving, inferior equipment, poorly maintained roads, overcrowded passenger boxes, and overloaded trucks.[39] To the discouraging conditions already presented by low wages, cotton workers had to add the possibility of being hurt, maimed, or even killed by cotton trucks. Reports of accidents, like the one in Marion, Arkansas, confirmed their worst fears and deterred workers from risking life and limb in the fields.

In the Marion disaster fifty-three cotton pickers were being transported from Kirkville and Marietta, Mississippi, across the Magnolia State to Lepanto, Arkansas. Shortly after crossing into Arkansas, the twenty-six-foot trailer broke loose from the cab and rolled over a six-foot embankment, killing six people and injuring thirty-three others. "We were crowded in the truck like hogs," a twenty-five-year-old survivor explained. "The bedding, stoves, and furniture were packed on the floor, and 53 of us were crowded on top," he continued, as he stood guard over the household effects of friends. "We had been on the road since 4 P.M. Wednesday, having made only 180 miles—this was on account of bad roads and detours. Even the women were unable to sleep, due to the crowded conditions and the roughness of the roads." When community memorial services for the victims were announced, laborers flocked into Memphis from miles around the tri-state area. So poor were the pickers that the funerals had to be postponed in order to enable families to raise money to cover the barest burial expenses.[40]

The Danger of High-Hatting

To recruit sufficient workers to harvest the cotton, growers were forced to go beyond their traditional labor force of tenants and seasonal contract workers and to appeal to transient labor for assistance. Planters perceived the thousands of unemployed people milling around towns throughout the cotton belt as a wellspring of untapped farm labor. As long as demands for pickers persisted, communities felt there was no excuse for any able-bodied person to be unemployed. Any person turning a deaf ear on the help-wanted pleas of growers was accused of "high-hatting." "A dollar and a half a day. Not a princely sum, but it seems some unemployed worker can at least be self-supporting," the *American-Statesman* of Austin, Texas, caustically commented. "'Unemployment?' There wouldn't be any if Austin unemployed were willing to go to work in the cotton fields."[41]

The unemployed, however, stubbornly refused to cooperate. Even after planters offered to increase the wage scale, idle laborers remained adamantly opposed to work in the fields. "We have assembled the Houston Negroes in bunches and begged them to come and pick cotton for 40 and 50¢ a 100, but they all refuse," a planter dejectedly complained to the chamber of commerce. "When we point out to them that it is better to pick cotton for this amount than to starve they tell us the City of Houston won't let them starve, that the city will always take care of them."[42]

Having suffered through the devastating hardships caused by the flood of 1927 and drought of 1930, hard-pressed communities were highly intolerant toward anyone who used low wages as an excuse to refuse to go into the fields. In an official proclamation, Governor Parnell informed the unemployed of Arkansas that the state would not condone their refusal to work while the harvest was ready and further delays might mean deterioration or the loss of the crop if unfavorable weather set in. "There are those who do not care and are loitering, idle, hoping that they will be supported," Parnell declared. "I am appealing to the officials of the various communities to make a complete survey, ascertain the names of those who are and should be in the fields, and to organize and make it possible for the unemployed at this time to be busily engaged. . . . There should be no idlers, loiterers in the towns."[43]

Agreeing wholeheartedly with this sentiment, public charity agencies attempted to induce unemployed people to work by threatening to withhold food, clothing, and other assistance during the hard months of winter. In community after community the word went out that social service aid would be cut off to anyone refusing the opportunity to work in the cotton fields. "No organization connected with the Community Chest will feed any able-bodied men who are capable of picking cotton," the Federation of Community Work of Shreveport, Louisiana, announced. "Families seeking food and shelter this Winter from the Community Chest will be thoroughly investigated. Those who refuse work will not be extended help. Our records show that 98% of beggars in the street and at private homes are transients. We must cooperate in driving outsiders out of Shreveport."[44]

To reinforce and supplement the appeals made by charitable agencies and philanthropic organizations, communities enlisted the support of the clergy. Speaking on behalf of the Houston Unemployment Relief Committee, the general manager of the Houston Chamber of Commerce told Negro ministers: "There is an immediate demand for not less than 7,000 cotton pickers, and the unemployed Negroes of the city should accept that work." Negro ministers subsequently amplified the message from the pulpit and through literature distributed at the churches. "We're telling them that they can't expect any help from the white folks unless they are first willing to help themselves," the head of the Negro Baptist Ministers Association of Houston explained. "We're urging them to go out and pick cotton wherever they can." Negro ministers went beyond the confines of their pastorates to speak at various points around the city and to preach in other cities and crossroad towns as well.[45]

Forced Labor Practices

The attempts at cowing the unemployed and cajoling them into the fields initially failed. For some time, rather than accept the same menial wages that had been offered to their forebears and relatives, blacks had been migrating within the South from rural areas into the nearest city and from the region into the border states and beyond. "Thousands have tramped or hitch-hiked their way from one big city to another in the South and have failed to read or heed the signs by the roadside, 'Cotton Pickers Wanted,'" T. E. Sharp, editor of the *Memphis Press-Scimitar*, complained. "If one drives to St. Louis he will pass scores of people going toward St. Louis 'looking for work'; he will meet scores of people coming toward Memphis 'looking for work,'" Sharp stated on another occasion. "And the work-hunters, whether bound for St. Louis or for Memphis, are passing field after field of cotton, paying no attention to the signs, 'Cotton Pickers Wanted.'"[46]

The desire of idlers to remain out of work rather than accept employment beneath their dignity so infuriated cotton growers that they issued the unemployed an ultimatum—either join the harvest or go to jail on vagrancy charges. In the past both public and private employers had responded to threats posed by various natural disasters with forced labor. In the West the lumber barons conscripted men to fight forest fires; in the South such "acts of God" as floods and hurricanes afforded various interests opportunities for forcing labor to build levees, clear fields, salvage crops, restore city streets, and perform other emergency work.[47]

The use of vagrancy as a pretext for jailing people and then assigning them to work details was a long-standing practice in America. In the South, however, the variety of the laws to force people to work was greater than that of any other region. The black codes that southern legislatures enacted in the aftermath of the Civil War provided the model. Now once again Southerners exhibited a special genius for adding new wrinkles to old unconstitutional procedures.[48]

Heeding the requests of growers, local agencies went out arresting as vagrants people who could not prove gainful employment. "There is too much cotton to be picked and too many Negroes hanging around doing nothing. We've had pleas for pickers from farmers," a member of the Shreveport police department explained. "We get several requests daily for cotton pickers, but are unable to furnish them help. To our knowledge there are dozens of Negroes who loaf about and will not work, but are depending on charitable organizations for help. We are going to ask these organizations to turn them over to us and we will see that they get employment in the cotton fields."[49]

Contributing to the climate that made this hard-line position against the unemployed acceptable, mayors and police chiefs reported that most of the difficulties encountered among the unemployed were caused by transients. "Evidently there is something radically wrong about the unemployment situation for at least the colored people when the Federal Employment Bureau can use at least several thousand of them, and when you take into consideration that we have a great many vagrants in the city, it is evident that they do not want to work," Walter A. Scott, mayor of Jackson, Mississippi, observed. "You are hereby directed to begin at once a drive on all vagrants in the city and see that they either go to work or leave the city."[50]

Of course, no one—not the planters, the police, or the mayors—ever tried to define the categories of transient and vagrant with any degree of precision and care. These classifications were deliberately kept vague so that everyone from local unemployed residents to drifters and casual laborers from other areas would be liable to impressment. This way local authorities could provide whatever the situation demanded. Today it was the cotton planters who needed help; tomorrow it could be sugar, rice, lumber, or some other southern commodity in dire straits.[51]

When the Business Men's Association of Caruthersville, Missouri, circulated a citation among the unemployed signed by the city attorney, chief of police, sheriff, and constable warning that those refusing work would be treated as vagrants, the following day more than four hundred persons were scared into the cotton fields.[52] Support for this reactionary action could be found among many organizations, like the Young Business Men's Association of Little Rock, which actually passed resolutions requesting city and county authorities to prevent transient unemployed from remaining in the town.[53]

Clarksdale, Mississippi, offers an outstanding example of how public officials went about implementing demands for forced labor. On the basis of complaints from planters in Coahoma County regarding their inability to secure a sufficient number of pickers, Mayor L. A. Ross and Police Chief L. N. Knight told idle laborers in Clarksdale either to pick cotton or to go to jail on vagrancy charges. Unemployed persons were subsequently warned that no able-bodied individual would escape a contemplated dragnet. Within three days Clarksdale officials had rounded up more than fifty blacks for the hard-pressed cotton growers.[54]

As other communities in the cotton states issued their edicts of "go to work or go to jail," laborers attempted to escape by fleeing to other counties and states. Frequently they were met by guards posted at local and state boundaries and forced back, or they experienced even stiffer fines and sentences to labor in the fields in the places they eventually reached. Newspapers waged campaigns to caution unemployed workers against moving from one area to another and pointing out the dire consequences and penalties others had already suffered. One could avoid being forced into the cotton fields in one locality only to be impressed for other menial work elsewhere—maintaining city streets on a chain gang in Abilene, hammering a rock pile in Texarkana, or toiling in rice fields around Devalles Bluffs.[55]

Labor Dragnets

Once southern communities had squeezed as many field hands as possible from the ranks of the unemployed on city streets, officials descended with considerable force on railroad yards to apprehend other transient laborers. In the rural South, with the incomplete highway networks of most states, it was extremely difficult for the destitute to hitchhike through the region, and unemployed persons often hitched rides on freight trains. The Missouri Pacific Railroad recorded 23,892 trespassers in 1930. By 1931 the volume of trespassers had jumped astronomically to 186,028.[56] As the Great Depression spread and intensified, it became common practice in the South to "strip" trains of transients. For picking coal along the railroad right-of-way, crossing railroad property, hitching a ride on a freight train, or committing one of a number of other infractions, individuals risked being classified as transients, convicted of trespassing, and farmed out to planters and private contractors to work on roads and in mines and cotton fields.[57]

The severe economic dislocation following the stock market crash forced thousands out of jobs and homes and onto the road in search of daily sustenance. Although thrust into a condition of transiency, these people were not, as future New Deal administrator Harry L. Hopkins carefully pointed out, bums, hoboes, or professional migratory workers. They were people from many different racial, regional, and occupational backgrounds who were forced by necessity to leave their settled lives and seek employment elsewhere.[58] By playing on the negative images of the hobo, gypsy, and fugitive from justice, however, southern officials made transients out to be vagrants and marshaled support for repressive policies.[59]

Among the transients providing a heartrending description of those hard times was the dynamic Maury Maverick. Destined to become in the Depression decade an outstanding congressman from the Twentieth Texas District, Maverick decided to "scrape around on the bottom and find out if the people really had any idea of 'revolution,' or just disorder, or change." Maverick assumed the role of a transient, eating, sleeping, and riding the "rods" with poverty-stricken people across the South. In Dallas and Fort Worth, this free southern spirit observed the wanderings of as many as two thousand transients a day; New Orleans and Oklahoma City he believed experienced even greater numbers. "I found that a very large proportion of those riding the freight trains were tenant farmers, sharecroppers, and agricultural workers. The old-time tramp constituted a negligible portion, say ten or fifteen percent of the whole."

When southern authorities were not stripping trains to secure workers, they were dishing out other forms of hospitality. In many places the refuse was sprayed with noxious substances to prevent the hungry from seeking to use waste food to ward off starvation. Should these forlorn souls seek refuge in some mission, they might be preyed upon by racketeers operating under the guise of preachers or dehumanized still further by religious zealots demanding conversion. "Promiscuity, filth, and degradation," Maverick felt, characterized their existence. The effects were unmistakable. "Undernourishment and malnutrition suffered by the transient population, unemployed and their children, will be indicated in bad health, insanity, and tuberculosis, for generations. It will be like the aftermath of a war," a disbelieving Maverick observed. "The depression has marred the race."[60]

While most transients were critical of an economic system that permitted such want in the midst of plenty, many accepted such economic dislocations as a normal feature of the capitalist system. When Maverick established the cooperative Diga Colony on the edge of San Antonio to assist transients until government relief programs began, he learned of their basic faith in the capitalist system and simple desire for a chance to compete. "None had ever heard of socialism—except as some vague thing that was 'bad.' As for Communism, all they knew was that it was Russian, unpatriotic, and sinful. As for the word 'collectivism,' it was just a word that had gotten misplaced," Maverick observed. "In many contacts, I found that their idea of 'capitalism' was a state of society in which you can go hungry for a while, but you will finally get a good job, and possibly have others that can either go hungry or work for you." Despite widespread and deep-seated privations, most transients, in Maverick's experience, were neither proselytizing radicals nor incipient criminals.[61]

Periodically social comment would surface from influential tribunals indicating that a good many Southerners were troubled by the repressive and exploitive actions urban and rural communities had taken. When the city of San Antonio carried out a mass deportation of transients the *Houston Post-Dispatch* publicly confronted the issue. Admittedly, the huge crop had forced farmers in counties around San Antonio to grovel for help, and whenever possible laborers rubbed salt in the wounds by shunning the wages offered.[62] This did not justify, however, the city police lumping all the indigent together, escorting one hundred alleged vagrants to the city limits, and forcing them to move on. "It is fair enough for a city to discourage indigent tourists from coming in, but when they have entered, and they are not found to be criminals, they should not be driven out by force," the *Houston Post-Dispatch* reprimanded San Antonio. "If their only defense is involuntary idleness, they should be assisted in escaping from starvation or death from exposure. To drive homeless, hungry men out of an American city in times like these is to give the lie to our boasted regard for humanity."[63]

Agricultural Elites Remain in Control

The agricultural disruptions of the 1920s intensified the grievances of field hands against cotton planters. Although protests by field hands were more extensive and intensive in 1931 than ever before, local agricultural elites were able quickly to contain and extinguish rebellions. The hard line taken was hailed across the South. Commenting on Mississippi's sense of labor justice, the *Daily Clarion-Ledger* of Jackson observed: "If they were victims of any conspiracy to force them to work at inadequate pay, that the planters might profit excessively, they could reasonably refuse. But they are not and those who won't work are not entitled to sympathy or charity. Adherence to this decision by the charitable agencies, and enforcement of the vagrancy laws and statutes by municipal and county authorities, is timely, necessary, and just."[64] Southern ruling oligarchies cracked down harder during the crisis year of 1931 than ever before, and for a variety of reasons.

World War I had created a variety of employment opportunities in defense-related industries, and many workers had left the fields to take these steady jobs. When the boll weevil drove cotton production down with its destruction of crops during the 1920s, more field workers left the rural South for life in the cities and jobs in the North. These migrations seriously disrupted and depleted the agricultural work force of the South.[65] "When the boll weevil reached the Delta country of Louisiana and Mississippi the large planters simply lost their heads and permitted the negroes to scatter," J. B. Meriwether of the Riverview Plantation near Forkland, Alabama, observed. "For years in traveling through that section I noticed deserted plantations one after another. If they have ever gotten their plantations filled with labor again I doubt it." The only crop that Meriwether found he could ever raise to meet a note with was cotton. In a sabbatical year he visualized his two hundred Negroes scattering to the four winds and his lands becoming worthless without labor to work them. Throughout the South planters were determined to deny their workers a chance to migrate, out of fear that they would never be able again to recapture this work force.[66]

Planters were not only concerned about losing their labor to other occupations and regions but also fearful that the unemployed might turn on them. Landlords visualized their tenants and wage hands becoming marauding bands during any sabbatical year. "I grow around 100 bales of cotton and if it is outlawed then I am to become guardian of some 50 Negroes now living on my farm and care for them until some adjustment is made," a tax specialist and farmer from Trenton, South Carolina, protested. "From what I have lost as a consequence of the depression, I am not able to take care of all these negroes who know nothing but cotton. If turned loose they would run wild and crime will result."[67]

Southern agriculture had suffered severe economic losses in the cotton crisis of 1926, the great Mississippi River flood of 1927, and the drought of 1930. Planters felt that their field hands had been ungrateful for assistance accorded them in those troubled times. "We served you with our money and our brains and our strength and, for all we did, no one of us received a penny. We white people could have left you to shift for your-selves. Instead we stayed with you and worked for you, day and night," planter William Alexander Percy of Greenville, Mississippi, lectured a group of reluctant workers. "During all this time you Negroes did noth-ing, nothing for yourselves or for us." The refusal by field hands to work was seen as simply the most recent and most outrageous example of in-gratitude by truculent laborers.[68]

During the agricultural dislocations of the 1920s, the South had had to accept aid from the federal government, Red Cross, Salvation Army, and other charitable organizations. Many people felt that the unskilled agri-cultural workers had come to believe public and private agencies would support the able-bodied as well as the disabled in good times as well as bad. "Dissatisfaction with the picking price does not account for all the laggards. Arkansas had to accept Red Cross aid last Winter, but on part of the population it inevitably had a bad psychological effect," the *Arkansas Gazette* observed. "In the minds of a certain element, the assumption exists that 'the government' will feed rural Arkansas again next Winter. That being the case, why broil in the cotton field? That assumption needs immediate erasure." In forcing Negroes off social service rolls into the fields, southern officials saw an opportunity for not merely assisting the agricultural interests of the region but also blocking the intrusion of social welfare into their communities.[69]

Although agricultural labor appeared to have several forces working in its favor, revolt against the South's ruling oligarchies was virtually a hope-less situation. Politicians, civic organizations, newspaper editors, law en-forcement officials, and other elitist elements combined to force labor back into the fields on the planter's terms. Commenting on the possibility the disorganized and spontaneous protests of the cotton pickers had in overthrowing the "big mules," the Reverend Claude Williams perceptively observed: "They didn't have the chance of a one-legged man at an ass-kicking."[70] While the vested interests effectively suppressed the challenge of wage laborers to their authority, they still had the holiday to contend with.

Texas Abandons the South

The campaign to bring Texas into the holiday fold commenced concurrently with Long's bedside signing of the Louisiana measure into law on 29 August. Long instructed O. K. Allen, his handpicked candidate to be the next governor of Louisiana, to charter a plane and personally deliver a certified copy of the prohibition law to Governor Ross Sterling. Setting out for Texas during the early morning hours, Allen arrived in Austin around 10 A.M. that same hectic Saturday morning, only to be informed that Governor Sterling had departed the capital for a weekend in Houston. Not deterred by this apparent attempt at evasion, Allen took off again, this time in the company of J. E. McDonald, Texas commissioner of agriculture. Catching up with Governor Sterling at the airport in Houston, Allen handed him the law encased in a cotton wrapper. "Here is Governor Long's baby, all washed, powdered, and wrapped in a cotton dress," Allen reportedly said. "I'm instructed to lay it before you in person, and you'll hear it cry: 'Daddy, take me up.'"[1]

Right on the heels of the Allen trip, James Thompson printed and distributed to Texas and the rest of the South a special drop-a-crop edition of the *New Orleans Item-Tribune*. The Sunday morning edition detailed the day-by-day history of the holiday movement from its inception among cotton farmers in north Louisiana right up to the overnight delivery of the Louisiana law to the governor of Texas. The New Orleans publisher sent Sterling 150 complimentary copies of the paper for whatever distribution the governor felt would be most useful. "During all of my life in the South I have regretted the inability of this section to properly control cotton," Thompson disclosed. "I feel that out of this emergency, we may finally solve this problem and make cotton a blessing instead of something of a curse to the section in which you and I live, and in which both of us try to serve."[2]

The action of Louisiana in pursuing drop-a-crop to legislative fiat placed Sterling in an unenviable position. He had acted wisely in insisting that Louisiana be the first to make the holiday state law. But he had made a bad mistake in thinking either that Long could not put the holiday over in Louisiana or that sentiment in the South in favor of a holiday would subside. Now his reckless words came back to haunt him. "Long has washed the baby. I think it your duty to dress it," a resident of New

Boston, Texas, needled Sterling. The lieutenant governor of Texas kidded with Long. "You have proven yourself the go-getter I have called you," Edgar E. Witt wrote. "To conceive and then give birth to such a baby in a week's time is some fast work." All humor and wisecracking aside, there were a lot of politicians in Texas who were starting to squirm over the implications of Louisiana's action.[3]

Whether Sterling endorsed the cotton holiday personally, the state of Texas, as the industry's largest and most influential producer, had a responsibility to its growers, and to the other cotton-producing states as well. While Governor Sterling might have preferred to sidestep this responsibility, Long held him accountable. "Your state needs leadership as much as any state I know of," Long cabled the Texas governor, "and it is going to be up to you to save your people and to help save the people of the balance of the country."[4] The showdown that Long insisted upon between himself and Governor Sterling, the South and Texas, the holiday and acreage reduction, promised to be one of the most emotional and significant affairs in southern history. Out of this clash of contrasting personalities and philosophies of relief would come a decision affecting millions of people and billions of dollars.

Governor Ross Sterling Surveys the Showdown

Standing well over six feet tall and weighing in the vicinity of two hundred and fifty pounds, Ross S. Sterling was not just a big man but one of the most successful big businessmen Texas ever produced. A founding father and president of the Humble Oil Company, Sterling expanded his business interests in the 1920s to include ownership of the *Houston Post-Dispatch*, banks, railroads, and real estate developments.[5] Appointed chairman of the Texas Highway Commission by Governor Dan Moody, Sterling moved up to the governorship in 1930. Although an aggressive and adventuresome businessman, Sterling proved to be a conservative and plodding politician. He interpreted the governor's role as advising the legislature, rather than trying to control and direct it; with no strong direction from the executive the state drifted during perilous times.[6]

Sterling acted most decisively in regard to oil. The discovery of new oil fields and increased production at old wells had glutted the market for crude. He called a special thirty-day session to enact proration legislation and used martial law to enforce oil limitation edicts. Since cotton farmers were experiencing a similar situation of overproduction and falling prices, they expected Sterling to take equally decisive and bold action for them.

On the same morning that O. K. Allen hand delivered a copy of the

Copyright *Time*, 21 September 1931. Reprinted by permission.

holiday law to Governor Sterling, mass meetings were held in Texas. Disturbed by Sterling's malingering on the cotton question, the Vernon
Chamber of Commerce had commenced a drive through more than four
hundred local chambers to hold mass meetings on Saturday, 29 August. In
all, meetings were held in seventy-seven Texas towns, and the Vernon
chamber reported that twenty-eight town meetings favored prohibition,
twenty-one indicated a preference for acreage reduction, nineteen held
miscellaneous views, and only nine took no action. The report indicated,
moreover, that some 11,954 people favored the holiday idea, as compared to 7,330 for acreage reduction in varying degrees.[7] "The demand is
almost unanimous for a special session to reduce cotton acreage, and the
feeling is strong that delay in announcement of call is costing the farmers
thousands of dollars daily," Lieutenant Governor Witt informed Governor Sterling. "I never before urged a special session of the legislature. I do
not believe the farmers ever before urged one, but they certainly are doing
so now."[8]

While cotton farmers urged legislative reform, special interests whose
livelihood depended on handling, processing, and manufacturing cotton
advised Sterling to continue to ignore the call. Representatives of these
interests informed the governor that the farmers were allowing emotions
to run away with events. The Texas Cotton Ginners' Association reported
on a tour covering fourteen thousand miles and thirty-two districts in
Texas. "I found the farmers in all sections willing to try anything. A great
undercurrent of unrest is sweeping over the country, a great many agitators are taking advantage of the stress of the times," the executive secretary reported. "I appeal to you as a friend, as one of your staunchest
supporters, and as head of our great state, to use your high authority and
save the farmer from himself." Sterling concurred that there was too much
hysteria, and he reassured troubled authorities that he would not buckle
under. "Yes, I have been bombarded with thousands of telegrams and
letters. I feel that the people are unduly excited," he told the chairman of
the Texas Prison Board. "I will work it out some way."[9]

Long utilized the radio virtually every night now to press the case for
holiday action by Texas. On Thursday evening, 3 September, he criticized
members of the Texas legislature for withholding comment and, thereby,
assisting Sterling in delaying matters. Long said he had no desire to place
Sterling's head in a halter and lead him around. But he asked the residents
of Texas to ask themselves whose voices members of the legislature were
listening to. In Long's opinion the members were harkening more to the
"whispering voice of cotton speculator and mill buyer than to the woes of
the downtrodden farmer." "It is always in the state senate that the big
corporations and nefarious interests get in their work. This is because it is

Copyright *Dallas Morning News*, 1 September 1931. Reprinted by permission.

easier to work with a small group of men than a big group. If any of you Texans are listening in as far as Houston or Austin, ring up your legislators on the telephone and tell them to do something right away. Ring 'em up quick."[10]

Among the people taking Long's advice on contacting politicians in Texas were the public officials of several southern states. Governor Richard B. Russell offered the opinion that the legislators of Georgia could act just as fast as those of any other state, and announced that he would convene the Georgia assembly just as soon as Sterling issued his special call. Ibra C. Blackwood wired his counterpart in Texas about the overwhelming decision of South Carolina's mass meetings. And Seth P. Storrs, commissioner of agriculture for Alabama, told Sterling: "All organized agricultural forces of Alabama will follow Texas in supporting legislation totally prohibiting growing cotton in 1932. We confidently believe that Alabama legislature will by a large majority follow Texas in prohibition legislation. Will you please pass this information to all members of your legislature."[11]

If Sterling's strategy was to wait for federal assistance, that way out was destroyed when Carl Williams announced, after meeting with a delegation of cotton state senators, that the Federal Farm Board would not under any circumstances buy any more cotton. The board's decision was the clearest and most emphatic indication by the Hoover administration that the cotton states were on their own. "The recent announcement of the Federal Farm Board, and the apparent disposition of the present national administration to let matters drift," Governor Russell observed, "lead to the conclusion that we cannot expect any succor from Washington."[12]

The Texas Legislature Convenes in Special Session

Late on Saturday, 5 September, Sterling issued his special call. He announced that he was reconvening the Forty-second legislature for a "farmers' session" commencing at twelve o'clock on Tuesday, 8 September.[13] Just as Long had called Sterling's bluff in guiding the holiday through the tangles of the Louisiana legislature, so Sterling's announcement brought other states another step closer to having to take action themselves. Governor Blackwood rose to the challenge by issuing an executive proclamation instructing South Carolina's general assembly to meet in extra session at noon on Monday, 14 September.[14] "Texas the greatest cotton producing state, must be party to any plan to curtail or prevent growing of cotton next year," Governor Parnell of Arkansas observed. "Whatever plan the Texas legislature adopts will be submitted to the farmers of Arkansas for approval."[15] But several other politicians were not so enthusiastic about the choice being forced on them. "I haven't made up my mind about what is best for the farmers of this country," Governor Miller of Alabama stated. "We should sit steady in the boat, for there's danger ahead. I never knew prosperity generally to be produced by legislative action."[16]

Commissioner McDonald lost no time in encouraging farmers and representatives of allied industries to come to Austin to spur the Texas legislature on. Leaders of the movement for acreage control in Texas met at the Driskill Hotel in Austin on Sunday, 6 September, to organize a mass meeting for Wednesday night on the grounds surrounding the capitol. "Oil people pre-empted last session and got a bill through that is bringing oil out of the gutter," McDonald observed. "Why should not the farmers come down to Austin by the thousands and let their members of the legislature know their wishes?" The commissioner asked all farmers to lay down their cotton sacks and travel to Austin to personally impress their demands on the legislature. He announced that motorcades and special cars would be arranged to bring people from cotton-growing areas to Austin, and farmers should plan to spend at least one whole day and night at the capitol. "Interests that have covertly fought the movement bitterly will no doubt array themselves against legislation that limits their profits on excessive production," the commissioner warned. "Friends of the cotton restriction movement must be on guard. Our opportunity has come and with it a responsibility to fight."[17]

Several prominent politicians immediately extended to Long an invitation to visit Governor Sterling and the Texas legislature on Wednesday, 9 September, and address the mammoth mass meeting scheduled for Wooldridge Park that evening. Organizers of the Austin mass meeting confidently predicted the event would be the largest of its kind in history and climax the movement for acreage control that had swept the South. "Every part of Texas will send delegations and everything portends success with active leadership. Our governor and six ex-governors to honor the occasion of your visit to the state capitol in defense of the South's leading product, our homes, and our families," A. A. Allison, a member of the Texas legislature from Corsicana, wrote Long. "Your coming is heralded as an omen of certain success. . . . You must not fail us."[18]

Whether Long would accept the invitation and appear in Austin became a matter of considerable suspense. The governor was engaged in a bitter feud with his lieutenant governor, Paul N. Cyr. Long had been elected to the United States Senate in 1930, but he refused to assume the seat until O. K. Allen could be elected in 1932 his successor as governor.

Cyr broke with Long over his selection of Allen and Long's refusal to commute the conviction of a white woman sentenced to be hanged. At the time of the cotton crisis the lieutenant governor was just sitting back and waiting for Long to leave the state so that in the governor's absence he could have himself sworn in as Louisiana's chief executive.[19]

Long had always fashioned himself as a champion of the common man, and addressing the concerns of the downtrodden made tremendous demands on his time. He had already conceived and carried out many programs for the forgotten man in Louisiana, but his promotion of the cotton holiday occasioned, as nothing else had ever done before, requests for him to leave Louisiana and lead the fight South-wide. "If you could only come here and make a few speeches, I believe you could render a service to the South that no man, living or dead, has ever before rendered or will ever render," a Gainesville, Texas, resident passionately appealed to him. "My people are, and have been for more than 120 years, cotton planters in the Mississippi delta, and now, we are facing more than a crisis, in fact, our financial souls are face to face with obliteration."[20]

When the Texas legislature convened on Tuesday, 8 September, legislators set about drafting acreage control legislation, committees commenced hearings on the various bills, and the floor of the legislature was thrown open to the public. In the lobby farmers clad in their everyday work overalls milled around and a hillbilly band played the appropriately titled tune "Whooping It Up." For the next several days a continuous line of farmers filed past a microphone erected in the House chamber to speak their piece. The emotional tone of the farmers' session was set by the very first speaker. "I'm not down here for any foolishness," a Fannin County farmer said. "It's a matter of living or death for me. I'm just a poor renter and heavily in debt. But I say to you men that I have as much right to live as any man who every drew breath," the old man stated as his voice cracked under the emotion and the House burst into applause. Regaining his composure, he quickly concluded: "Men, if you'll just show us farmers as much respect—if you'll just treat us as kindly as you did the oil men, we'll go home and not say a word." And so it went. One impassioned plea after another.[21]

The Wooldridge Park Mass Meeting

Since his rift with Cyr, Long had dared only to sneak out of the state for a few hours at a time and without any notice to his enemies. He complained that the dispute made him a prisoner in his own state. The Louisiana governor asked Cyr either to accompany him to Austin or to sign a pledge promising to refrain for two days from trying to seize the reins of government. The *New Orleans Item* pleaded with the lieutenant governor to allow humanitarian considerations to prevail over petty politics. "In war, in flood control legislation, in all cases of epidemics, it pays all citizens to subordinate personality and factionalism. This is particularly true as relates to public officials who seek popular suffrage," the *Item* editorialized. "Louisiana cotton growers who elected both the governor and lieutenant governor should not suffer in their advocacy of their cause because friction has arisen between them." Cyr refused to sign anything, insisting his word was his bond.[22]

On Wednesday morning, not being able to wait until the absolute last second for Cyr's assurance that he could leave the state without fear of tampering, Long dispatched O. K. Allen, Seymour Weiss, and his son, Russell B. Long, to Austin to act as his personal representatives. While holiday forces were of course upset and disappointed over being denied the presence of their leader, they saw his absence as the kind of sacrifice that had to be endured when championing a cause that threatened entrenched interests. Although Long was prevented from appearing in person, he made arrangements to address the Austin mass meeting over KWKH, and sent his radio technician to Wooldridge Park to supervise the erection of amplifiers and other speaking equipment.[23]

A crowd approaching twelve thousand people gathered on the lawns of Wooldridge Park to hear the speakers go at each other and to voice their own sentiments.[24] Austin radio station KUT broadcast the meeting locally, permitting members of the Texas House and Senate to listen to the proceedings in the safety of their homes and legislative chambers. Lieutenant Governor Witt presided over what would prove to be the largest and most tumultuous event in Wooldridge Park history. Witt complimented the politicians for taking the issues to the people. "It will be woe to the legislator," the lieutenant governor observed, "who does not do what his people want him to do at this time." Witt invited Eugene Talmadge to address the crowd, and the Georgia commissioner of agriculture filled the time until Long's scheduled appearance with reasons why he favored a cotton holiday.

Long had left Baton Rouge at one o'clock that afternoon for the grueling $5\frac{1}{2}$-hour ride to Shreveport for the evening's broadcast. An audience of over five hundred people had gathered in the auditorium of KWKH to witness firsthand what promised to be a fiery address. Long strode into the studio, stopping to shake hands and acknowledging the congratulations of onlookers. He took off his collar and necktie, scattered notes about the table, and even spilled water over himself as he got ready to speak.

A few minutes after 8:00 P.M., Long began to speak, his voice booming over the loudspeakers loud and clear. Dispensing with amenities, he went right after the opposition. Long bitterly denounced Hoover and the Federal Farm Board for failing to relieve the cotton situation. He charged that large corporations, not the mass of cotton farmers, had the ear of Washington bureaucrats. "Will Clayton of Anderson Clayton Company is in Washington today talking with Hoover. He wasn't interested in the welfare of the cotton farmers until it looked like the cotton states were going to pass strict laws," Long charged. "Well, watch out. They're going to give you a sugar tit." In southern parlance, a sugar tit was a piece of cloth soaked in sugar water that mothers suckled their babies with during political speeches to keep the infants quiet and to put them to sleep. Long was cautioning the public not to be fooled by the pacifiers that speculators and large corporations were presently trying to offer them.

Long claimed he was only trying to keep the song of hard times from being sung all over the South. He recalled a conversation he had with Texas Congressman Wright Patman back at the New Orleans cotton conference. Patman reportedly told the Louisiana governor that he had seen people in Texas crying because they couldn't buy the things they needed. "We'll dry every tear in Texas in less than a week's time," Long promised, "if Texas passes this no cotton law." Long reviewed for his audience the essential objections to the holiday that various interests had raised—foreign competition, unemployment, and constitutionality—and he outlined ways the mass meetings had discussed for handling those problem areas. "A fight for modern civilization is on in the South, and is on all over the world," Long declared, "to see if a handful of men shall have everything while our women folk cry because their cotton will not bring enough to put clothes upon their backs."

Toward the end of his impassioned speech, Long polled the crowd. He asked all those in favor of the holiday to demonstrate their support by standing, and nearly the whole audience got to its feet. As Long addressed the mass meeting in Austin from KWKH's studio in Shreveport, he had at his ear a long distance telephone connection with the speaker's platform in Wooldridge Park. Long's delegation in Austin kept him constantly apprised of what the crowd was doing. "That's the spirit. You all stood," Long responded a few seconds after the action had actually taken place. "The members of your legislature ought to know now what the cotton farmers of Texas want." Throughout the broadcast there was this intimate interplay between speaker and audience, even though over three hundred miles separated them. Seasoned politicians present at the mass meeting could not help but marvel at the way Long demonstrated that he was as adept at rabble rousing by remote control as he was in person. It was an awesome display of intelligence and ability.[25]

Governor Sterling spoke directly after Long finished. Whatever debating advantage he might have enjoyed by going last the crowd took away through spirited heckling. Sterling attempted to dissipate Long's hold over the audience by appealing to the sense of history he felt all Texans shared. "What would Stephen F. Austin think if he should awake from his blissful sleep and see the legislature thinking of passing a law to prevent a man from growing cotton on his farm?" Sterling asked. "What would Sam Houston think if he would suddenly return to life and see the governor of Louisiana telling the people of his beloved Texas what to do?" Shouts of "Hurrah for Long" rang out from the audience.

Sterling tried to ignore the affront by forging right ahead. "When you get too much government in business you won't be a free people very long," the governor admonished. "We are not free now," some boisterous voices shot back as the interruptions grew louder and more frequent. "These are times of great unrest. Everything seems to be upside down. Confidence is scattered to the four winds. I urge you," Sterling implored, "to think for yourselves. Don't let one man do your thinking for you. Don't get excited."

Sterling admitted there was something drastically wrong with a distribution system that permitted hunger in a world of surpluses. But he placed the blame on the Republican party and Washington and urged farmers to insist on changes in federal policies. "It seemed like there was going to be trouble during Sterling's talk. The crowd all but hissed him down. Really we hung our heads in shame to think we had a governor of whom so many of our citizens had no respect," a resident of Buda, Texas, reported on her experience. "When Sterling referred to Hoover our spineless President causing this trouble, the crowd went wild and yelled 'who did you vote for? Give us the Long plan for relief.' I begged Uncle Sherman to go home I was afraid of a fight."

The crowd grew more surly as Sterling persisted. Several times the clamor of the stormy mass meeting drowned out the governor's words and forced him to stop speaking altogether. Sterling tried to take out after Long, charging he had more pajamas than any man in the country, and none of them cotton. The audience became so revulsed by his performance that they threatened to hurl rotten eggs. "I frankly say," a resident of Leonard, Texas, remarked, "that I believe I could of taken the crowd and hung Sterling to a tree." Sterling finally gave in and sat down, a thoroughly defeated and dejected man.[26]

Holiday Forces Pressure Texas

Long returned to Baton Rouge by automobile on Thursday morning, 10 September. Along the way he savored the tremendous demonstration dis-

ciples of the holiday movement had put on the previous night in Wooldridge Park. "We've got the lobbyists and paid grafters of the big interests
on the run," he observed. "If those cotton farmers who voted almost to a
man Wednesday night for my plan will get behind their senators and
representatives, the Texas legislature will be compelled to pass a law prohibiting the planting of cotton in 1932." Governor Sterling had prepared
a message to deliver to the Texas legislature that day, but with the memory
of the epochal mass meeting still fresh and painful in his mind, he destroyed it. When pressed to comment on the outpouring in favor of a
holiday, Sterling sternly replied: "I'm not going to let any children get
burned in a fire if I can help it."[27]

Sterling had to launch some kind of counterattack. In a press conference held on Friday afternoon, 11 September, Sterling claimed he had
communicated with almost all the governors of the cotton states and
could not find any of the sentiment among chief executives that Long had
been talking about. Sterling alleged that he found only one chief executive
who favored the cotton holiday. He declined, however, to identify for the
press the individual in question. Sterling preferred to talk about the unemployment, the damage to the port of Houston and Galveston, and the
roving bands of brigands the Long Plan would cause. He warned the
Texas legislature he would veto any bill prohibiting the planting of cotton
next year. "The Southern states are looking to Texas for leadership to save
the cotton industry. I accept the challenge. I offer cotton acreage reduction and soil conservation—nothing radical or dangerous like the Long
plan which would do far more harm than good," Sterling asserted. "My
feet are on the ground. I have not been swept off my feet yet. There is too
much hysteria in Texas and the South. I have not lost my equilibrium and
there is no influence in Texas that can make me lose it."

Southerners knew Sterling's charges didn't comport with the facts. Both
governors Parnell and Blackwood had already gone on record as favoring
the holiday. Upon hearing of Sterling's remarks, adherents elsewhere accused their officials of lying and secretly trying to jettison the plan. But
several politicians denied ever having been in contact with Sterling. "I
have not been approached by Governor Sterling for an expression of my
views on the Long plan," Richard B. Russell of Georgia asserted, "and
have made no statement regarding the plan, either for or against."[28]

Long came right back at Sterling's press conference threats later that
same evening in his radio broadcast. "The people are not hysterical.
That's the wail of the hungry, the crying of children. It's people wanting to
pay their debts, to send their children to school, and to pay the land
banks," Long declared. "Your feet may be on the ground, but if you veto a
cotton prohibition bill passed by the Texas legislature, something other
than your feet will be on the ground!"[29] Long warned lawmakers in Texas

again the next evening that electoral defeat might be the price they would pay for going against the holiday. He indicated that a list of legislators voting against drop-a-crop would be compiled and widely distributed.[30]

As Long hurled his accusations and charges at Texas from a distance, other holiday forces bore in on the opposition from positions inside the Texas capitol. On Saturday, 12 September, Governor Parnell appointed a committee of six and dispatched the delegation to Austin to apprise the Texas legislature of Arkansas's position.[31] In a formal address before both houses of the Texas legislature, the head of the Arkansas delegation told Texas solons that he had heard more speeches against the no-cotton plan than for it. But he had also seen twenty thousand farmers in Arkansas vote on the question, and less than one hundred of them opposed it. From the Texas capitol the Arkansas delegation proceeded to cable the governors of cotton states for increased assistance. "Position of other states will influence Texas. We urge that you wire House Committee on Agriculture at Austin that your state favors Louisiana act and cannot assure passage of any partial reduction law for 1932."[32]

State Senator Margie E. Neal of Carthage, secretary of the Joint Committee on Agriculture for the Texas House and Senate and cosponsor of the holiday bill in the Texas Senate, polled the governors of the cotton states on Sunday, 13 September. Neal asked if the Texas legislature passed a cotton holiday law contingent upon other states following suit, would the governors of the other cotton-growing states immediately convene their legislatures to undertake similar action. Doubting both the constitutionality and practical wisdom of the holiday, Governor Benjamin M. Miller cautioned against injuring the farmer and called for more careful consideration of the situation. "We must help the farmer and not hurt him by legislation," the Alabama governor warned. "I have never seen general prosperity produced by legislative action." Governor Bilbo also continued adamantly to oppose drop-a-crop. "Personally, I fail to see much good in the no-cotton plan," the Mississippi governor wrote. "I rather favor an acreage reduction for 1932 and 1933." But Governor Russell joined Parnell of Arkansas in promising to convene his legislature immediately upon Texas's enacting holiday legislation. "In my opinion the majority of Georgia cotton farmers and members of Georgia general assembly favor the cotton holiday for 1932," Russell cabled. "I have not polled the assembly on partial reduction. But seriously doubt whether the legislature would pass any partial reduction law."[33]

The most encouraging news for holiday hopefuls came from Blackwood. Once the South Carolina general assembly had convened in special session on Monday, 14 September, legislators steered holiday bills expeditiously through both houses. By the time Blackwood found the time to reply to Neal, the South Carolina Senate had already advanced the holiday to a third, and final, reading. The legislature was moving so rapidly toward officially dropping a crop in 1932 that it appeared South Carolina would reach a conclusion before Texas could act. "Indications are that the House will pass 3 to 1," Blackwood advised. "Believe legislature will pass total prohibition act, and adjourn this week."[34]

Heartened by the comments and commitments she had received, State Senator Neal asked Texas not to desert Arkansas, Georgia, South Carolina, and Louisiana in the cotton matter as it had the South in the presidential election of 1928 by swinging over to the Republicans. "If you again fail to stand with your sister states," she warned, "then it is fair that your name be spoken with derision in the rest of the Southland."[35]

Lobbyists Protect Their Interests in Austin

Just when the holiday movement appeared to have gained the upper hand, special interest groups that had been lurking in the background launched their counterattack. Holiday forces had surmised right from the inception of the movement that every processing, handling, and manufacturing industry affected by a sabbatical year would sooner or later hire lobbyists to protect their interests in legislative halls throughout the South and throw into the fray whatever resources necessary to win. By having the legislatures of several states meet simultaneously, holiday forces had hoped to prevent the oil mills, ginners, railroads, brokers, chambers of commerce, and other vested interests from ganging up on them in any one place. "They cannot be at Austin, Texas, and Atlanta, Georgia, at the same time. Let's overcrop these lobbyists and have the Georgia legislature in session at the same time the Texas, South Carolina, Arkansas, and Oklahoma legislatures are in session," Eugene Talmadge once urged. "If all of these legislatures are in session at the same time, they will need more than aeroplanes to visit them." When mass meetings failed to force several simultaneous special sessions, however, the strategy of thinning out the ranks of lobbyists by spreading them around went by the boards, permitting the special interests to concentrate their efforts on Austin.[36]

The holiday movement had been able to turn out large and vociferous crowds at local mass meetings in the principal cotton-growing states because both the county seat and the single morning or afternoon of debate were convenient for cotton farmers. Although thousands upon thousands of cotton farmers participated in mass meetings and contacted local, state, and federal officials by mail and telephone, few of these individuals could afford to travel to their state capital and remain there for an extended period of time. With their money running out and the harvest in full swing, most farmers had to remain in their fields to salvage whatever they could from the present crop. Farmers who had made great personal sacrifices to travel to Austin to attend the Wooldridge Park mass meeting and file before the House microphone complained that the Texas legislature was only going through the motions of listening to them. Often, they charged, only a handful of legislators were present, and some members slept with their boots propped up on desks while others just marked time by making paper airplanes and sailing them around the chamber. "There are only about 50 members that have the farmers interests at heart," a resident of Cotulla, Texas, insisted. "The balance are with the railroads, compresses, and large operators."[37]

When the swarm of lobbyists descended on the Texas legislature, A. A. Allison, chairman of the coalition for the Long Plan in Texas, was prompted to call a meeting for 14 September to express the farmers' indignation and to alert the public to what was taking place. About one hundred holiday supporters gathered in the hearing room of the State Railroad Commission. "This session was called as a farmers' session," Allison declared, "but it looks as though the ginners, cotton mill men, and all others interested in cotton, except the farmers, are to be the first beneficiaries." Concurring in Allison's charge that special interests were trying to out-muscle holiday supporters, the assembled farmers and legislators framed a resolution calling for renewed efforts by the folks back home. "As the bulk of the farmers moved out last week," the resolution declared, "all those interests conspiring against cotton moved in and are apparently in high glee over the prospect of winning their fight, unless the farmers of Texas come to the rescue our fight will be lost." To counter the rising influence of cotton buyers, carriers, shippers, exporters, and others, farmers were urged to deluge their senators and representatives once again with telegrams and telephone calls upholding the holiday idea.[38]

The growing menace of lobbyists prompted Long to make in New Orleans on 15 September some bombshell accusations. Governor Long charged that big money was being spent in Austin to keep the Texas legislature from declaring a cotton holiday. "It would be hard to understand why the Texas legislature would refuse to heed the request of Arkansas, South Carolina, Georgia, Alabama, Louisiana, and other Southern states, as well as the people of Texas, were it not for the fact that we know large sums of money are being lavishly used in Austin in an effort to sway the Legislature." Long accused lobbyists of plying legislators with, among other blandishments, cash payoffs, women, and parties. It was simply an out-and-out sale to deprive the people of the South of something they wanted and needed.[39]

The accusations of bribery that Long so casually threw around provoked the Texas legislature into an uproar. Legislators were thoroughly incensed and outraged by what they considered Long's cheap smear tactics. Representative Temple H. McGregor of Austin rose in the House to offer an acrimonious defense of his state's honor and integrity. Calling Long everything from an "intellectual pervert" to "an arrogant ass which brays from Louisiana," a livid McGregor contended that the legislature had not seen a single lobbyist all session. McGregor's name-calling struck such a responsive chord that the Senate asked him to repeat his cutting remarks before the upper house that afternoon, and then ordered his speech printed in the legislative journal.[40]

The press had a field day with McGregor's strident attack. For the past few weeks Long had been doing a pretty good job of cutting down hostile editors, doing it, no less, over radio, the rival communications medium. McGregor's condemnation afforded those smitten by Long's charges the opportunity to get back at him. The Sterling-owned *Houston Post-Dispatch* led the onslaught. The editor admitted that the Travis County legislator had used some awfully strong language, but the paper insisted Long deserved every word. "Mr. McGregor merely answered him in the only kind of language that Huey Long can understand—words smacking of the barnyard. And how he poured it on! That fiery speech . . . clarified the atmosphere. It placed Louisiana's colorful and noisy governor in the true light of a meddler."[41]

Texas Kills the Holiday

On Wednesday, 16 September, the Texas legislature vented its anger against Long on the pending holiday legislation. The Texas House of Representatives killed the holiday bill sponsored by Victor B. Gilbert of Cisco, 92–38, and followed this show of strength with another vote that conclusively advanced the acreage reduction bill of J. J. Olsen of Yoakum, 95–34. The initial reaction of the cotton market to the defeat of the Gilbert-sponsored bill was a price decline. Holiday adherents pointed out that this meant the cotton market had absolutely no confidence in acreage reduction.[42]

Shortly after the House had decisively defeated drop-a-crop legislation, John Hornsby of Austin introduced in the Senate a resolution calling Long "a consummate liar." The resolution contended Long's charges were nothing more than "the venom of a liar." Senator Margie Neal opposed the resolution on the grounds it was "unkind and un-Christian," and Senator T. J. Holbrook of Galveston declared it was "beneath the dignity

Copyright *Dallas Morning News*, 17 September 1931. Reprinted by permission.

of the Senate to spread the resolution on its minutes." But Long's enemies stood firm and refused to allow the indictments to be either watered down or couched in more dignified language. State Senator Walter Woodul insisted on the acrimonious tone. "Long is a coward and afraid to come to Texas," Woodul maintained, "and this is the only way we can reach him." Representative G. J. Cox of Paris asked the legislature to appoint him a committee of one so that he could go to Louisiana to "bring back that 'pinhead governor' and make him eat what he said."[43]

Rejection of the Long Plan by Texas served only to spur on the lawmakers of South Carolina. The South Carolina general assembly paused momentarily to consider the options: they could advance legislation to reduce acreage, comporting with the decision arrived at by Texas; they could adjourn for two to three days to provide time for more thought; or they could forge ahead with holiday legislation. Scorning any change in the course already settled upon by the public, the South Carolina Senate passed the holiday that same Wednesday afternoon, 16 September, on a third and final vote, 21–13, and sent the measure to the lower house for action.[44]

When Long took to the airwaves that night, he stunned his audience by announcing he was giving up the fight. Characterizing the evening's broadcast as his "swan song," Long said that, despite the loyalty and confidence exhibited by the South Carolina Senate, Texas had delivered the fatal blow. He ridiculed the resolution of the Texas Senate condemning him and continued adamantly to insist that lobbyists hired by vested interests turned the tide. "We know the scalawags who had already sold the crop, and were trying to keep the price down, were going to bribe, buy, or get hold of the Texas legislature by any means they could. Of course, these influences were not going to let the farmers get all that money if by spending a few million they could prevent it. They combed hell with a fine-toothed comb to get the lowest type of lobbyists, skunks, and lowdown thieves they could get to work on the Texas legislature."

Long insisted he had no regrets about the way he had conducted himself. He felt that he had pursued the best strategy possible. His only regret was that the farmers had lost out. Long advised his listeners in Texas to make a list of senators and representatives and to remember on election day how they voted on cotton. "To the people of Texas, hereafter, see that you are represented by legislators who won't turn a deaf ear to the people." It was for holiday forces a most depressing sign-off.[45]

In the days to come, Long was asked to temper his remarks and try for some sort of rapprochement with Texas. J. H. Fisher, a Texas legislator who supported the holiday, was just one of many who pleaded with the governor of Louisiana to apologize in order to "allay bitterness." Representative Fisher believed that lobbyists had not actually paid any money to lawmakers, but "only urged their point of view." Long refused to smooth over his charges and chided Fisher for his naiveté. "How the point of view of these foreign lobbyists could have appealed to the legislators of Texas more strongly than the unanimous urging of their own fathers can be explained by only one theory," Long cynically insisted. "If you think lobbyists were just there to reason with their eloquence and persuasive qualities you are still looking for what has happened in Austin."

Long compared the Texas legislature to a gang of highwaymen who went out and robbed cotton farmers of $375 million. "I consider it a compliment to be denounced by a gang like that. It is almost a certificate of good character for them to say that I don't belong to such a crowd. For them to have said about me what they did is just like if Capone would say I don't belong to his crowd," Long commented. "Every half-dressed woman and every barefoot child in Texas this Fall and Winter will owe the credit for their condition to Governor Sterling and the Texas legislature."[46]

Cause of Death

In the wake of the holiday's demise in Texas, editors and politicians across the South became coroners in the case. All of the inquests conducted by adversaries of the holiday identified Long's behavior as the cause of death. Francis Williams, chairman of the Louisiana Public Service Commission, voiced one of the most devastating indictments. Williams argued that from Long's very first speech, when he branded anyone opposing the holiday a crook, the governor locked himself into a course of conduct that was destined to make more enemies than converts. "Having bought so many votes like a sack of potatoes, in the Louisiana legislature, when justice was about to overtake him and expel him from the governorship, Long foolishly imagined that the plague of dishonesty and indecency he started in our legislature had spread to Texas," Williams announced. "His success in Louisiana at branding bankers, businessmen, politicians, and mayors as thieves and then making them kiss him for his insults is probably responsible for most of Huey's mistakes in handling the Texas no-cotton crop situation."[47]

These attacks only served to rally support around Long. The *New Orleans Item* praised Long for the "vitality and substance and force" that he gave to the holiday, and for placing the interests of the region before his own welfare. The paper was gratified by the way Louisianians hung together on the holiday and stood for something that was progressive and constructive. "The idea was defeated, not through lack of intelligence and aggressiveness on the part of the farmers," publisher Thompson charged, "but largely because of the inertia and cowardice of politicians, gentlemen comfortably situated themselves, who wanted to 'let well enough alone.' "[48]

Whether any money or women actually changed hands, as Long charged, only those directly involved knew for sure. Opponents of the cotton holiday vehemently denied that their votes had been purchased. Dennis Ratcliff, a member of the Texas House of Representatives from Haskell, told Long his statement was "an insult to every citizen of Texas" and called upon Long "to produce proof or retract same." Clarence E. Farmer, another member of the Texas House, readily conceded that Sterling was not a popular and masterful politician. "The people have just as good a government as the majority of those who vote want to have," Farmer pointed out. "The majority voted for Hoover and Sterling. They are now taking their own mixed drinks." Although agreeing that Sterling badly misjudged and mishandled the entire situation, Farmer vigorously professed his own innocence, and absolved his colleagues from any malfeasance whatsoever. "Get out of your mind that there was any money used in the Texas legislature on the cotton bill," Farmer told a friend in Louisiana who had been riding him on the point. "There was no need to use money." Foreign competition, unemployment, and the Supreme Court were sufficient deterrents to the holiday.[49]

Long had received reports all along that special interests were flooding lobbyists into Austin. No less an authority than the lieutenant governor of Texas confidentially told him that Sterling was listening to the representatives of special interests rather than to the representatives of the people. "My guess is that he is being influenced by city folks who have not attended the farmers meetings and do not know their best wishes," Witt confided. "There are some folks who profit by quantity who are doubtless selling the governor on the idea that the farmers are merely hysterical and do not know what is to their best interests."[50]

As part of the legislative process representatives of special interests regularly met with individual legislators and spoke before hearings on matters affecting the welfare of their industries or groups. And at election time those interests contributed heavily to the campaigns of friendly candidates. With the holiday striking directly at their daily operations, special interests prevailed on the legislative contacts they had cultivated over the years in Austin and painted the gravest picture imaginable of the holiday.

The Port Arthur Chamber of Commerce was just one of many special interests that had Sterling's ear and knew exactly how to frighten and alarm a public official whose political and financial fortunes depended on big business. The general manager of the Port Arthur chamber impressed on Sterling that the city had a population of over fifty thousand, water shipments of more than 8 million tons, and an annual payroll of $30 million. "I hesitate of thinking what would happen to the railroads, the truck lines, the gins, the compresses, the Texas ports, and the other instrumentalities that depend largely upon the production of cotton for their operations," a horrified Harve H. Haines wrote. "If all of these facilities were to suddenly go out of business in the handling of cotton the unemployment that would result would be so tremendous in volume as to shock the commercial world of Texas into almost insensibility."[51]

Long's daily ranting did not scuttle drop-a-crop in Texas. From the outset it was evident that Texas politicians opposed the holiday, and were looking for some way to save face in denying their constituents something they wanted. Long's emotional outbursts merely provided Texas legislators with an excuse for their own conservatism. "I do not believe that in the long run, Long's statements or his position had very much to do with the decision of the Texas legislature," W. R. Poage, a member of the Texas Senate from Waco, wrote. "Legislators had made up their minds that the whole idea was too radical."[52]

The special session had placed legislators under intense emotional strain and required much personal sacrifice. Time spent in Austin meant absences from families, jobs, and other duties requiring attention in those hard times. For the forces of acreage reduction, triumph made these sacrifices at least bearable. But for those supporting the cotton holiday, defeat was an emotionally crushing experience. "I thought I saw an opportunity for the South to rehabilitate itself as independent of commercial and industrial interests that have fed upon us for more than half a century," A. A. Allison of Corsicana reminisced. "But interests that have fattened upon cotton right here at home had their forces at Austin to hammer the movement all they could, and cotton farmers had wedges driven into their army from every angle imaginable. . . . If I were young, how I would like to lead the hosts of my fellows who have been the butt end of social, educational, and economic discrimination since the Civil War out of such enforced dependence."[53]

South Carolina Leads Holiday Forces down the Stretch

Long was besieged with appeals urging him to continue the crusade. Holiday believers absolutely refused to concede defeat. "You have made yourself a hero in the minds of the masses of the South, and probably the West," a general merchandise merchant from Pleasant Hill, Louisiana, observed. "Don't let a little thing like Texas cause you to give up such a noble fight. Victory will come . . . for all the common people are with you." "Texas has not absolutely closed the door against the cotton farmer," the *Shreveport Times* declared. "It has made his lot harder, darkened his future, and almost shattered his faith. But the fight is still on. . . . The South has no thought of raising the white flag of surrender."[54]

Nowhere was faith in the holiday stronger than in South Carolina. During the debate on the holiday legislation Representative Neville Bennett of Clio argued that it was pointless to proceed to a vote on the issue, for events in Austin had made the holiday a dead letter. "Our action was to be predicated on the action of Texas. Texas has now acted. Why should we pass something that is already dead before we pass it?" The majority of the South Carolina general assembly, however, felt that South Carolina farmers had expressed themselves so overwhelmingly in favor of a holiday that they were obligated to continue to push for it and to bring other states around to that viewpoint. "Why change your position now?" Representative Randolph Lee of Summerville, Dorchester County, asked. "My constituents have not changed." The South Carolina House approved holiday legislation in a final vote on Saturday, 19 September, by a solid 75–22 vote.[55]

Although Long withdrew from an out-front public role, he remained active behind the scenes in holiday affairs. As the holiday movement cranked up its media machines for one last blitz, Will Henderson reminded Long that radio time, newspaper space, out-of-town guests, and personal excursions did not come cheap. "I am taking a chance on spending money every day like a drunken sailor to take care of an unavoidable situation that you ought to relieve me of without regard to any cause whatsoever and do it at once. You take care of the cotton people in this matter and the cotton people will take care of you in any other situation." Long promptly had the Louisiana State Board of Liquidation ask the legislature for an appropriation of fifty thousand dollars to sustain holiday activities down the stretch.[56]

At 11:44 on the morning of Tuesday, 22 September, Governor Sterling signed into law the Texas acreage control bill. Commissioner McDonald, senators Oliver Cunningham of Abilene and Clint Small of Wellington, and representatives J. J. Olsen of Yoakum and Lawrence Westbrook of Waco witnessed the signing. The law limited cotton acreage in 1932 and 1933 to 30 percent of the land in cultivation in 1931. After 1933 there would be no percentage limit, but no land could be planted to cotton in successive years. The chief weapon of enforcement would be the injunction. District attorneys would have to bring suit to enjoin a violator from raising an excessive amount of cotton. Penalties ranged from $25 to $100 for each acre, and the fines would be paid into county road and bridge funds.[57]

The signing was delayed several times, some observers thought prophetically, as the camera of the official photographer failed to function three times in succession. "This law is the farmers' law; they wanted it and they will respect it," Commissioner McDonald optimistically predicted. "We do not expect any sensational rise in the price of cotton, but common sense dictates that if the supply is curtailed the prices will be stabilized. Others were not so confident about the law's impact on cotton markets and its chances of passage elsewhere in the South. "A lot of the senators voted for the cotton acreage bill thinking they were jumping on a band wagon," State Senator Tom Deberry of Red River County remarked. "I think they jumped on a hearse."[58]

The Hearse Makes Its Rounds

As public officials from Texas began to press other states to jump on the acreage reduction wagon, they soon discovered a serious omission in their acreage reduction law. Texas legislators had been so intent on assaulting Long's personality and politics that they had neglected to incorporate an escape clause in their legislation. In both Louisiana and South Carolina holiday laws set a date beyond which drop-a-crop would become null and void. But Texas politicians had concentrated so passionately on striking back at Long that they had failed to make acreage reduction contingent on similar action by other states. They now faced the distinct possibility that Texas farmers would be forced to reduce acreage while those of other states went right along planting as before. From the largest cotton-producing state a plea went out for early legislative action and spirited cooperation.[1] Mississippi was the first to respond, and the reaction of the Magnolia State would indicate whether there was any life remaining in the cotton holiday.[2]

On Sunday afternoon, 27 September, Theodore G. Bilbo unexpectedly issued his special call, directing the Mississippi legislature to convene in special session at Jackson at twelve o'clock on 29 September. While Bilbo's decision to call a special session was cause for considerable relief among Texas officials, it was also cause for exultation among his supporters. Ever since the cotton crisis had emerged in mid-August as the principal preoccupation of the southern states, some persons had indicated to Bilbo that his taking a leadership role on the issue would go a long way toward making up for the shortcomings of previous years.[3] These men were motivated more by selfish political considerations than concern over the economic plight of the farmers. "Leave nothing of any real importance for the incoming administration so that history will only record his administration as that of one who never fought for anything except office," the chairman of the state Democratic executive committee advised. "Should you succeed in this, I am sure your political future will loom large on the horizon."[4]

When the Mississippi legislature convened on Tuesday afternoon, Bilbo rose to the dramatic pitch of the occasion by insisting that no less than nine areas of relief and assistance be considered. The governor declared

Copyright *New Orleans Item,* 29 September 1931. Reprinted by permission of
New Orleans Times-Picayune/States-Item.

that the public interest required, first of all, that the legislature consider
regulating cotton acreage by legislation. He then proceeded to enumerate
eight other largely depression related recommendations: authorization of
$3 million in bonds for payment of bank guaranty certificates of all failed
banks up to March 1930; issuance of $5.5 million in state notes to pay off
the present deficit; repeal of nuisance taxes; issuance of bonds to pay for
road construction projects; passage of provisions that payment of the poll
tax, insofar as taxes are concerned, qualified a resident to exercise the
franchise; extension of the time for redemption under tax sales; reorganization of the governing boards of schools to satisfy accrediting associations; and, finally, reduction of government expenses.[5]

   Although a new sense of harmony characterized the relationship between the governor and the legislature, legislators remained divided over
what plan would be enacted, and at least three schools of thought were
discernible in their arguments. Bilbo had indicated in his special address
that he believed Mississippi would follow the Texas plan, since the nation's largest producer had decided to go that route, and there were many
legislators who felt the cotton holiday was now a moot question.[6] "The
Long plan has already been decisively rejected," Representative Walter
Sillers of Bolivar County declared. "What's the use of worrying about

something that is dead?" Many of the legislators who had previously championed the holiday were ready to concede the point. Moreover, by having all the cotton-producing states fall into line behind Texas, the South could influence federal agencies and these could, in turn, reach accommodation with foreign producers.[7]

Even though Texas had thoroughly repudiated the holiday, many people still urged Mississippi not to forsake the cause and to enact drop-a-crop legislation. "Acreage limitation may be a slow working remedy but it will not be a cure for present conditions in the South," a merchant in Plain Dealing, Louisiana, informed Bilbo. "I am confident that no acreage limitation legislation will be worth the paper on which it is written not to take into consideration the expense of enacting it. Cotton and cottonseed are worth less in the market than when Texas passed the acreage limitation bill."[8] Some persistent Mississippi legislators still agreed and argued that total abstinence was the only plan offering immediate relief and hope in the long run for the South. "The Texas plan will not serve the purpose intended, and the Long plan is the only sure proposition to establish balanced agriculture in the state," Lawrence T. Kennedy said in revealing that he would introduce a bill patterned on the holiday idea. "If five states adopt the Louisiana measure, Texas is almost sure to reconsider and favor that law in preference to Governor Sterling's proposal."[9]

Other legislators continued to oppose all cotton legislation, regardless of its sponsors or intentions. "Too long we have fooled ourselves with the magic formula of be it enacted," Representative Tom V. Anderson of Greenville, Washington County, complained. "The greatest cotton state in America 30 days ago passed a curtailment bill and cotton has gone down 3 cents a pound." According to the antilegislation bloc, cotton would take care of itself through its own "suicidal tyranny." "That's just the point," Anderson underscored. "Nickel cotton is the best cure for nickel cotton."[10]

Bills emulating the Texas and Louisiana plans touched off a considerable tug-of-war in the Mississippi legislature.[11] A delegation of prominent Louisianians, headed by Will K. Henderson and W. H. Hodges, spent several days in Jackson addressing the legislature and buttonholing prominent residents on behalf of the holiday. Still wanting to save the holiday from extinction, an estimated six hundred farmers from around the state converged on the capitol over the weekend of 3 and 4 October. Granted the use of the House chamber, the farmers adopted a resolution memorializing the Mississippi legislature "to enact laws relating to cotton in harmony with the cotton laws recently enacted by the legislatures of Louisiana and South Carolina."[12]

Despite the strong and persistent sentiment in favor of a sabbatical year, a coalition of representatives from delta and hill counties, picturing the holiday as producing night riding and mob rule and charging that only speculators stood to benefit, was able to beat back the surge.[13] On 13 October, Bilbo signed a cotton reduction bill into law that required present acreage to be reduced by 30 percent for both 1932 and 1933; the law would become operative just as soon as states producing 75 percent of the cotton crop enacted similar laws. "I congratulate you on the action which you, yourselves have done," Carl Williams told a joint session of the legislature. "I believe that cotton will remain king because I have complete faith in the willingness and ability of the Southern people to tackle and successfully conquer any problem when they know what it is."[14]

When the Mississippi legislature finally adjourned on Saturday, 31 October, it could point with considerable pride to several steps taken to alleviate the distress of the national depression. Governor Bilbo had seized on the special session to submit some 175 measures for consideration, and the legislators had turned 35 recommendations into law. Among the more significant were a cotton reduction law; a $5 million bond bill to redeem guaranty bank certificates; a $6 million short-term note to take care of the state deficit; a $5 million road bond issue; and a law for the quarterly payment of taxes.[15]

Southern Banks Enter the Fray

Although Arkansas joined Mississippi in passing an acreage control law, governors Parnell and Bilbo protected themselves by including escape clauses in their legislation, and Texas found itself still very much on the hook.[16] Other cotton-growing states were not flocking to sign up. Unless Texas could induce states like Alabama and Georgia to join in before a January deadline, the whole acreage control movement threatened to collapse, with Texas left holding the bag.

Just as Texas approached the toughest sledding, however, the Hoover administration made a move to grease the way. Members of the Federal Farm Board met with representatives of the American Cotton Cooperative Association and southern banking associations in New Orleans on Monday, 12 October, to work out arrangements for withholding from market some of the present crop and reducing the potential total of the next. Ever since Hoover had conferred in mid-September with prominent cotton industry figures, federal officials had been quietly urging southern financial institutions to assume responsibility for enforcing production cutbacks. At New Orleans, James C. Stone and Carl Williams officially extended to southern bankers a formal proposition.

The Farm Board and the American Cotton Cooperative Association promised to hold 3.5 million bales until 31 July 1932 provided southern banks would make loans enabling farmers to withhold 3.5 million bales. Nathan Adams, a Dallas banker, was credited by federal officials with having formulated the idea and promoting it to southern financiers. Not surprisingly, southern bankers were receptive to the offer. In New Orleans representatives of southern banking associations offered to extend loans to farmers who would sign a contract observing the guidelines set down by Texas's acreage control law. The various banking associations called for members to gather in their own states on 20 October to either ratify or reject the proposal. Moreover, if southern legislatures continued to approve laws substantially reducing acreage, the Farm Board offered to sweeten the pot still further by withholding its cotton stocks from market for another year.[17]

Chairman Stone submitted a report to Hoover on 16 October which credited the New Orleans meeting with taking "the most encouraging and constructive move in connection with cotton which has been taken this year." He was particularly enthusiastic about the renewed cooperation between the federal government and the private sector. "The job of restoring prosperity to American agriculture is necessarily a partnership job between the government and the people themselves, and it is tremendously encouraging to see the government's efforts along this line backed up in such a very practical way by Southern business leadership." Stone insisted that the rejoining of the financial leadership of the South and the Federal Farm Board meant "a very material reduction in the acreage of cotton is thus made inevitable next Spring" and "the accumulation of surplus cotton will gradually work down to normal."[18]

Even before state banking associations could assemble their members to collect pledges, the agricultural councils of Arkansas, Tennessee, and other southern states came out strongly in favor of the proposed arrangement. Hoover broke his silence on cotton matters to laud the cooperative effort as "constructive action of the type the country needs."[19] When banking associations convened in their respective cotton belt states on 20 October, southern bankers committed themselves so thoroughly to the venture that they pledged to hold five hundred thousand bales more than originally promised.[20] "The really able bankers of the South know perfectly well that they are able to handle and control the cotton problem in the South," the *Atlanta Constitution* declared. "They hold the whip hand over it every year before a cotton plow is struck into the ground. They can, by concert of plan and action, say more surely than 10 legislatures how much cotton acreage should be financed."[21]

The Jackson Cotton Conference

Once southern banking associations had secured the pledges necessary to carry out the proposed withholding offer, southern politicians got back into the act to try to complete their part of the bargain. On 2 November, governors Parnell and Bilbo issued a joint invitation to every cotton-growing state to send a delegation to a cotton convention to be held at the Edwards Hotel in Jackson, Mississippi, on 23 November to establish a uniform cotton acreage reduction plan for the entire South. Parnell and Bilbo underscored in the invitation that the proposed conference was necessary because the continuing support of the Farm Board and southern banks depended upon the cotton states' agreeing on a binding, common policy.[22]

For the next few weeks organizers of the Jackson cotton convention kept hammering home the need for a spirit of compromise and conciliation in the South. Speaking over station KWKH on 19 November, Governor Parnell told listeners that the Jackson convention constituted the last chance for southern states to save themselves from further social and economic disintegration.[23] Leaders of the holiday movement revealed a willingness to place the welfare of the region ahead of personal preference. Once again Will Henderson not only made his radio facilities available but also personally contacted many complacent politicians and reminded them that the Louisiana legislature had allocated fifty thousand dollars to the Cotton Relief Association to see the movement through to fruition.[24]

When Bilbo called the Jackson cotton convention to order on 23 November, ten southern states—Alabama, Arkansas, Georgia, Louisiana, Mississippi, Missouri, Oklahoma, South Carolina, Tennessee, and Texas —were officially represented by delegates numbering over one hundred. Parnell presided over the proceedings, and the Arkansas governor paid tribute to holiday forces for the initiative shown in originating and sustaining the movement for acreage control. "Mr. James Thompson, publisher of the *Item* and *Tribune*, has forgotten that he has a business of his own to tend to and has devoted himself completely to the interest of the Southern cotton farmer," Parnell said in singling out just one of many for praise. "Louisiana, Texas, Arkansas, Mississippi, and all the other delegations are here today fighting not for any one plan but for an agreement which will save us from ruin. Low as the price of cotton is, it is propped-up today. The props that hold it is the conference that was held in New Orleans. If we leave Jackson without doing something definite, cotton will go to 4¢ a pound, provided you can sell it at all." Parnell proceeded to invite delegates to the speaker's table to address the conference.[25]

Copyright *Dallas Morning News*, 23 November 1931. Reprinted by permission.

Governor Blackwood brought exciting financial news. The South Carolina governor informed delegates that he had discussed the cotton crisis with Bernard M. Baruch, noted New York financier and confidant to presidents. On his way from New York City to South Carolina's Waccamaw peninsula, where he owned the Hobcow barony, Baruch stopped in Washington on 21 November for a visit with Hoover and then proceeded to Columbia, South Carolina, where on 22 November he had breakfast with Blackwood and "Cotton Ed" Smith. "He told me," Blackwood related, "that he has encouragement amounting practically to assurance that if we make a substantial and real reduction in our cotton producing the Federal government will step in and help hold off the market 4,000,000 bales more than is already held."

To assure every state a voice in the convention's decisions equal to the amount of cotton it produced, the convention adopted a voting rule that provided every state with one guaranteed vote, plus one additional vote for every five hundred thousand bales of cotton produced. Texas had the largest bloc of votes with twelve; followed by Arkansas and Mississippi with five each; Alabama, Georgia, and Oklahoma, four each; Louisiana, South Carolina, and Tennessee, three each; and Missouri, two.

Delegates to the Jackson convention unanimously recommended that an acreage control law similar in effect to the law enacted in Texas be adopted by all cotton-producing states. To place the law before the public officials of every cotton state that had not already passed some form of acreage reduction, the Jackson convention selected an executive committee comprising Dr. Tait Butler, editor of the *Progressive Farmer*; E. F. Creekmore, head of the American Cotton Cooperative Association; Harry D. Wilson, Louisiana commissioner of agriculture; W. H. Hodges, president of the North Louisiana Cotton Growers Association; and J. E. McDonald, Texas commissioner of agriculture.

Everyone seemed in high spirits as the Jackson cotton convention disbanded. The *Daily Clarion-Ledger*, which had covered the hometown proceedings most thoroughly, hailed the convention as a declaration of independence from the tyranny of cotton. "Action by governors' delegates from ten Southern states for cotton reduction by a uniform law was a stroke that has been heard around the world," editor T. M. Hederman declared. "It was one of the most significant days in the history of the South. It struck the mightiest blow ever attempted against the fetters of King Cotton."[26]

Alabama Holds the Key

The Jackson executive committee departed for Montgomery, Alabama, to start right at the beginning of the alphabetical list of states that had not as yet acted. Just as Texas had decided the difference between reduction and no cotton, now Alabama would largely determine whether the South would enjoy cooperation or suffer from continued discord. "If the South is to be saved from smothering itself with cotton, then, it must be by legislation," Commissioner McDonald told Governor Miller. "For we have tried the plan of voluntary reduction and it will not meet such an emergency as we now face." Miller, however, remained unconvinced and as intractable as ever. "I don't believe that Alabama is the key state as everyone is telling me," Governor Miller told the delegation. "A plan to restrict a farmer from planting cotton would be unconstitutional, impracticable, and unenforceable. It would break the State of Alabama to enforce such a law if it were passed."[27]

Texas officials had too much at stake to be deterred by an initial rebuff. Commissioner McDonald continued to try to soften the stance of the Alabama chief executive. He expressed appreciation to Miller for consenting to an audience with the Jackson delegation and expressed faith that Alabama would eventually come around. "President Hoover advised Senator Ed Smith of South Carolina," McDonald added, "that if the South would cooperate in passing adequate cotton acreage reduction laws that he would assure the holding of some 4 million bales off the market for an indefinite period."[28]

McDonald contacted everyone in any position of power in Alabama to use his influence toward getting Governor Miller involved. Alabama was holding up a parade, he said, and other states were growing impatient with Alabama's "delay in evidencing a cooperative spirit." The feedback that McDonald received was pessimistic. Parnell reported that it took him several days just to get a telephone call through to Miller. Judge N. S. Carmichael of Montgomery notified the Texas commissioner that "some of the governor's close friends appeared interested," but Miller remained as detached as ever. Seth P. Storrs indicated that from his ongoing conversations with Miller he gathered that a special session was only a "very remote" possibility at best.[29]

Although McDonald privately despaired that Miller "just doesn't realize the gravity of the situation," the Texas commissioner of agriculture tried to keep up a hopeful public front. In desperation, McDonald made virtually every kind of appeal imaginable. He personally felt that much of the increase in cotton acreage in Texas and Oklahoma had been the work of immigrants from the older states of the South within the past twenty years. "We were very glad to have these good people adopt Texas as their home; in fact that is just what my good old Daddy did. He came from Coose County, Alabama, and married a Fort Payne, Alabama, girl," Mc-Donald told Frederick Thompson, a publisher in Mobile, Alabama. "So, you see Alabama is very near and dear to me, and I am just betting that Alabama will be found in the columns with the other states."[30]

The Court Rescues Texas

As days turned into weeks and Texas failed to line up additional states behind its reduction law, cotton farmers in Texas complained bitterly that they were being sacrificed for the benefit of the remainder of the South. Various politicians and farm organizations in Texas commanded Governor Sterling either to secure commitments from states producing 75 percent of the crop by 20 December or to call the legislature back into session to repeal acreage control. "Why should I threaten the governors of the states that have not yet enacted cotton acreage reduction statutes?" Governor Sterling asked. "We ought to let well enough alone. The farmers asked for the law the legislature gave them. They wanted to go farther than that and call a 1932 cotton holiday." Commissioner McDonald agreed that repeal of the law would further depress the price of cotton and possibly "break the South." "Have we heard any of the same organizations heading a movement for the repeal of the oil proration law, which, everyone knows, transferred that major industry from despair and ruin into one of business stability?" McDonald asked.[31]

Failing the cooperation of the other states, the only hope Texas had for extricating itself from its dilemma was to file a court case that would declare acreage control illegal. No sooner had the new year dawned than the state launched a test case. On 5 January 1932, T. L. Tyson, Robertson County attorney, filed a suit asking for an injunction against Fred L. Smith, a cotton farmer near Calvert. The county attorney charged that Smith intended to plant cotton on 1,100 acres out of a 1,300-acre tract, or nearly 85 percent of the land under his control. Attorney Tyson contended that the farmer had revealed his intention to violate the law in the amount of land he had begun to prepare, a crop mortgage filed with the Calvert State Bank, and contracts signed with tenants and seasonal workers. If Tyson could prove the case, Smith stood to be assessed a maximum of $110,000 in fines.[32]

County attorneys in virtually every cotton-growing district in Texas could have filed the same suit. While many Texas cotton farmers planned to disregard the law, some were already circumventing it so openly and

Copyright *Dallas Morning News*, 3 February 1932. Reprinted by permission.

extensively that state officials had to be embarrassed. After harvesting the
1931 crop, farmers in south Texas cut off the stalks from cotton plants on
acreage that would have to be set aside in 1932 and waited for a second
growth of cotton to rise from the old roots in the coming year. The 1931–
32 winter proved quite mild, and in January many south Texas fields
already had cotton plants twelve to fifteen inches high and with fifteen to
twenty sprouts from each root. Although the cotton would be quite bushy
and of inferior quality, it would nonetheless be a crop. Farmers contended
they could not help it if cotton volunteered to grow on idle land.[33]

Some three hundred farmers packed the district court in Franklin on 20
January 1932 as Judge W. C. Davis of Bryan heard arguments in the case.
County Attorney Tyson based his suit chiefly on the police power clauses
of the state constitution. Tyson argued that the constitution gave the legislature the power to protect "the convenience, safety, property, and general
welfare of the people." He produced testimony from experts in the field
that root rot was spreading, the soil was being depleted, and erosion was
destroying the value of land. Defense attorneys countered with demurrers
charging that the acreage control law impaired the obligation of contracts, constituted a deprivation of property without due process of the
law, set aside private property for public benefit without just compensation, and represented price fixing rather than conservation. "It's a fraud
on its face, a lie, a deception," attorney R. E. L. Knight of Dallas argued.
"It was created in a frenzy of hysteria, and passed by a weak-kneed legislature."[34]

Demands that Texas repeal acreage control peaked as the laws of other
states expired. On 21 January 1932 Mississippi's cotton reduction law
died. Just before departing for Washington on 28 January to assume his
seat in the United States Senate, Huey Long repealed by executive proclamation his state's holiday law. Representative J. R. Donnell of Hillsboro,
Texas, himself a cotton farmer, called Sterling's attention to a resolution
adopted at the Jackson convention providing for repeal of acreage control
by 20 January if sufficient states did not come through. "As you know, not
a single other state has, as yet, enacted any law in regard to cotton acreage
reduction since the Jackson conference. The laws of those states that had
previously been enacted have died by limitation. I now express the hope
that you may see fit to call the legislature in session to repeal or amend the
law, so that the farmers of Texas may not be penalized by being forced to
cut their production in half that other states may profit."[35]

District Judge W. C. Davis ruled on 1 February that the acreage control
law passed by the special session of the Forty-second legislature was "unconstitutional, null, and void." Judge Davis said the question that confronted the court was whether the state had the authority under the con-

stitution to deny a citizen the right to use his privately owned lands as he desired. Judge Davis decided that the police powers of the state could be invoked only when the use of property rights endangered either public health, safety, or comfort. "The fundamental principles and guarantees of life, liberty, and property, vouchsafed under the constitution of the United States and the State of Texas, should never be abrogated during the stress of depression," Judge Davis declared. "Precedents by law or otherwise, destructive of these rights, no matter what be the occasion, eventually will destroy our system of free government. Depression and economic ills are, as a rule, of brief duration, but precedents endure."[36] County Attorney Tyson immediately appealed Judge Davis's decision to the Tenth Court of Appeals at Waco. On 5 March 1932 the appeals court sustained Judge Davis's decision, and Tyson chose not to carry the case to the Texas Supreme Court.[37]

Epilogue

Attempts to raise the price and improve the quality of agricultural staples by restricting production can be traced in the South back to colonial times. In 1665 tobacco-producing colonies proposed a one-year moratorium on the planting of the crop. When Lord Baltimore of Maryland refused to go along, the scheme of planned scarcity fell apart.[1] Although plans advocating layoffs have surfaced from time to time since in the United States, the cotton holiday constituted the most comprehensive movement of its kind.[2]

The cotton holiday movement contained many of the ingredients necessary for successful agricultural reform. The people who had the closest contact with the staple and the most to gain or lose—the cotton farmers themselves—were intimately involved in the decision-making process. Huey Long used the new communications medium of the radio to mold and mobilize public opinion throughout the region and to keep everyone informed of rapidly unfolding developments just as soon as they occurred. Concerned parties came together in the most convenient and expedient forum possible, the countywide mass meeting, and debated the pressing issues—the constitutionality of various measures, the impact of the proposals on employment and income, the challenge of foreign competition and substitute products, and the possibility of diversifying southern agriculture. As mass meetings analyzed approaches to the agricultural crisis, the cotton holiday emerged in the minds of many as a feasible vehicle for agricultural reform, and a wide variety of people called for their state legislatures to be summoned into special session to make a sabbatical year binding.

The cotton holiday received widespread and intensive support where others had failed because it promised immediate price relief and the chance to ameliorate the negative influences of cotton on the social, economic, and political life of the South. "Regardless of the outcome," the lieutenant governor of Texas wrote to Long early in the battle, "the people of the Southern states are under a great debt to you for bringing to the attention, in a way never done before, the necessity of reducing production of cotton. I believe," Edgar E. Witt continued, "in the long run—over the years to come—the result of your effort will mean millions of dollars to the people of the South."[3]

The cotton holiday movement was, however, doomed from the start to defeat. The cotton crisis of 1931 provided another classic reminder of the weaknesses and divisions that plague farmers when competing for reforms and favors with other special interest groups from the state to the national level. Cotton farmers were not able to achieve and enjoy the bargaining position that their numbers and contributions to the national economy warranted because of their independent and headstrong nature, dispersed and differing interests, inability to control certain market situations, and lack of political power.[4]

Farmers had no control over the price that they received for their product. Cotton farmers found themselves in a take-it-or-leave-it situation. When farmers took the cotton from the field to the gin, they had to take the price offered or store the bales and seed at additional cost. The price agents offered was based not on the farmer's cost of production but on market conditions at the time of harvest. Likewise, farmers were unable to bargain for machinery, fertilizer, and other necessary supplies. Manufacturers, dealers, and retailers expected the farmers to sell at wholesale, but buy at retail. This meant that farmers had to shoulder the markups made by the manufacturer, wholesaler, and retailer. Cotton farmers were caught in an ever-tightening cost-price squeeze.[5]

In advocating agricultural holidays of one sort or another, farmers were attempting to improve their position in the marketplace. The nation reaped the rewards for overproduction, while the farmer paid the penalties. Just as manufacturing enterprises controlled output and stockpiles through management tactics such as reduced hours, layoffs, and shutdowns, so cotton farmers hoped to influence production and price through acreage controls and planned scarcity. Cotton farmers learned, however, that they could not turn production on and off. Farmers were obligated by contracts to seeing a crop through once it was in the ground. The weather, insects, and disease could dramatically and unpredictably change output. And, finally, there were market conditions beyond the farmers' control. During periods of recession and depression, the demand for farm products declined, and farm prices fell, usually further than the prices of other products. Cotton farmers were in an especially precarious position because a substantial amount of the crop was exported. International crises, ranging from economic downturns to diplomatic hostilities, could seriously influence worldwide consumption.[6]

Of course, farmers were constantly alert to ways to improve their bargaining position in both the marketplace and legislative halls. For example, they organized cooperatives to reduce their costs and bypass a wide range of middlemen both in the purchase of necessary supplies and in the marketing of farm products. These cooperative ventures failed, however, because of the lack of capital, overexpansion and mismanagement, and the cutthroat tactics of competing business, banking, and retail interests.[7]

Cotton farmers recognized the significant role that government could play in improving their welfare. After all, government dictated the rules under which such mundane agricultural matters as credit, currency, and the tariff operated. By the 1920s, various farm groups had established lobbyists in Washington. The National Grange, National Farmers Union, National Board of Farm Organizations, and American Farm Bureau reflected the growing political consciousness of farmers and constituted a vigorous agricultural lobby on Capitol Hill.[8]

These farm organizations were, however, frequently divided over how to support farm prices and control crop surpluses. Farm organizations speaking for midwestern grain and livestock interests usually favored the protective tariff, but southern cotton interests opposed protection because most of the staple was sold abroad. Some farm spokesmen advocated inflationary monetary policies to help farm prices, while others insisted that government should guarantee the cost of production or make parity payments to equalize the price inequities between farm and nonfarm products. Although farmers recognized the benefits that could be secured through unity, organization, and persistence, the wide variety of commodities raised, the dispersion of these crops across a region or the nation, and the many different solutions proposed kept farmers divided and their influence fragmented.[9]

Cotton farmers were, moveover, unable to improve their bargaining position by forming coalitions with other special interest groups. Some of the best-organized and most powerful special interests in the country—labor, manufacturing, and consumer groups, for example—were, farmers believed, the very groups that had been in collusion with government at the expense of agriculture. Although farmers admired the high wages and fringe benefits that unions secured for their members, they felt that such wages and protective tariffs added to the cost of machinery and other operating materials and were partly responsible for the cost-price squeeze in which they found themselves. Farmers believed that residents of cities, especially those in the North and East, wanted only cheap food and clothing, and that Congress heeded the demands of the large urban electorate by either watering down or rejecting aid to agriculture, in order to keep the cost of living down. Manufacturing groups, they felt, were equally insensitive to hard times in the countryside because workers driven off the farm into the city would provide a ready supply of inexpensive labor for mills and factories.[10]

State and federal officials knew only too well the many weaknesses of agricultural protest movements, as revealed in the experiences of the

Grange, Greenbackers, Populists, and a host of other farm groups. From southern statehouses to the nation's capital authorities who opposed drop-a-crop exploited every division and pulled every string to scuttle the holiday idea.

The Hoover administration recognized that farmers were not free and independent. Having raised the crop on credit and accumulated bills due many different middlemen, cotton farmers were at the mercy of the financial structure. "No one ever attempted to organize an army without first getting a general; in the cotton producing business the generals are the creditors," an adviser perceptively informed President Hoover. "By withholding credit, the big people at the top can enforce their edict without any legislation, and without putting the Government in the business as super cotton-merchants of the world." Hoover implemented the advice of his confidant to "put the screws on the strata below."[11]

The White House forced cotton interests to concentrate on the domestic scene by scuttling attempts at international conferences and cooperation. The State Department informed foreign countries by cable that the Federal Farm Board, the Department of Agriculture, and the Department of Commerce had decided it was "undesirable to discuss either the reduction of cotton acreage by legislation or any restriction on the exportation of American cotton."[12] Pushing foreign countries off the stage and into the wings was a shortsighted action on Hoover's part because international competition was very much a part of the overall cotton crisis. Hoover, however, wanted conservative money managers, not southern politicians or foreign diplomats, orchestrating a resolution to the cotton crisis.

The Hoover administration moved to minimize federal involvement and compel the financial system to assume enforcement responsibilities by refusing to seek further appropriations from Congress, buy any more surplus cotton, or develop emergency agricultural relief programs. "Before any credit or financial assistance is extended to any bank, corporation, cooperative association, or other unit in the financial structure," the president's game plan read, "they should be required to sign an ironclad agreement that they will give no credit or financial assistance to any other unit in the structure unless they also bind themselves to refuse all credit unless cotton acreage is reduced 50%."[13] Beginning with the Federal Reserve Board and the Federal Farm Board, pressure was exerted downward through credit and cooperative institutions until it reached the local level of banks, merchants, and cotton farmers with cumulative impact. While corporate and commercial interests held sway in critical legislative chambers, such as Texas, local elites forced striking cotton workers back into the fields and holiday disciples back into the credit line.

Although the cotton holiday movement went down to defeat, it nevertheless made substantial contributions on several fronts. Traditionally, political defeats tarnish a politician's record. Many politicians steered clear of involvement in the cotton holiday out of fear of discrediting themselves politically. The collapse of the holiday, however, instead of devaluating Long's political stock, actually strengthened and enhanced his image as a champion of the forgotten man. He was seen as a person always on the side of the common man in his struggle against the railroads, banks, fertilizer companies, jute-bagging trust, and other vested interests. "Your great fight for the downtrodden cotton farmers of the South has made you the idol of 95% of our people," wrote E. C. Glover, a member of the Alabama House of Representatives. "I mean, of course, the common people, and not the cotton gamblers, cottonseed oil kings, grafters and parasites who live by fleecing the common folks."

As Long fulfilled his promises of roads, bridges, hospitals, schoolbooks, and other public services in Louisiana, he launched a social service welfare state well in advance of Franklin D. Roosevelt's New Deal. Long recognized that state and federal governments were the only institutions with the power and resources to redress deep-seated inequities in society. He consequently used government in a bold and adventuresome manner on behalf of society's have-nots, and he became for the lower social and economic classes throughout the South a messianic figure. "It is my opinion," a resident of Hagen, Arkansas, declared, "that you are the Moses that will finish the work that Abe Lincoln started, and that is to free the white as well as the black slaves of our dear Southland."[14]

The mass meetings and special legislative sessions that spread through the South prepared the region psychologically for mandatory production control and paved the way for regulation on the national scene.[15] The first stepping-stones had been put into place during the 1920s. Long capitalized on the curtailment sentiment the Memphis cotton conference of 1926 had revealed and carried the case a step forward to a holiday. In the 1930s, a group of eminent social scientists from the University of North Carolina and Fisk University studied the cotton situation in the United States and concluded that the cotton holiday movement had a significant impact on the crop reduction and recovery programs of the New Deal. "The legislation passed by Louisiana, Texas, and South Carolina in the Fall and Winter of 1931–32 . . . indicated the South's demand for some form of acreage control," the commission concluded. "Once the allotment was agreed upon, the plow-up campaign and the 1934 acreage reduction followed as a matter of course."[16]

Virtually every issue central to the production control programs of the New Deal was thoroughly discussed in the mass meetings that were held across the South during the cotton crisis of 1931. Holiday forces had analyzed the role that the courts, employment, alternative crops, overseas producers, and many other issues might play in production control and spelled out the contingencies that would have to be met to make legislation constitutional, financial compensation acceptable, diversification feasible, and regional cooperation possible. As Theodore Saloutos has underscored, farmer movements in the South have always contributed more to the formation of national policy than most people recognize.[17]

The election of Franklin D. Roosevelt opened the way for new and experimental approaches to agricultural reform. Instead of attempting to dispose of surplus crops after they were produced, the New Deal decided to raise the price of commodities by restricting output. The Agricultural Adjustment Act, which was passed in May 1933 as part of the "First Hundred Days," provided farmers with benefit payments for limiting production. The New Deal proceeded to establish the federal government's role in agricultural planning by passing legislation that provided for emergency farm mortgage relief, soil conservation, and the distribution of surplus agricultural products to the destitute. The New Deal also attempted to raise the standard of living of southern farmers through projects like the Tennessee Valley Authority, which provided cheap fertilizer and inexpensive power for rural electrification, among other benefits.[18]

Once Long assumed his Senate seat in Washington, agricultural reform became only part of his broader program to redistribute wealth nationally. Through a combination of income, inheritance, and capital levy taxes, Long hoped to create a mammoth fund that would be used to provide needy families with a minimum annual income of two to three thousand dollars; a family homestead worth five thousand dollars; a college education for persons demonstrating ability; and a pension in old age. Long felt that in this country which had been blessed with certain natural resources farmers should be encouraged to produce at full capacity and the federal government should market the fruits of their labors to the less fortunate around the world. "The government will always keep a surplus, if it can get enough products to do so," Long said, "in order to prepare for any emergency or distress that may threaten." If government wanted farmers to restrict their productive capacities, then government should compensate them for the loss.[19]

Long protested against many of the New Deal's agricultural proposals because he felt that they either did not go far enough or failed to incorporate sufficient safeguards for the common man. "One day here we vote an appropriation of several billion dollars . . . to take land out of cultivation, and the next day we vote a few billion dollars to get it back into cultivation. One day we vote a few billion dollars to kill all the hogs, and then the next day we vote a few billion dollars to raise hogs," Long said in a

typical critique. "Where in the hell are we going?" By criticizing or opposing the provisions of various bills, Long actually assisted in their passage
because, as T. Harry Williams has pointed out, some senators feared he
might arouse support for something even more drastic and extreme.[20]

In the mid-1930s, the New Deal moved leftward. During the "Second
Hundred Days," Roosevelt introduced must pieces of legislation involving
social security, banking, public utilities, labor relations, and taxation. In
making these requests, Roosevelt was responding to a number of conditions, including recent Supreme Court decisions that struck down early
New Deal legislation, growing criticism from the business community, a
Congress of more liberal interests and ideology, and, of course, Huey
Long. From a group of political dissidents that included Father Charles
Coughlin, Dr. Francis Townsend, and Upton Sinclair, Long had emerged
as the most dangerous and serious challenger to Roosevelt's leadership. The president undercut the burgeoning popularity of these radicals
through legislative counteroffers. "Huey Long seemed a dangerous individual, and some maneuvering had to be arranged to contain his spreading influence," Rexford G. Tugwell has written. "He helped in his way . . .
to pass the Social Security Act, the bill for an increase in corporate taxes,
and the huge (as it was then regarded) appropriation to combat unemployment."[21]

Although the New Deal provided agricultural relief, recovery, and reform, commercial agriculture was the main beneficiary and corporate
interests remained entrenched. The agricultural price-cost squeeze compelled cotton farmers to increase size and cut expenses to stay in business.
The emphasis on growth and cost cutting forced small-scale operators to
give way to commercial agriculture. Since the large operators had the
most influential voice in agricultural matters, the programs and policies
that emanated from legislative chambers most favored the commercial
farmer.[22]

New Deal programs were rife with abuses and marked by exploitive
incidents. The federal government offered landowners production credit
at 4½ to 6½ percent interest, but tenant farmers could not secure such
low interest unless the landlord waived his first lien on the crop. Planters
plowed under more than ten million acres of cotton and farmers slaugh-
tered over six million young pigs and pregnant sows to raise the prices,
but in the process perhaps as many as one hundred thousand tenants were
displaced and countless millions of Americans remained undernourished.
Benefit payments were supposed to trickle down the agricultural ladder,
but insurance companies, oil mills, landlords, merchants, lawyers, and
other vested interests grabbed off their share and more before it ever
reached the bottom rung. Parity benefits, rent payments, low-interest

loans, and other federal funds were used by commercial farmers to purchase more land, machinery, and scientific agriculture at the expense of the family farm. "The depression caught cotton growers at just the wrong point between feudalism and modernization," Pete Daniel has written. "One disaster after another—boll weevil, flood, drought, the AAA program, tractors, war, and picking machines—swept croppers, wage hands, and small owners from the land." Indeed, the cotton crisis of 1931 represented in many ways a tragic last gasp by the family farmer before he was overwhelmed by the advance of agribusiness in America.[23]

Notes

Abbreviations

Bilbo MS	Theodore G. Bilbo Papers
Blackwood MS	Ibra C. Blackwood Papers
Connally MS LC	Thomas T. Connally Papers
Hoover MS	Herbert H. Hoover Papers
Hunt MS	George W. P. Hunt Papers
Long MS	Huey P. Long Papers
McKellar MS	Kenneth D. McKellar Papers
Miller MS	Benjamin M. Miller Papers
Parnell MS	Harvey Parnell Papers
RG 16 NA	General Correspondence of the Secretary of Agriculture
RG 83 NA	General Correspondence of the Bureau of Agricultural Economics
Sterling MS	Ross S. Sterling Papers
USDA	United States Department of Agriculture
USDC	United States Department of Commerce

Introduction

1. Molyneaux, *The Cotton South and American Trade Policy*, 7–11.

2. Woodman, *King Cotton and His Retainers*, throughout.

3. Memorandum for the President, 9 September 1931, Hoover MS.

4. Hubbard, *Cotton and the Cotton Market*, 49–59; Haystead and Fite, *The Agricultural Regions of the United States*, 107–13; Fite, "Southern Agriculture since the Civil War," 13–15.

5. Crowther, "The Cotton Crisis," 4–5.

6. S. L. Sandford to Hatton W. Sumners, 26 September 1925, RG 16 NA. Interpolation in original.

7. USDA, *The Crop and Livestock Reporting Services of the United States*; USDA, *A History of Agricultural Experimentation and Research in the United States, 1607–1925*; USDA, *The Agricultural Estimating and Reporting Services of the United States Department of Agriculture*.

8. Howard L. Taylor to William M. Jardine, 17 October 1927, RG 16 NA. Interpolation in the original.

9. Link, "The Cotton Crisis, the South, and Anglo-American Diplomacy, 1914–1915," 122–38; McCorkle, "Louisiana and the Cotton Crisis, 1914," 303–21.

10. From time to time institutes of public affairs have sponsored symposia on the problems of cotton, and foundations have subsequently made the proceedings available in anthology form. See, for example, Myres (ed.), *The Cotton Crisis*.

11. Fite, "Voluntary Attempts to Reduce Cotton Acreage in the South, 1914–1933," 486–89.

12. Helms, "Just Lookin' for a Home," throughout; Vance, *Human Factors in Cotton Culture*, 89–107.

13. For statistical information on cotton consult the appropriate years of USDA, *Yearbook of Agriculture*.

14. W. N. Malone to Calvin Coolidge, 13 October 1926, Earle Helm to Coolidge, 9 October 1926, RG 16 NA.

15. G. L. Pattilo to Ross S. Sterling, 26 August 1931, Sterling MS. The chronic poverty of the region receives treatment in Mertz, *New Deal Policy and Southern Rural Poverty*, 1–19.

16. Francis G. Tracy to Huey P. Long, 22 August 1931, Long MS.

17. Long, *Every Man a King*, 263–64.

18. M. S. Carmichael to John Peach, 10 December 1931, Miller MS.

Chapter 1

1. *New Orleans Times-Picayune*, 8 August 1931, 21, and 9 August 1931, 1:1, 6; *New York Times*, 2 August 1931, 3:5, 6 August 1931, 33, and 7 August 1931, 30.

2. USDA, *Cotton Prices and Markets*; USDA, *Factors Affecting the Price of Cotton*.

3. *Montgomery Advertiser*, 13 August 1931, 2; *Houston Post-Dispatch*, 3 August 1931, 4.

4. *New York Times*, 9 August 1931, 2:14; *New Orleans Times-Picayune*, 9 August 1931, 1:1.

5. USDC, *Cotton Production and Distribution, 1925–1932*; *Wall Street Journal*, 10 August 1931, 1, 4.

6. *New York Times*, 8 August 1931, 1, and 11 August 1931, 2; *New Orleans Times-Picayune*, 9 August 1931, 1:1, 6.

7. *New Orleans Times-Picayune*, 9 August 1931, 8; *Memphis Commercial Appeal*, 9 August 1931, 4:4.

8. *Chicago Tribune*, 9 August 1931, 1:9, 2:8, and 11 August 1931, 27; *New York Times*, 9 August 1931, 1:9; *Washington Post*, 9 August 1931, 1:9; *New Orleans Times-Picayune*, 10 August 1931, 21.

9. *New Orleans Times-Picayune*, 9 August 1931, 4:8; *Chicago Tribune*, 9 August 1931, 2:7; *Wall Street Journal*, 10 August 1931, 4; "Cotton and Wheat Lead Commodities to New Lows," 8; "Wheat and Cotton Are Steadier but Not by Farm Board Aid," 15–16.

10. *Dallas Morning News*, 9 August 1931, 1:12.

11. *Arkansas Gazette*, 11 August 1931, 11; *Wall Street Journal*, 11 August 1931, 2; *Chicago Tribune*, 11 August 1931, 25.

12. *New York Times*, 11 August 1931, 2; *New Orleans Times-Picayune*, 11 August 1931, 1, 4, 21; *Manchester Guardian Weekly*, 14 August 1931, 121, 123, 126; *Chicago Tribune*, 11 August 1931, 25.

13. *New York Times*, 11 August 1931, 1, 2; *New Orleans Times-Picayune*, 11 August 1931, 1, 4, 21; *Wall Street Journal*, 11 August 1931, 1, 2; *Arkansas Gazette*, 10 August 1931, 11.

14. *Houston Post-Dispatch*, 13 August 1931, 1, 6; *Memphis Commercial Appeal*, 11 August 1931, 1, 3; *Wall Street Journal*, 11 August 1931, 1, 2.

15. Smith, "Ellison Durant Smith," throughout; Lander, *A History of South Carolina, 1865–1900*, 77–78.

16. Ellison D. Smith to Arthur M. Hyde, 3 August 1931, RG 16 NA; *Memphis Commercial Appeal*, 4 August 1931, 1.

17. C. Marvin to Ellison D. Smith, 4 August 1931, RG 16 NA.

18. *Shreveport Times*, 14 August 1931, 2; *Montgomery Advertiser*, 18 August 1931, 4; *Atlanta Constitution*, 8 August 1931, 12; *State*, 9 August 1931, 1:2.

19. *Atlanta Constitution*, 8 August 1931, 12.

20. R. R. Claridge to Thomas T. Connally, August 1931, Connally to Claridge, 17 August 1931, Connally MS LC.

21. Lafayette L. Patterson to Arthur M. Hyde, 10 August 1931, RG 16 NA.

22. *Memphis Commercial Appeal*, 10 August 1931, 6; *Greenwood Commonwealth* editorial reprinted in *Memphis Press-Scimitar*, 18 August 1931, 4. For some of the department's previous statistical errors consult Smith, "The Statisticians' Error Cost Cotton Growers $100,000,000," 15, 36.

23. C. Marvin to Thomas T. Connally, 12 and 14 August 1931, Marvin to Lafayette L. Patterson, 12 and 14 August 1931, RG 16 NA.

24. "Cotton Crisis," 10; *Memphis Commercial Appeal*, 12 August 1931, 11.

25. *Atlanta Constitution*, 31 August 1931, 4.

26. Ron L. McKellar to Kenneth D. McKellar, 28 August 1931, McKellar MS.

27. Kenneth D. McKellar to Arthur M. Hyde, 17 August 1931, C. Marvin to McKellar, 25 August 1931, RG 16 NA. Since the Crop Reporting Board was not formed until 1912 and did not start making cotton forecasts until 1915, McKellar revealed exactly how unfamiliar many southern politicians actually were with the system.

28. Kenneth D. McKellar to Ron L. McKellar, 29 August 1931, McKellar MS.

29. Robert D. Pope, "Senatorial Baron," 145–211.

30. R. T. Fant to Kenneth D. McKellar, 24 August 1931, McKellar MS.

31. Kenneth D. McKellar to R. T. Fant, 31 August 1931, McKellar MS.

32. Throughout the 1920s southern politicians registered numerous complaints on a wide variety of issues with federal agricultural officials. These letters are filed under either individual names or cotton folders in RG 16 and RG 83 NA; "Representative Black Plans Legislation to Abolish Cotton Forecast of Department of Agriculture," 1826–27.

33. William F. Callander to Dunlap, 6 July 1925, RG 16 NA.

34. John E. Rankin to Calvin Coolidge, 4 October 1928, RG 16 NA.

35. Charles E. Gage to Cooper, 24 November 1925, RG 83 NA.

36. Thomas T. Connally to Arthur M. Hyde, 9 August 1931, RG 16 NA; *New York Times*, 10 August 1931, 17.

37. *Houston Post-Dispatch*, 12 August 1931, 1:6.

38. Clarence D. Cade to Thomas T. Connally, 13 August 1931, Connally MS LC.

39. D. A. Bandeen to Thomas T. Connally, 19 August 1931, Connally MS LC.

40. L. W. Dongres to Thomas T. Connally, 11 August 1931, Connally to Dongres, 17 August 1931, Connally MS LC. Recent research suggests that the Farm Bloc in Congress during the 1920s was far less stable and disciplined than previously believed. Although Democrats from the South joined western and midwestern Republicans on various agricultural issues, Patrick G. O'Brien has concluded through quantitative techniques that "an idealized agrarian bloc seldom was a reality because legislation could not be equally advantageous to all farmers" (O'Brien, "A Reexamination of the Senate Farm Bloc, 1921–1933," 248–63).

41. See, for example, Thomas T. Connally to William M. Jardine, 30 November 1925, Connally to Arthur M. Hyde, 30 September 1929, RG 83 NA.

42. Robert M. Gates to Thomas T. Connally, 13 August 1931, Connally MS LC.

43. Thomas T. Connally to Robert M. Gates, 10 September 1931, Connally MS LC.

44. Nils Olsen to Arthur M. Hyde, 17 August 1931, RG 16 NA; William F. Callander to Paul L. Koenig, August 1931, RG 83 NA.

45. *Wall Street Journal*, 13 August 1931, 13; *New York Times*, 12 August 1931, 13; *Washington Post*, 12 August 1931, 13; *Memphis Press-Scimitar*, 11 August 1931, 14.
46. Paul L. Koenig to William F. Callander, 17 August 1931, RG 83 NA.

Chapter 2

1. Hoover, *The New Day*, 12–24; Hoover, *The Memoirs of Herbert Hoover*, vol. 2, *The Cabinet and the Presidency, 1920–1933*; Romasco, *The Poverty of Abundance*, 20–22, 97–106.
2. U.S., Congress, *Congressional Record*, 71st Congress, 1st Session, 16 April 1929, vol. 71, pt. 1, 42–43; Hoover, *Memoirs*, 2:253–54; Wilbur and Hyde, *The Hoover Policies*, 149–51.
3. Fite, *George N. Peek and the Fight for Farm Parity*, 12–15, 38–42, and throughout; Fite, *American Farmers*, 41–48. Benedict, *Farm Policies of the United States, 1790–1950*, 207–38; Hicks, *Republican Ascendancy, 1921–1933*, 193–201.
4. Fite, *George N. Peek*, 92–93, 95, 151–68, 170–71, 177, 188–90; Hicks, *Republican Ascendancy*, 197–98; Saloutos, *Farmer Movements in the South, 1865–1933*, 265–72; Grant, "Southern Congressmen and Agriculture, 1921–1932," 338–51.
5. Wilson, *Herbert Hoover*, 102–10; Wilson, "Hoover's Agricultural Policies, 1921–1928," 335–61; Fausold, "President Hoover's Farm Policies, 1929–1933," 362–77; Koerselman, "Secretary Hoover and National Farm Policy," 378–95; Shideler, "Herbert Hoover and the Federal Farm Board Project, 1921–1925," 710–29.
6. The origins and functions of the Agricultural Marketing Act and Federal Farm Board are covered by Stokdyk and West, *The Farm Board*. Several unpublished studies of the Farm Board have also been consulted: Miller, "Origins and Functions of the Federal Farm Board"; Moe, "The Federal Farm Board"; Norman, "The Federal Farm Board."
7. Myers and Newton, *The Hoover Administration*, 393–94; Wilbur and Hyde, *The Hoover Policies*, 151–52; Fausold, "Hoover's Farm Policies," 368.
8. Hoover, *Memoirs*, 2:255; Miller, "Federal Farm Board," 136–37.
9. Further information on Carl Williams can be found in: U.S., Congress, Senate, Committee on Agriculture and Forestry, *Hearings: Confirmation of the Federal Farm Board*, 71st Congress, 1st Session, pt. 4, 181–86; Hard, "Hoover Picks His Men," 46–51; *Who's Who in America* (Chicago: A. N. Marquis, 1930), 16:2363.
10. Commenting on cotton's shift westward: Becker, "Regional Shifts Large in Major Crop Acreages During Decade 1919–1929," 485–86; Chambliss, "Cotton Growing in the West," 507–10; W. J. Spillman, "Changes in Type of Farming, 1919–1924," 203–7; Stern, "Cotton Goes West," 29–30.
11. Vance, Ivey, and Bond, *Exploring the South*, 89–90; "King Cotton's Throne Moves Westward," 45–46.
12. *New York Times*, 27 June 1929, 2.
13. "The Men Who Will Tackle the Big Farm Relief Task," 8–9; Murphy, "President Hoover's Cabinet," 269–75; Saloutos, *Farmer Movements in the South*, 272–73. Southern expectations regarding regional appointments to the cabinet and Farm Board are discussed by Ginzl, "Herbert Hoover and Republican Patronage Politics in the South, 1928–1932," 130–35.
14. U.S., Congress, *Hearings: Confirmation of the Members of the Federal Farm Board*, 204–7; *New York Times*, 5 October 1929, 32, and 7 October 1929, 20.
15. U.S., Congress, *Congressional Record*, 71st Congress, 1st Session, 1929, 81, pt. 4, 4593. Letter from Williams in ibid., 4309, and U.S., Congress, *Hearings: Confirmation of the Members of the Federal Farm Board*, 263–64.

16. U.S., *Congressional Record*, 71st Congress, 1st Session, 1929, 81, pt. 4, 4600, 4611, 4587; *New York Times*, 12 October 1929, 9, and 17 October 1929, 1, 8.

17. Romasco, *Poverty of Abundance*, 109–14; Benedict, *Farm Policies*, 257–60.

18. Myers and Newton, *The Hoover Administration*, 24; Wilbur and Hyde, *The Hoover Policies*, 152; Romasco, *Poverty of Abundance*, 114–15; Benedict, *Farm Policies*, 241–42, 247–48.

19. Federal Farm Board, *First Annual Report*, 10–12, 37–40; Benedict, *Farm Policies*, 259–60; Saloutos, *Farmer Movements in the South*, 273–75.

20. Myers and Newton, *The Hoover Administration*, 37–39; Wilbur and Hyde, *The Hoover Policies*, 153–54.

21. Federal Farm Board, *First Annual Report*, 40; Federal Farm Board, *Second Annual Report*, 48; Benedict, *Farm Policies*, 260.

22. Federal Farm Board, *Second Annual Report*, 48–49; Wilbur and Hyde, *The Hoover Policies*, 154–56; Benedict, *Farm Policies*, 263.

23. Federal Farm Board, *Second Annual Report*, 53–57; Federal Farm Board, *Third Annual Report*, 60–61; Myers and Newton, *The Hoover Administration*, 148.

24. Federal Farm Board, *Second Annual Report*, 57–58; Federal Farm Board, *Third Annual Report*, 60–61.

25. Theodore G. Bilbo to Governors of the Cotton States, 10 August 1931, Bilbo MS; *Daily Clarion-Ledger*, 11 August 1931, 1, 8.

26. *Wall Street Journal*, 12 August 1931, 2.

27. Kenneth B. McMicken to George W. P. Hunt, 12 August 1931, M. C. Stevens to Hunt, 12 August 1931, H. A. Thompson to Hunt, 12 August 1931, W. S. Prouty to Hunt, 14 August 1931, G. M. Bridges to Hunt, 12 August 1931, Bilbo MS; *Daily Clarion-Ledger*, 12 August 1931, 1.

28. The fourteen cotton states cabled by Chairman Stone were Alabama, Arizona, Arkansas, California, Florida, Georgia, Louisiana, Mississippi, New Mexico, North Carolina, Oklahoma, South Carolina, Tennessee, and Texas.

29. The telegram to southern governors can be found in several manuscript collections. See, for example, James C. Stone to Huey P. Long, 12 August 1931, Long MS. *New York Times*, 13 August 1931, 1, 13.

30. *New Orleans Times-Picayune*, 14 August 1931, 1; *Memphis Commercial Appeal*, 14 August 1931, 3.

31. Stone's telegram to Long et al., 12 August 1931, Long MS.

32. F. G. Salter to Benjamin M. Miller, 15 August 1931, Miller MS.

33. *New York Times*, 14 August 1931, 1, 9; *New Orleans Times-Picayune*, 14 August 1931, 3.

34. E. P. Ruhman to Ross S. Sterling, 14 August 1931, Sterling MS; W. C. Lankford to Theodore G. Bilbo, 13 August 1931, Bilbo MS.

35. *Memphis Commercial Appeal*, 21 August 1931, 24, and 3 October 1931, 3.

36. Editorial of the *Abilene Morning News*, reprinted in *Houston Chronicle*, 14 August 1931, 2. Other complaints along similar lines: *Atlanta Constitution*, 15 August 1931, 8; *Houston Post-Dispatch*, 15 August 1931, 1:5.

37. W. G. McIntyre to Arthur M. Hyde, 29 September 1931, Hyde to McIntyre, 10 October 1931, RG 16 NA.

38. *Houston Post-Dispatch*, 22 August 1931, 1:1, 6.

39. *Daily Clarion-Ledger*, 13 August 1931, 1; *Jackson Daily News*, 13 August 1931, 1, 16.

40. *New Orleans Times-Picayune*, 14 August 1931, 3, 21; "Wheat and Cotton Are Steadier but Not by Farm Board Aid," 15–16.

41. "Salvation by Suicide," 48; B. W. Bailey to Huey P. Long, 13 August 1931, Francis G.

Tracy to Arthur Seligman, 20 August 1931, Long MS; Thomas C. McReynolds to George W. P. Hunt, 14 August 1931, Bilbo MS; *Daily Clarion-Ledger*, 21 August 1931, 11.

42. J. M. M'Kean to Editor, *New Orleans Times-Picayune*, 23 August 1931, 1:18.

43. *Atlanta Constitution*, 15 August 1931, 8.

44. Federal Farm Board, *Third Annual Report*, 81–83.

45. Hoover, *Memoirs*, 3:152; Myers and Newton, *The Hoover Administration*, 224, 235, 528.

46. *New York Times*, 21 August 1932, 1:2.

47. Federal Farm Board, *Third Annual Report*, 84; Miller, "Origins and Functions of the Federal Farm Board," 289–91.

48. *Atlanta Constitution*, 19 August 1931, 6.

49. Benjamin M. Miller and Seth P. Storrs to Arthur M. Hyde, 15 August 1931, Miller and Storrs to Herbert Hoover, 15 August 1931, Miller MS; *Montgomery Advertiser*, 16 August 1931, 1:1; *Atlanta Constitution*, 16 August 1931, 1:2; *New Orleans Item-Tribune*, 16 August 1931, 1:9.

50. Carl Williams to William H. Beatty, 20 August 1931, Beatty to Benjamin M. Miller, 22 August 1931, Miller MS; J. F. Woodward to Kenneth D. McKellar, 10 February 1931, McKellar MS.

51. *Atlanta Constitution*, 14 August 1931, 1, 8, and 19 August 1931, 8; *New Orleans Item*, 14 August 1931, 1; *New York Times*, 14 August 1931, 16; *Jackson Daily News*, 1 September 1931, 1; *Memphis Commercial Appeal*, 2 September 1931, 2; *Shreveport Times*, 30 September 1931, 12; *Houston Post-Dispatch*, 5 September 1931, 1:8, and 12 November 1931, 8.

52. *New York Times*, 14 August 1931, 9; *New Orleans Times-Picayune*, 14 August 1931, 21; *Washington Post*, 14 August 1931, 2; *Houston Post-Dispatch*, 16 August 1931, 1:12; "Cotton Crisis," 11.

53. Editorial survey in Hoover MS; "Destroy and Prosper," 198.

54. Blair Gimer to Thomas T. Connally, 15 October 1931, Connally MS LC.

Chapter 3

1. E. C. Pierce to Ross S. Sterling, 1 September 1931, Sterling MS.

2. Huey P. Long, *Every Man a King*, 263; Williams, *Huey Long*, 531; Molyneaux, *The Cotton South and American Trade Policy*, 20–22.

3. Undated typescript of Huey Long's telegram and announcement in Long MS; *New Orleans Item*, 17 August 1931, 1, 3; *Baton Rouge State-Times*, 17 August 1931, 1, 12, and 18 August 1931, 1, 4; *New Orleans Times-Picayune*, 19 August 1931, 1, 21; *New York Times*, 17 August 1931, 34.

4. *Birmingham News*, 18 August 1931, 8; *Dallas Morning News*, 19 August 1931, 2:4; *Houston Post-Dispatch*, 20 August 1931, 1:6.

5. Williams, "The Politics of the Longs," 20–33.

6. Long furnishes a running account of his performance on the commission in *Every Man a King*, 37–69, 78–93, and Williams provides a detailed description of how Long transformed an essentially moribund body into an effective modern agency in *Huey Long*, 119–80, 225–43. Long's activities on the commission also receive passing mention in: Beals, *The Story of Huey Long*, 41–54; Martin, *Dynasty*, 31–37; Sindler, *Huey Long's Louisiana*, 46–48.

7. Charles H. Franz to the Chairman of the Long Ouster Case, 11 February 1934, Franklin D. Roosevelt Papers, Franklin D. Roosevelt Library, Hyde Park, New York. Practi-

cally every orator who eulogized Long voiced a similar sentiment. See, for example, U.S., Congress, House Document 480, *Memorial Services Held in the House of Representatives of the United States, Together with Remarks Presented in Eulogy of Huey Pierce Long,* 74th Congress, 2d Session, 1936, and U.S., Senate Document 110, *Acceptance of the Statue of Huey Pierce Long, Presented by the State of Louisiana, Proceedings in the Congress and Statuary Hall,* 77th Congress, 1st Session, 1941.

8. *Shreveport Times,* 15 August 1931, 2, and 21 August 1931, 2; *New Orleans Times-Picayune,* 22 August 1931, 1, 3; Williams, *Huey Long,* 531.

9. George R. Bowman to Huey P. Long, 14 August 1931, Long MS.

10. John L. McLaurin to Editor, *Atlanta Constitution,* 16 August 1931, 1:13. Years earlier the South Carolina and Texas legislatures briefly flirted with the possibility of instituting a complete ban on cotton for one year. Tindall, *The Emergence of the New South, 1913–1945,* 35; Wallace, *South Carolina,* 664; "Suspension of Cotton Planting for One Year Proposed by Senator Smith," 1160–61.

11. T. N. Mauritz to Ross S. Sterling, 17 August 1931, B. S. Smith to Sterling, 13 August 1931, J. M. Henderson to Sterling, 14 August 1931, Sterling MS.

12. North Arkansas Ginners Association to Herbert Hoover, 11 August 1931, Sterling MS.

13. Pusateri, "The Stormy Career of a Radio Maverick, W. K. Henderson of KWKH," 389–407; Hall, "A Historical Survey of Programming Techniques and Practices of Radio Station KWKH, Shreveport, Louisiana, 1922–1950"; Williams, *Huey Long,* 201, 252.

14. Written interview of Cecil Morgan to author, 6 October 1975.

15. In 1933, Henderson was forced to sell his beloved station because the national depression, legal fees, operating expenses, and personal debts had placed him in severe financial straits. See Pusateri, "Radio Maverick," 403–6.

16. James M. Thompson to Huey P. Long, 17 August 1931, Long MS; *New Orleans Item,* 18 August 1931, 3:2, 20 August 1931, 16, and 21 August 1931, 6; *Shreveport Times,* 19 August 1931, 1, 4; Wilds, *Afternoon Story,* 204–11, 228–34; Williams, *Huey Long,* 445, 534–35.

17. James M. Thompson to Harvey Parnell, 19 August 1931, Parnell to Thompson, 20 August 1931, Parnell MS.

18. *New Orleans Times-Picayune,* 18 August 1931, 3.

19. Will K. Henderson to Benjamin M. Miller, 18 August 1931, James M. Thompson to Miller, 19 August 1931, Miller MS.

20. *New Orleans Item,* 21 August 1931, 1, 4.

21. James M. Thompson to Ross S. Sterling, 19 August 1931, Sterling MS; W. P. Hobby to Thompson, 20 August 1931, Long MS. For other private interest groups wiring Sterling to attend consult: Shreveport Clearing House Association to Sterling, 17 August 1931; Robstown, Texas, Chamber of Commerce to Sterling, 17 August 1931, Sterling MS.

22. Ross S. Sterling to Huey P. Long, 21 August 1931, Sterling MS.

23. *New Orleans Item,* 20 August 1931, 1, 3; *Houston Post-Dispatch,* 21 August 1931, 1:5.

24. Saloutos, *Farmer Movements in the South, 1865–1933,* 156–60; Watkins, *King Cotton,* 210–11.

25. The following account of the New Orleans cotton conference has been compiled from: *New Orleans Times-Picayune,* 22 August 1931, 1, 3; *New Orleans Item,* 21 August 1931, 1, 4, 22 August 1931, 1, 2, and 26 August 1931, 1, 4; *Baton Rouge State-Times,* 21 August 1931, 1, 4, and 22 August 1931, 1, 4; *Shreveport Times,* 22 August 1931, 1; *Atlanta Constitution,* 25 August 1931, 3; *Houston Post-Dispatch,* 22 August 1931, 1:2; *Memphis Commercial Appeal,* 22 August 1931, 12; "No More Cotton?" 11.

26. *Dallas Morning News*, 21 August 1931, 2:4; *Montgomery Advertiser*, 23 August 1931, 1:4; *Arkansas Gazette*, 21 August 1931, 4; *Shreveport Times*, 21 August 1931, 1.

27. *New Orleans Times-Picayune*, 22 August 1931, 3; *Atlanta Constitution*, 22 August 1931, 4.

28. "A Farmer" to Huey P. Long, 17 August 1931, Long MS. The ineffectiveness of voluntary measures has been well documented by Fite, "Voluntary Attempts to Reduce Cotton Acreage in the South, 1914–1933," 481–99.

29. *New Orleans Item*, 24 August 1931, 1, 2.

30. *New Orleans Item*, 25 August 1931, 10.

31. "Texas Tries," 14; "East Texas Prorated," 16.

32. J. M. Jones to Huey P. Long, 24 August 1931, Marvin H. Young to Long, n.d., Long MS.

33. *Austin American-Statesman*, 23 August 1931, 2; *Houston Post-Dispatch*, 23 August 1931, 1:14.

34. *Austin American-Statesman*, 24 August 1931, 1; *Dallas Morning News*, 25 August 1931, 1:1, 3; *Houston Chronicle*, 24 August 1931, 14; *Houston Post-Dispatch*, 24 August 1931, 1:1, 2.

35. *Houston Chronicle*, 24 August 1931, 4; *New Orleans Item*, 25 August 1931, 1, 2.

36. Huey P. Long to Ross S. Sterling, 24 August 1931, Long MS.

37. *New Orleans Item*, 22 August 1931, 1, 2. For Louisiana politicians pledging support see, for example, F. E. Delahoussaye to Huey P. Long, 20 August 1931, Paul H. Mahoney to Long, 17 August 1931, and John H. Overton to Long, 18 August 1931, Long MS.

38. Undated typescript of Long's announcement in Long MS; *New Orleans Times-Picayune*, 25 August 1931, 1, 3.

39. Sewall and Adger to Huey P. Long, 25 August 1931, Long MS.

40. Valuable discussions of this topic are provided in: Hair, *Bourbonism and Agrarian Protest*; Kirwan, *Revolt of the Rednecks*; Woodward, *Origins of the New South, 1877–1913*.

41. Key, *Southern Politics*, 159–60; Williams, *Huey Long*, 181–91; Reynolds, *Machine Politics in New Orleans, 1897–1926*; Kemp, *Martin Behrman of New Orleans*.

42. Sindler, *Huey Long's Louisiana*, 1–26; White, "Populism in Louisiana During the Nineties," 3–19; McWhiney, "Louisiana Socialists in the Early Twentieth Century," 315–36.

43. Long, *Every Man a King*, 122–25, 138–83; Williams, *Huey Long*, 347–410.

44. *New Orleans Times-Picayune*, 25 August 1931, 1, 3; *New Orleans Item*, 25 August 1931, 2.

45. Several quantitative studies of Louisiana electoral data and census statistics have indicated that the most consistent and intense electoral opposition to Huey P. Long came from larger cities and along alluvial deltas, namely, those geopolitical areas controlled by machine politicians headquartered in New Orleans and planting interests and courthouse groupings in the outlying parishes. See, for instance, Sindler, *Huey Long's Louisiana*, 48–57, 71–79, and Howard, *Political Tendencies in Louisiana*, 211–50. T. Harry Williams was the first to suggest that previously antagonistic planting and machine interests supported Long during the holiday (*Huey Long*, 530–33).

All of the following letters and telegrams to Huey P. Long are to be found in Long MS: W. D. Brown, 25 August 1931, T. B. Gilbert & Co., 12 September 1931, John Pullen, 4 September 1931, John O. Roy, 1 September 1931. Norris C. Williamson's comment in *New Orleans Times-Picayune*, 21 August 1931, 3.

46. Written interviews of C. P. Liter to author, 9 October 1975, J. Cleveland Frugé to

author, 9 October 1975, George Healy to author, 14 October 1975, Cecil Morgan to author, 6 October 1975; Reuben T. Douglas to Huey P. Long, 18 August 1931, Long MS; *Shreveport Times*, 20 August 1931, 1, 2.

47. Louisiana, *Official Journals*; *New Orleans Times-Picayune*, 26 August 1931, 1, 2; *Baton Rouge State-Times*, 25 August 1931, 1, 4, 26 August 1931, 1, 2, 4, and 27 August 1931, 1, 4.

48. Louisiana, *Official Journals*; *New Orleans Times-Picayune*, 26 August 1931, 1, 2, and 27 August 1931, 1, 2.

49. *New Orleans Item*, 27 August 1931, 4.

50. *Shreveport Times*, 29 August 1931, 16.

51. *New Orleans Times-Picayune*, 28 August 1931, 1, 3; *New York Times*, 28 August 1931, 1:2; *Wall Street Journal*, 28 August 1931, 2.

52. *New York Times*, 30 August 1931, 1:2; *New Orleans Item*, 29 August 1931, 1, 2; Long, *Every Man a King*, 263; Williams, *Huey Long*, 532.

53. Typical of the many letters written in support of prohibition by different economic concerns were those of E. C. Fortenbury Co., Osyka, Mississippi, and Farmers Gin Co., Sunset, Louisiana; cotton merchants and buyers, Allen Douglas & Co., New Orleans, Louisiana, Planters Mercantile Co., Greenville, Alabama, and Benson Plantation, Anguilla, Mississippi; marketing cooperatives, Delta Cotton Seed Cooperative, Clarksdale, Mississippi; fertilizer companies, McLaughlin Co., Raleigh, North Carolina, Millen Fertilizer Co., Millen, Georgia, and Arlington Manufacturing Co., Arlington, Georgia; and dealers in planting supplies, J. W. Ramsey, Pleasant Hill and Pelican, Louisiana. All of these communications to Huey P. Long in 1931 can be found in Long MS: E. C. Fortenbury, 24 August; C. A. Mardiner, 13 September; Allen Douglas, 22 August; L. A. Harrison, 24 December; W. M. Corbett, 22 September; J. S. Camart, 18 August; J. W. Ramsey, 20 August; W. C. Coker to J. E. McDonald, 14 September; and I. D. Benson to Editor, *Jackson Daily News*, 13 September 1931.

54. For out-of-state legislators consult, for example, from Arkansas, E. E. Alexander, 9 September, Carl Munn, 9 September, and Lawrence L. Mitchell, 9 September; from South Carolina, Louis Cary, 5 September, D. H. Dantzler, 31 August, and Edgard A. Brown, 3 September; from Georgia, J. Scott Davis, 9 September; from Texas, Victor B. Gilbert, 31 August; and from Oklahoma, R. B. Bryant, 22 August, all for 1931 and in Long MS.

55. Thomas P. Gore (U.S. Senate, Oklahoma) to Huey P. Long, 17 September 1931, Long to Gore, 21 September 1931, D. D. Glover (U.S. House of Representatives, Arkansas) to Huey P. Long, 28 August 1931, Long MS.

56. "Cotton Paper," 13.

57. Huey P. Long's cotton letter, n.d., Long to Mrs. McDuffie, 6 September 1931, Long MS.

Chapter 4

1. R. M. Mickle to Ross S. Sterling, 24 August 1931, Sterling MS.

2. *Houston Chronicle*, 24 August 1931, 14; *Houston Post-Dispatch*, 24 August 1931, 1:2.

3. Lafayette L. Patterson to Arthur M. Hyde, 29 August 1931, Hyde to Patterson, 31 August 1931, RG 16 NA.

4. For further information on the evolution of mass meetings consult Snyder, "The Cot-

ton Holiday Movement in Mississippi, 1931."

5. Thomas H. Maxwell to Benjamin M. Miller, 20 September 1931, D. Hardy Riddle to Miller, 29 August 1931, Lafayette L. Patterson to Miller, 31 August 1931, Miller MS.

6. Robert K. Ewing to Huey P. Long, 4 September 1931, Long MS.

7. See, for example, Eino Peaspanen to Huey P. Long, 9 September 1931, George J. Becknell to Long, 9 September 1931, Ralph S. DesGranges to Long, 10 September 1931, Luther Barker to Long, 11 September 1931, F. M. Thompson to Long, 16 September 1931, and Ray S. Gibson to Long, 13 September 1931, Long MS.

8. Written interview of Courtney Pace to author, 12 May 1975; Bormann, "This is Huey P. Long Talking," 121–22.

9. W. L. Dyer to Huey P. Long, 11 September 1931, Long to Dyer, 14 September 1931, E. E. Newton to Long, 7 September 1931, J. W. Bolton to Long, 10 September 1931, Thomas P. Gore to Long, 17 September 1931, I. I. Femrite to Long, 2 September 1931, Long MS.

10. George A. Ripley to Huey P. Long, 9 September 1931, H. E. Park to Long, 4 September 1931, Long to Park, 9 September 1931, Long MS.

11. J. E. Bryan to Huey P. Long, 5 September 1931, W. H. Houston to Huey P. Long, 3 September 1931, Long MS.

12. Wright Patman to Huey P. Long, 10 September 1931, Long to Patman, 14 September 1931, Bryant to Long, 2 September 1931, Long MS.

13. W. D. Hayman to Benjamin M. Miller, 28 August 1931, Miller MS; B. M. Cooper to Ross S. Sterling, 3 September 1931, Robert Swann to Sterling, 1 September 1931, Sterling MS.

14. *New Orleans Item*, 2 September 1931, 2. Southern senators refused to bring acreage control legislation before the Congress because they felt not only would it fail to pass but the courts would consider it unconstitutional. "I think you are entirely right," Kenneth D. McKellar wrote to his senatorial colleague John H. Bankhead. "There is no way under our Constitution for the Congress to limit production" (Kenneth D. McKellar to John H. Bankhead, 6 September 1931, McKellar MS).

15. *Austin American-Statesman*, 4 September 1931, 14; *Houston Chronicle*, 4 September 1931, 29; *Dallas Morning News*, 5 September 1931, 1:1, 8.

16. *Daily Clarion-Ledger*, 3 September 1931, 7.

17. Joseph R. Bryson to Huey P. Long, 10 September 1931, Long to Bryson, 12 September 1931, Long MS.

18. Robert Arrington to Benjamin M. Miller, 24 August 1931, T. O. Harris to Long, 4 September 1931, Long MS.

19. J. A. Grant to Huey P. Long, 20 August 1931, Long MS.

20. T. N. Mauritz to Huey P. Long, 25 August 1931, Long MS.

21. *Shreveport Times*, 27 August 1931, 5; *Memphis Press-Scimitar*, 25 August 1931, 9. For editorials exploiting the anxiety of cotton's vulnerability to substitute products consult *Dallas Morning News*, 8 September 1931, 2:4, and 9 September 1931, 2:1, 10.

22. *Daily Clarion-Ledger*, 11 September 1931, 1.

23. Lemmon, "The Public Career of Eugene Talmadge: 1926–1936," 58–63; Lemmon, "The Agricultural Policies of Eugene Talmadge," 22, 24–25; Anderson, *The Wild Man from Sugar Creek*, 53, 57.

24. Charles B. Carson to Huey P. Long, 9 September 1931, B. W. Bailey to Long, 17 August 1931, Long MS; McKay and Company, Inc., to Harvey Parnell, 3 September 1931, W. F. Hancock to Ross S. Sterling, 27 August 1931, Sterling MS.

25. Carl Williams to Huey P. Long, 25 August 1931, Long MS.

26. Leeming, "Dixie Versus the British Empire," 66; "The Development of Cotton Growing in the British Empire," 749–51.

27. For articles discussing impediments to overseas expansion consult: Bader, "British Colonial Competition for the American Cotton Belt," 210–31; Bean, "Changing Trends in Cotton Production and Consumption," 442–59; Cox, "New Cotton Areas for Old," 49–60; McBride, "Cotton Growing in South America," 35–50; Reed, "Competing Cottons and United States Production," 282–98.

28. J. B. Preston to Clarence Farmer, 1 May 1931, Sterling MS.

29. *New Orleans Times-Picayune*, 19 August 1931, 1, 21; *Baton Rouge State-Times*, 20 August 1931, 1, 4; *New Orleans Item*, 20 August 1931, 3.

30. "The Brussels Sugar Convention of 1931," 391–401; "The International Sugar Accord," 422–23; *New York Times*, 23 August 1931, 2:7, 11; Chadbourne, "The International Stabilization of the Sugar Industry," 383–85; Brucher, "A Cure for Too Much Sugar," 49–51.

31. William Jardine to Secretary of State, Telegram No. 92, 25 August 1931, Jardine to Secretary of State, Telegram No. 93, 26 August 1931, Hoover MS; *New York Times*, 11 August 1931, 2, 27 August 1931, 10, and 29 August 1931, 3.

32. Seostris Sidarouss to William R. Castle, 28 August and 31 August 1931, Castle to Herbert Hoover, 1 September and 3 September 1931, Jardine to Secretary of State, Telegram No. 96, Hoover MS.

33. "Governor Long's Drop-A-Crop Plan," 8; *New Orleans Item*, 2 September 1931, 2; Louis E. Foster to Ibra C. Blackwood, 4 September 1931, Blackwood MS.

34. Lemmon, "The Ideology of Eugene Talmadge," 233–34; Lemmon, "The Public Career of Eugene Talmadge," 58–79; Lemmon, "The Agricultural Policies of Eugene Talmadge," 22–23; Anderson, *The Wild Man from Sugar Creek*, 50–61.

35. J. E. Hollan to Ross S. Sterling, 2 September 1931, J. M. Boothe to Sterling, 25 August 1931, M. E. Harwell to Huey P. Long, 26 August 1931, J. J. Summers to Sterling, 26 August 1931, Sterling MS.

36. Dabney White flyer in Sterling MS.

37. Paul Jones, Jr., to Harvey Parnell, 12 September 1931, Henry Buist, Jr., to Ibra C. Blackwood, 28 August 1931, Blackwood MS; Peck Welhausen to Ross S. Sterling, 25 August 1931, W. C. Conrads to Sterling, 1 September 1931, E. G. Hoskinson to Sterling, 24 August 1931, M. E. Harwell to Huey P. Long, 26 August 1931, William B. Moss to Sterling, 24 August 1931, Sterling MS; "Cotton Prohibition," 38.

38. *Atlanta Constitution*, 11 September 1931, 10; *New York Times*, 11 September 1931, 7.

39. R. A. Meek to Kenneth D. McKellar, 3 September 1931, McKellar MS; C. M. Harley to Benjamin M. Miller, 7 September 1931, Miller MS.

40. *Houston Post-Dispatch*, 20 November 1931, 6.

41. Robert A. Beeland, Jr., to Benjamin M. Miller, n.d., Miller MS.

42. *Jackson Daily News*, 13 August 1931, 15.

43. *Memphis Commercial Appeal*, 18 October 1931, 4:6; *Houston Post-Dispatch*, 20 November 1931, 6.

44. J. W. Howell to Ross S. Sterling, 30 August 1931; Dabney White flyer to Sterling, n.d., Sterling MS; Ezell to Huey P. Long, 18 August 1931, Long MS.

45. *New Orleans Item*, 2 September 1931, 2.

46. McCorkle, "The Louisiana 'Buy-A-Bale' of Cotton Movement, 1914," 133–52; Gray, "Embattled Cotton," 30; Saloutos, *Farmer Movements in the South, 1865–1933*, 242.

47. "Gum for Cotton," 18; "Cotton's Week," 17; E. A. Cudahy, Jr., to G. E. Robertson, August 1931, Robertson to Huey P. Long, 1 September 1931, Long MS.

48. Adams, "Helping Out 'King Cotton,' " 8–9, 44; *Houston Chronicle*, 5 August 1931, 6.

49. Harold C. Booker to Huey P. Long, 9 July 1931, Long MS; *State*, 11 August 1931, 9, and 9 September 1931, 7; *Wall Street Journal*, 13 August 1931, 4; *Daily Clarion-Ledger*, 31 August 1931, 10.

50. "New Jobs for King Cotton," 24; "New Roles for Cotton," 42; "New Uses for Cotton," 50–51.

51. *Daily Clarion-Ledger*, 31 August 1931, 10.

52. *State*, 9 September 1931, 7.

53. *State*, 4 September 1931, 14.

54. W. E. Talbot to Lawrence Richey, 16 September 1931, Richey to Talbot, 19 September 1931, "The Texas Five Year Plan" by W. E. Talbot in Long MS; McKay, *Texas Politics, 1906–1944*, 215–16.

55. Saloutos, *Farmer Movements in the South*, 276; Elmo Thomas to Huey P. Long, 12 September 1931, Long MS.

56. J. E. Yates to Arthur M. Hyde, 4 December 1931, Hyde to Yates, 7 December 1931, RG 16 NA.

57. "Cotton Paper," 13; *New York Times*, 22 July 1931, 35.

58. Morris Sheppard to Herbert H. Hoover, 13 September 1931, Long MS; Fulton Bag and Cotton Mills to Ross S. Sterling, 10 August 1931, Sterling MS; R. N. Dunlap to Arthur M. Hyde, 6 October 1931, RG 16 NA.

59. L. W. Krueger to George W. P. Hunt, 17 August 1931, Hunt MS.

60. William H. Barker to Huey P. Long, 15 September 1931, Long MS.

61. W. W. West to Huey P. Long, 27 June 1931, Long MS; *Wall Street Journal*, 18 August 1931, 3.

62. E. L. Evans to Huey P. Long, 3 October 1931, Long to Evans, 5 October 1931, Long MS.

63. R. S. Bohn to Huey P. Long, 14 September 1931, C. Doorn to Long, 16 September 1931, Long MS.

64. George W. P. Hunt to All State Department and Institutions State of Arizona, 2 November 1931, Miller MS; Letters of Georgia Department of Agriculture in RG 83 NA.

65. R. L. Jurney to Ross S. Sterling, 2 September 1931, Sterling MS; J. B. Risher to Huey P. Long, 18 August 1931, Long MS.

66. M. W. McDuff to Huey P. Long, 19 August 1931, Long MS.

67. Allen Douglas & Company to The Cotton Trade, n.d., Sterling MS.

68. J. D. Duke to Huey P. Long, 3 September 1931, Long MS.

Chapter 5

1. Hopkins, *Changing Technology and Employment in Agriculture*, 127–31.

2. For a more detailed description of the tenantry system consult: USDA, *A Study of the Tenant Systems of Farming in the Yazoo-Mississippi Delta*, 6–10; USDA, *Relation of Land Tenure to Plantation Organization*, 19–38 passim; Goldenweiser and Truesdell, *Farm Tenancy in the United States*; Johnson, Embree, and Alexander, *The Collapse of Cotton Tenancy*, 1–33; Taylor, *Agricultural Economics*, 270–304.

3. USDC, *Fifteenth Census of the United States: 1930, Agriculture*, 3:62, 4:890.

4. Raper, *Preface to Peasantry*, 39–41, 152–56; Mitchell, *Mean Things Happening in This Land*, 17–21; Vance, *Human Factors in Cotton Culture*, 73–75; Holley and Arnold, *Changes in Technology and Labor Requirements in Crop Production: Cotton*, 19–21, 48.

5. The figures are for the 1937 season. South Carolina, *Sharecroppers and Wage Laborers on Selected Farms in Two Counties in South Carolina*, 7, 29; USDA, *Perquisites and Wages of Hired Farm Laborers*, 2, 35–36, 46–48.

6. Raper, *Preface to Peasantry*, 155; "Police and Planters Hunt for Pickers to Save an Early Crop in Mississippi and Arkansas," 10.

7. *Austin American-Statesman*, 1 August 1931, 4; *Houston Post-Dispatch*, 28 September 1931, 1:1.

8. *Houston Chronicle*, 7 September 1931, 7; *Houston Post-Dispatch*, 4 October 1931, 1, and 16 October 1931, 1, 7.

9. *Daily Clarion-Ledger*, 1 September 1931, 2, and 17 September 1931, 2; *Jackson Daily News*, 1 September 1931, 10; *Austin American-Statesman*, 5 September 1931, 6, and 21 September 1931, 8.

10. F. J. Sparke to Harvey Parnell, 23 September 1931, Parnell MS.

11. *Arkansas Gazette*, 25 August 1931, 4, 9; *Houston Post-Dispatch*, 16 August 1931, 2:3; *Daily Clarion-Ledger*, 17 September 1931, 2.

12. *Arkansas Gazette*, 12 September 1931, 1.

13. C. N. Tony to Harvey Parnell, 14 September 1931, Parnell MS.

14. *Memphis Press-Scimitar*, 19 September 1931, 1.

15. *Memphis Press-Scimitar*, 26 August 1931, 1; *Dallas Morning News*, 26 August 1931, 2; *Houston Chronicle*, 27 August 1931, 2.

16. *Houston Post-Dispatch*, 2 October 1931, 2:7.

17. *Arkansas Gazette*, 11 September 1931, 1, 5, 12 September 1931, 1, and 17 September 1931, 2; *Jackson Daily News*, 16 September 1931, 10; *Daily Clarion-Ledger*, 22 September 1931, 5; *Memphis Press-Scimitar*, 18 September 1931, 1, and 19 September 1931, 1; *Memphis Commercial Appeal*, 18 September 1931, 7, and 22 September 1931, 9.

18. *Arkansas Gazette*, 11 September 1931, 1.

19. *Atlanta Constitution*, 29 August 1931, 6.

20. *Jackson Daily News*, 13 September 1931, 1.

21. *Memphis Press-Scimitar*, 19 September 1931, 1.

22. *Memphis Press-Scimitar*, 19 September 1931, 1.

23. *Atlanta Constitution*, 12 September 1931, 6, and 27 September 1931, 1:1.

24. *Arkansas Gazette*, 11 September 1931, 1, 5.

25. *Arkansas Gazette*, 12 September 1931, 12.

26. *Montgomery Advertiser*, 12 September 1931, 1.

27. *Houston Post-Dispatch*, 6 August 1931, 1:6.

28. *Daily Clarion-Ledger*, 1 October 1931, 4.

29. *Arkansas Gazette*, 12 September 1931, 1, 12.

30. *Arkansas Gazette*, 12 September 1931, 1, 12, 13 September 1931, 1:4, and 17 September 1931, 10.

31. *Arkansas Gazette*, 13 September 1931, 1:4.

32. *Memphis Press-Scimitar*, 30 September 1931, 12, and 6 October 1931, 4; *Dallas Morning News*, 21 September 1931, 1:7.

33. *Austin American-Statesman*, 20 August 1931, 1.

34. *Daily Clarion-Ledger*, 5 September 1931, 3.

35. *Memphis Press-Scimitar*, 5 October 1931, 9.

36. *Memphis Press-Scimitar*, 7 October 1931, 12; *Houston Post-Dispatch*, 16 August 1931, 1, 9, 19 August 1931, 1:9, and 21 August 1931, 1:6; *Arkansas Gazette*, 8 November 1931, 1:6; 10 November 1931, 6, and 5 November 1931, 20.

37. *Memphis Commercial Appeal*, 18 September 1931, 2.

38. *Arkansas Gazette*, 10 October 1931, 12, 16, 16 October 1931, 18, and 5 November 1931, 20; *Shreveport Times*, 15 September 1931, 7; *Houston Chronicle*, 2 September 1931, 4, and 3 September 1931, 16.

39. *Austin American-Statesman*, 18 October 1931, 1:1, and 29 October 1931, 10; *Houston Post-Dispatch*, 16 October 1931, 1, and 22 November 1931, 1, 6.

40. *Memphis Press-Scimitar*, 29 October 1931, 2, 30 October 1931, 19, and 31 October 1931, 9.

41. *Austin American-Statesman*, 20 August 1931, 1.

42. *Houston Chronicle*, 2 September 1931, 4; *Houston Post-Dispatch*, 11 October 1931, 3:3.

43. *Arkansas Gazette*, 8 October 1931, 1. Speaking before an unemployment conference in Houston, Governor Sterling hit hard against the idea of Texas tolerating a relief system. "I do not believe in a dole system," the governor said. "Old John Smith was right when he said those that did not work should not eat." *Houston Post-Dispatch*, 17 October 1931, 1; *Houston Chronicle*, 25 September 1931, 2.

44. *Shreveport Times*, 1 October 1931, 1, 3; *Houston Post-Dispatch*, 4 September 1931, 1:6, 4 October 1931, 1, and 16 October 1931, 1, 7; *Memphis Commercial Appeal*, 18 September 1931, 2.

45. *Houston Chronicle*, 23 September 1931, 21, and 1 October 1931, 5; *Houston Post-Dispatch*, 1 October 1931, 2:4; *Memphis Press-Scimitar*, 19 October 1931, 10.

46. *Memphis Press-Scimitar*, 29 October 1931, 4, and 6 October 1931, 6.

47. Daniel, *The Shadow of Slavery*, 150; Wilson, *Forced Labor in the United States*, 22–23; Shofner, "The Legacy of Racial Slavery," 411–26.

48. Wilson, *Forced Labor in the United States*, 84–99; Ezell, *The South since 1865*, 47–49.

49. *Shreveport Times*, 18 September 1931, 2 and 30 September 1931, 2; *Austin American-Statesman*, 6 October 1931, 1.

50. *Jackson Daily News*, 1 September 1931, 10.

51. An excellent overview of the plight of transients is presented by Whisenhunt, "The Transient in the Depression," 7–20.

52. *Memphis Commercial Appeal*, 7 October 1931, 6.

53. *Arkansas Gazette*, 3 November 1931, 14.

54. *Daily Clarion-Ledger*, 24 September 1931, 4, 25 September 1931, 8, and 26 September 1931, 6. In the forefront of forced-labor practices in the early 1930s, the growers of Clarksdale would become by the mid-1940s outstanding practitioners of mechanization. Through the use of delinted seed, flame weeders, airplane dusting, and mechanical pickers, among other scientific advances, the Hobson brothers' plantation near Clarksdale harvested in 1944 what is believed the first commercial crop ever produced entirely by machinery (Street, *The New Revolution in the Cotton Economy*, 130).

55. *Daily Clarion-Ledger*, 29 September 1931, 1, 2; *Austin American-Statesman*, 29 September 1931, 1, and 6 October 1931, 1; *Houston Chronicle*, 28 September 1931, 2.

56. U.S., Congress, Senate, Subcommittee of the Committee on Manufacturers, *Hearings, on S. 5121, Relief for Unemployed Transients*, 2:23–24, 35–36, 111–12; Webb, *The Transient Unemployed*, 14–16.

57. Reed, *Federal Transient Program*, 26, 17.

58. Hopkins, *Spending to Save*, 126.

59. Bernstein, *The Lean Years*, 323–27.

60. Maverick, *A Maverick American*, 160–64.

61. Ibid., 155–56, 170. Federal studies conducted during the 1930s tended to confirm many of Maverick's observations. Whether cotton pickers, mill hands, or farmers, transients were usually among the most enterprising and energetic people of their former communities. Better than two-thirds of the unattached persons studied during the period October 1934 through April 1935 gave the search for work as the single most important reason for migrating. Reed, *Federal Transient Program*, 28–29; Webb, *The Transient Unemployed*, 59, 90–91.

62. *Houston Post-Dispatch*, 16 August 1931, 1:9, 19 August 1931, 1:9, and 21 August 1931, 1:6.

63. *Houston Post-Dispatch*, 12 December 1931, 4.

64. *Daily Clarion-Ledger*, 1 October 1931, 4.

65. Higgs, "The Boll Weevil, the Cotton Economy, and Black Migration, 1910–1913," 335–50.

66. J. B. Meriwether to Benjamin M. Miller, 10 September 1931, Miller MS.

67. J. H. Courtney to Ibra C. Blackwood, 8 September 1931, E. N. C. to Blackwood, 2 September 1931, Blackwood MS.

68. Percy, *Lanterns on the Levee*, 267–68.

69. *Arkansas Gazette*, 25 September 1931, 4.

70. Written interview of the Reverend Claude Williams to author, 24 January 1976.

Chapter 6

1. *New Orleans Times-Picayune*, 30 August 1931, 1:1, 11; *Austin American-Statesman*, 30 August 1931, 1, 2; *Houston Post-Dispatch*, 30 August 1931, 1:1, 3; *Dallas Morning News*, 30 August 1931, 1:1, 11.

2. James M. Thompson to Ross S. Sterling, 31 August 1931, Thompson to Private Secretary of Governor Sterling, 2 September 1931, Sterling MS.

3. Joe White to Ross S. Sterling, 28 August 1931, A. V. Simpson et al. to Sterling, 29 August 1931, Sterling MS; Edgar E. Witt to Huey P. Long, 28 August 1931, Long MS.

4. Huey P. Long to Ross S. Sterling, 1 September 1931, Sterling MS; *New Orleans Times-Picayune*, 2 September 1931, 3.

5. Bissett, "The Public Life of Ross Shaw Sterling"; Paul, "Ross Shaw Sterling"; and Mills, "A Biography of Ross Shaw Sterling."

6. Political scientist Fred Gantt, Jr., classifies Sterling as a "moderate rightist," *The Chief Executive in Texas*, 204, 225, 304–6, 327; McKay, *Texas Politics*, 217–22.

7. L. A. Wilson to Ross S. Sterling, 23 August 1931, Sterling MS; Wilson to Huey P. Long, 24 August 1931, Vernon Chamber of Commerce to Long, 4 September 1931, Long MS.

8. Edgar E. Witt to Ross S. Sterling, 3 September 1931, Long MS.

9. John C. Thompson to Ross S. Sterling, 30 August 1931, W. A. Paddock to Sterling, 1 September 1931, Sterling to Paddock, 2 September 1931, Sterling MS.

10. *Shreveport Times*, 4 September 1931, 1, 2; *New Orleans Times-Picayune*, 4 September 1931, 3.

11. Ibra C. Blackwood to Ross S. Sterling, 31 August 1931, Seth P. Storrs to Sterling, 1 September 1931, Sterling MS.

12. *Atlanta Constitution*, 3 September 1931, 1; *New Orleans Item*, 4 September 1931, 10.

13. *Austin American-Statesman*, 6 September 1931, 1, 2; *Houston Chronicle*, 6 September 1931, 1:1, 8; *Houston Post-Dispatch*, 6 September 1931, 1:1, 4, and 7 September 1931, 2.

14. *State*, 10 September 1931, 1; *New York Times*, 10 September 1931, 4.

15. *Arkansas Gazette*, 6 September 1931, 1, 4.

16. *Memphis Commercial Appeal*, 6 September 1931, 1:1; *Houston Post-Dispatch*, 6 September 1931, 1, 4; *Dallas Morning News*, 6 September 1931, 1:1, 12.

17. *Austin American-Statesman*, 7 September 1931, 1, 2, and 8 September 1931, 1, 2; *Houston Post-Dispatch*, 7 September 1931, 1:1, 2; *Dallas Morning News*, 7 September 1931, 1:1, 8.

18. J. E. McDonald to Huey P. Long, 6 September 1931, A. A. Allison to Long, 7 September 1931, Long MS.

19. Long, *Every Man a King*, 126–32, 250–51, 279–80, 287–88; Williams, *Huey Long*, 336–40, 540–43; "Who's Huey Now," 13.

20. Owen Saunders to Huey P. Long, 12 September 1931, Tom Tanner to Long, 11 September 1931, S. S. Pittman to Long, 28 August 1931, Erle Pettus to Long, 2 September 1931, Long MS; *New Orleans Times-Picayune*, 27 August 1931, 1, and 31 August 1931, 1; *Austin American-Statesman*, 8 September 1931, 1, 2; *Houston Post-Dispatch*, 8 September 1931, 1:7.

21. *Journals of the House of Representatives and Senate of Texas*, 2–7; *Austin American-Statesman*, 8 September 1931, 12; *Houston Chronicle*, 8 September 1931, 1:17; *Dallas Morning News*, 9 September 1931, 1:3.

22. *New Orleans Item*, 7 September 1931, 2, and 9 September 1931, 1; *Shreveport Times*, 10 September 1931, 13; J. W. Bolton to Huey P. Long, 9 September 1931, Long MS.

23. James M. Thompson to Harvey Parnell, 5 October 1931, Parnell MS; *New Orleans Item*, 9 September 1931, 1, 2.

24. The Austin mass meeting has been reconstructed from accounts in *Austin American-Statesman*, 10 September 1931, 1, 2; *Baton Rouge State-Times*, 10 September 1931, 1, 4; *New Orleans Item*, 10 September 1931, 1, 6, 7, 11; *New Orleans Times-Picayune*, 10 September 1931, 1, 6, 10; *Shreveport Times*, 10 September 1931, 1, 13; *Houston Chronicle*, 10 September 1931, 1, 28; *Houston Post-Dispatch*, 10 September 1931, 1, 2; *Dallas Morning News*, 10 September 1931, 1, 8; *Memphis Press-Scimitar*, 10 September 1931, 1, 8; "Drop-A-Crop," 12; and written interviews of W. R. Poage to author, 1 December 1975 and 16 December 1975.

25. Edgar E. Witt to Huey P. Long, 14 September 1931, Long MS.

26. Mrs. W. S. Birdwell to Huey P. Long, n.d., Wes Sudderth to Long, 17 September 1931, J. B. Preston to Long, 16 September and 18 September 1931, Long MS.

27. *New Orleans Item*, 10 September 1931, 1; *Dallas Morning News*, 11 September 1931, 1:3.

28. *Atlanta Constitution*, 13 September 1931, 1.

29. *Austin American-Statesman*, 12 September 1931, 1, 6; *Houston Post-Dispatch*, 12 September 1931, 1:1, 2; *Houston Chronicle*, 12 September 1931, 2; *Shreveport Times*, 12 September 1931, 1; *Dallas Morning News*, 12 September 1931, 1:1, 2.

30. *New Orleans Item-Tribune*, 13 September 1931, 1:13; *Arkansas Gazette*, 13 September 1931, 1:1.

31. Executive Dispatch, n.d., Parnell MS.

32. *Texas House Journal*, 56; *Texas Senate Journal*, 47; *Dallas Morning News*, 15 September 1931, 1:1, 2, 12; *New York Times*, 15 September 1931, 4; Richard B. Russell, Jr., to Harvey Parnell, 15 September 1931, Parnell MS; Arkansas Delegation to Benjamin M. Miller, 15 September 1931, Miller MS.

33. See, for example, Margie E. Neal to Harvey Parnell, 13 September 1931, Parnell to Neal, 14 September 1931, Parnell MS; Neal to Benjamin M. Miller, 13 September 1931, Miller to Neal, 14 September 1931, Miller MS; *Daily Clarion-Ledger*, 15 September 1931, 1; *Atlanta Constitution*, 15 September 1931, 6.

34. Margie E. Neal to Ibra C. Blackwood, 13 September 1931, Blackwood to Neal, 15 September 1931, Blackwood MS.

35. *Austin American-Statesman*, 15 September 1931, 8; *New Orleans Item*, 15 September 1931, 1, 4.

36. *Atlanta Constitution*, 14 September 1931, 4.

37. C. Youngkin to Huey P. Long, 17 September 1931, Long MS; *Dallas Morning News,* 12 September 1931, 1:2.

38. *Houston Post-Dispatch,* 15 September 1931, 1:7; *Dallas Morning News,* 15 September 1931, 1:2; *New Orleans Item,* 15 September 1931, 4.

39. *New Orleans Item,* 15 September 1931, 1; *Austin American-Statesman,* 15 September 1931, 1, 8; *Dallas Morning News,* 16 September 1931, 1, 2; *New York Times,* 16 September 1931, 2.

40. *Texas Senate Journal,* 55–59; *Houston Chronicle,* 15 September 1931, 1, 2; *Austin American-Statesman,* 15 September 1931, 1, 8; *Dallas Morning News,* 16 September 1931, 1:1, 12.

41. *Houston Post-Dispatch,* 17 September 1931, 1:8; *Dallas Morning News,* 17 September 1931, 2:2; *Memphis Commercial Appeal,* 17 September 1931, 6.

42. *Texas House Journal,* 108–13; James Thompson to Huey P. Long, 16 September 1931, Long MS.

43. *Texas Senate Journal,* 64–65; *Houston Chronicle,* 17 September 1931, 1; *Shreveport Times,* 17 September 1931, 1; *New York Times,* 17 September 1931, 1; *Houston Chronicle,* 18 September 1931, 1; *Texas House Journal,* 132–33.

44. *State,* 18 September 1931, 1, 10.

45. *Shreveport Times,* 17 September 1931, 1, 13; *Memphis Commercial Appeal,* 17 September 1931, 1; *New York Times,* 17 September 1931, 1.

46. J. H. Fisher to Huey P. Long, 17 September 1931, Long to Fisher, 17 September 1931, Long MS; *Shreveport Times,* 17 September 1931, 30; *New Orleans Item,* 17 September 1931, 30; *Houston Post-Dispatch,* 18 September 1931, 1:6.

47. *Shreveport Times,* 19 September 1931, 9. For other attacks on Long consult: "Drop-Half-A-Crop," 18; *Daily Clarion-Ledger,* 21 September 1931, 3; *Montgomery Advertiser,* 18 September 1931, 4; *Dallas Morning News,* 18 September 1931, 2:2.

48. *New Orleans Item,* 18 September 1931, 12.

49. Dennis P. Ratcliff to Huey P. Long, 15 September 1931, Clarence E. Farmer to M. T. Lewis, 22 September and 23 September 1931, Long MS.

50. Edgar E. Witt to Huey P. Long, 5 September 1931, Long MS.

51. Harve H. Haines to Ross S. Sterling, 1 September 1931, Sterling MS.

52. Written interview of W. R. Poage to author, 16 December 1975.

53. A. A. Allison to Thomas T. Connally, 20 September 1931, Connally MS LC.

54. P. M. Gaddis to Huey P. Long, 18 September 1931, Frank Grosgean to Long, 17 September 1931, V. B. Wosham to Long, 17 September 1931, Long MS; *Shreveport Times,* 18 September 1931, 4.

55. *State,* 18 September 1931, 1, 8, 19 September 1931, 1, 2, 20 September 1931, 1, 13, 24 September 1931, 1, and 25 September 1931, 1, 3; Huey P. Long to Ibra C. Blackwood, 22 September 1931, Blackwood to Long, 29 September 1931, Long MS.

56. Will K. Henderson to Huey P. Long, 25 September 1931, Long MS; *New Orleans Item,* 29 September 1931, 1; *Shreveport Times,* 30 September 1931, 1.

57. Ashburn, "The Texas Cotton Acreage Control Law of 1931–1932," 116–17; *Austin American-Statesman,* 22 September 1931, 1; *Houston Post-Dispatch,* 22 September 1931, 1:1, 2; *Houston Chronicle,* 22 September 1931, 1, 7; *Dallas Morning News,* 23 September 1931, 1:1, 4; *New York Times,* 22 September 1931, 45.

58. *Houston Post-Dispatch,* 23 September 1931, 1:1, 2; *Houston Chronicle,* 20 September 1931, 10.

Chapter 7

1. See, for example, Ross S. Sterling et al. to Theodore G. Bilbo, 22 September 1931, J. E. McDonald to Bilbo, 26 September 1931, Bilbo MS; *New York Times*, 23 September 1931, 2; *Austin American-Statesman*, 23 September 1931, 2; *Houston Chronicle*, 23 September 1931, 3; *Houston Post-Dispatch*, 23 September 1931, 1:1, 2.

2. A detailed account of events in Mississippi can be found in: Snyder, "The Cotton Holiday Movement in Mississippi, 1931," 1–32.

3. W. B. Roberts to Theodore G. Bilbo, 17 August 1931, Phil Stone to Bilbo, 29 September 1931, Bilbo MS.

4. E. G. Williams to Theodore G. Bilbo, 28 September 1931, Bilbo MS.

5. Undated typescript of Bilbo's call in Bilbo MS. Text of Bilbo's message in *Daily Clarion-Ledger*, 28 September 1931, 2. Other articles pertaining to announcement: *Daily Clarion-Ledger*, 28 September 1931, 1, 2, 4, and 30 September 1931, 2. The special session receives treatment in Balsamo, "Theodore G. Bilbo and Mississippi Politics, 1877–1932," 221–25; and Saucier, "The Public Career of Theodore G. Bilbo," 91–95.

6. *Daily Clarion-Ledger*, 28 September 1931, 1, 7, 29 September 1931, 1, and 3 October 1931, 1, 8; *Daily News*, 28 September 1931, 1, 10, and 1 October 1931, 1, 10.

7. *Daily Clarion-Ledger*, 29 September 1931, 1, 8, and 30 September 1931, 1, 10.

8. John H. Allen to Theodore G. Bilbo, 29 September 1931, Bilbo MS.

9. *Daily Clarion-Ledger*, 29 September 1931, 1, 8.

10. *Daily Clarion-Ledger*, 7 October 1931, 1, 8.

11. *Daily Clarion-Ledger*, 30 September 1931, 1, 10, 1 October 1931, 1, 14, and 2 October 1931, 1, 14; *Daily News*, 2 October 1931, 1, 2, 10, 12, and 16, and 3 October 1931, 1, 10.

12. *Daily Clarion-Ledger*, 4 October 1931, 16, 17, and 5 October 1931, 1, 7; *Daily News*, 1 October 1931, 1, 10, 2 October 1931, 1, 16, and 3 October 1931, 1.

13. *Daily Clarion-Ledger*, 8 October 1931, 1, 10.

14. *Daily Clarion-Ledger*, 14 October 1931, 1, 4, 8; *Daily News*, 13 October 1931, 1, 10, 14.

15. *Daily Clarion-Ledger*, 1 November 1931, 1, 17; *Daily News*, 1 November 1931, 1, 9, 21, 22, and 2 November 1931, 1, 6; Green, *The Man Bilbo*, 87–88.

16. On Saturday, 3 October Harvey Parnell issued his special call for the Arkansas general assembly to meet at noon on 7 October. On 14 October Governor Parnell signed into law an acreage reduction bill patterned on the Texas statute. See, for example, *Arkansas Gazette*, 4 October 1931, 1:6, 8 October 1931, 11, and 15 October 1931, 1.

17. *Wall Street Journal*, 12 October 1931, 7; *New Orleans Item*, 13 October 1931, 1; *Dallas Morning News*, 21 October 1931, 1:1, 2, and 22 October 1931, 1:1, 2, 2:2.

18. James C. Stone to Herbert Hoover, 16 October 1931, Hoover MS.

19. *Arkansas Gazette*, 17 October 1931, 14, 24. For other related articles consult: *Arkansas Gazette*, 20 October 1931, 1, 25 October 1931, 1:1, and 26 October 1931, 1.

20. *Arkansas Gazette*, 21 October 1931, 18, and 27 October 1931, 1.

21. *Atlanta Constitution*, 22 October 1931, 8; *Houston Chronicle*, 14 October 1931, 4; *Dallas Morning News*, 15 October 1931, 2:4; "Bankers, Not Legislators, Will Cut Cotton Acreage," 26.

22. *Daily Clarion-Ledger*, 3 November 1931, 1, 4 November 1931, 1, 5, 5 November 1931, 14, and 6 November 1931, 1.

23. *Daily Clarion-Ledger*, 20 November 1931, 1; *Arkansas Gazette*, 20 November 1931, 10.

24. Will K. Henderson to Thomas T. Connally, 10 November 1931, Connally MS LC; Henderson to Huey P. Long, 9 November 1931, Long MS.

25. The proceedings of the Jackson cotton convention have been compiled from: *Daily Clarion-Ledger*, 23 November 1931, 1, 7, 24 November 1931, 1, 5, 9, and 25 November 1931, 4; *Daily News*, 23 November 1931, 1, 10, and 24 November 1931, 1, 10; *New Orleans Item*, 23 November 1931, 1, 8; *Birmingham News*, 23 November 1931, 1.

26. *Daily Clarion-Ledger*, 25 November 1931, 4.

27. *Montgomery Advertiser*, 25 November 1931, 2, and 26 November 1931, 2; *Atlanta Constitution*, 26 November 1931, 7; *Birmingham News*, 1 December 1931, 19, and 3 December 1931, 6; Harvey Parnell to Benjamin M. Miller, 24 November 1931, Miller MS.

28. J. E. McDonald to Benjamin M. Miller, 28 November 1931, Miller MS.

29. Harvey Parnell to J. E. McDonald, 8 December 1931, McDonald to Parnell, 11 December 1931, McDonald to N. S. Carmichael, 28 November 1931, McDonald to Carmichael, 1 December 1931, Carmichael to McDonald, 4 December 1931, Seth P. Storrs to McDonald, n.d., McDonald to Storrs, 4 December 1931, Storrs to McDonald, 10 December 1931, Parnell MS.

30. J. E. McDonald to Frederick I. Thompson, 12 December 1931, McDonald to W. F. Fagan, 12 December 1931, Parnell MS.

31. *Houston Post-Dispatch*, 1 December 1931, 2:1, 4 December 1931, 6, 13, 7 December 1931, 1, 2, 8 December 1931, 2:1, 14 December 1931, 2:1, and 20 December 1931, 11; *Houston Chronicle*, 30 November 1931, 3, 6 December 1931, 1:3, 4:3, and 7 December 1931, 4.

32. *Houston Post-Dispatch*, 5 January 1932, 2:1, and 17 January 1932, 2:1; *Houston Chronicle*, 19 January 1932, 21; *Austin American-Statesman*, 17 January 1932, 1:2; Ashburn, "The Texas Cotton Acreage Control Law of 1931–1932," 124; Whisenhunt, "Huey Long and the Cotton Acreage Control Law of 1931," 153.

33. Ashburn, "Texas Cotton Acreage Control Law," 121–22.

34. *Austin American-Statesman*, 21 January 1932, 1, 5; *Houston Post-Dispatch*, 21 January 1932, 1, 7; *Dallas Morning News*, 21 January 1932, 1:1, 10, and 22 January 1932, 1:1, 2; *Houston Chronicle*, 21 January 1932, 2 and 22 January 1932, 7.

35. *Austin American-Statesman*, 22 January 1932, 1; *Houston Post-Dispatch*, 22 January 1932, 2:1, 24 January 1932, 2:2, and 25 January 1932, 1, 2.

36. *Austin American-Statesman*, 1 February 1932, 1, 3; *Houston Post-Dispatch*, 2 February 1932, 1, 2; *Houston Chronicle*, 1 February 1932, 1, 22; *Dallas Morning News*, 2 February 1932, 1:1, 3.

37. *Houston Post*, 6 March 1932, 1:1.

Epilogue

1. Billington, *The American South*, 16; Saloutos, *Farmer Movements in the South, 1865–1933*, 282–87.

2. Owen, "The Sabbatical Year," 32–45.

3. Edgar E. Witt to Huey P. Long, 14 September 1931, Long MS.

4. Fite, *American Farmers*, 50, 236, 241–42; Fite, "Voluntary Attempts to Reduce Cotton Acreage in the South, 1914–1933," 496–99.

5. Fite, *American Farmers*, 32, 39–40.

6. Saloutos, *Farmer Movements*, 277–81; Fite, *American Farmers*, 30–32, 42–46, 74–75.

7. Fite, *American Farmers*, 33.

8. Ibid., 33–34, 37.

9. Ibid., 4–5, 16, 41, 227, 230, 241–42.

10. Ibid., 45–46, 225, 227–28, 233.

11. Memorandum for the President, 9 September 1931, Hoover MS.

12. Federal Farm Board, *Minutes*, 9:589–90; a series of cables between the United States State Department and the Egyptian government, Minute Exhibit C-201, Hoover MS.

13. Memorandum for the President, 9 September 1931, Hoover MS.

14. E. C. Glover to Huey P. Long, 29 September 1931, W. E. Everett to Long, 17 September 1931, J. M. Black, Jr., to Long, 2 September 1931, T. N. Towns to Long, 10 September 1931, Long MS.

15. McCormick, "Cotton Acreage Laws and the Agrarian Movement," 302–3.

16. Johnson, Embree, and Alexander, *The Collapse of Cotton Tenancy*, 48.

17. Saloutos, *Farmer Movements*, 234–35, 282–87.

18. Fite, *American Farmers*, 50–66; Benedict, *Farm Policies of the United States, 1790–1950*, 276–401; Benedict and Stine, *The Agricultural Commodity Programs*, 3–46; Richards, *Cotton and the AAA*.

19. Long, *My First Days in the White House*.

20. Mertz, *New Deal Policy and Southern Rural Poverty*, 132–38; Williams, *Huey Long*, 709; Brinkley, *Voices of Protest*, 60, 126, 155, 212.

21. Tugwell, *The Democratic Roosevelt*, 348. Interpolation in the original.

22. Fite, *American Farmers*, 236–39.

23. Daniel, "The Transformation of the Rural South, 1930 to the Present," 236–48; Johnson et al., *The Collapse of Cotton Tenancy*, 50–57.

Bibliography

Manuscript Collections

Alabama, Department of Archives and History, Montgomery, Alabama
    Benjamin M. Miller Papers
Arizona, Department of Archives and History, Phoenix, Arizona
    George W. P. Hunt Papers
Arkansas, History Commission, Little Rock, Arkansas
    Harvey Parnell Papers
Herbert Hoover Library, West Branch, Iowa
    Herbert Hoover Papers
Library of Congress, Washington, D. C.
    Thomas T. Connally Papers
Louisiana State University, Baton Rouge, Louisiana
    Huey P. Long Papers
Memphis Public Library, Memphis, Tennessee
    Kenneth D. McKellar Papers
National Archives, Washington, D. C.
    Bureau of Agricultural Economics (Record Group 83)
    Office of the Secretary of Agriculture (Record Group 16)
Franklin D. Roosevelt Library, Hyde Park, New York
    Franklin D. Roosevelt Papers
South Carolina, Department of Archives and History, Columbia, South Carolina
    Ibra C. Blackwood Papers
Texas State Library, Austin, Texas
    Ross S. Sterling Papers
University of Southern Mississippi, Hattiesburg, Mississippi
    Theodore G. Bilbo Papers

Interviews

Frugé, J. Cleveland. Member of Louisiana House of Representatives, 1928–30; Assistant District Attorney 13th Judicial District, 1930–35; Judge, Louisiana Court of Appeals. Baton Rouge, Louisiana.
Healy, George. With the *New Orleans Times-Picayune* as reporter, 1926, city editor, 1931, managing editor, 1936, and editor, 1952. New Orleans, Louisiana.
Liter, C. P. With the *Baton Rouge State-Times* as reporter, 1922, managing editor, 1928, and executive editor, 1949; founder of Louisiana News Bureau. Baton Rouge, Louisiana.
Morgan, Cecil. Member of Louisiana House of Representatives, 1928–32, and Senate, 1932–34; Counselor to Standard Oil of New Jersey; Dean of Tulane University Law School. New Orleans, Louisiana.

Pace, Courtney. Member of Mississippi House of Representatives, 1928–40; Administrative Assistant of U.S. Senator James Eastland since 1941. Washington, D. C.

Poage, W. R. Member of Texas House of Representatives, 1925–29, and Senate, 1931–37; U.S. House of Representatives from Texas's 11th District since 1937. Washington, D. C.

Williams, Claude. Official of Southern Tenant Farmers Union; Cofounder of People's Institute of Applied Religion. Alabaster, Alabama.

Public Documents

Federal Farm Board. *First, Second, and Third Annual Reports*. Washington, 1930–32.

———. *Minutes*. Washington, 1929–31.

Louisiana. *Official Journals of the Proceedings of the House of Representatives and Senate of the State of Louisiana at the Seventh Extra Session of the Legislature, August 25–29*. Baton Rouge, 1931.

South Carolina. *Sharecroppers and Wage Laborers on Selected Farms in Two Counties of South Carolina*. Bulletin 328. Clemson, 1940.

Texas. *Journals of the House of Representatives and Senate of Texas, Second Called Session of the Forty-Second Legislature, Begun and Held at the City of Austin, September 8, 1931*. Austin, 1931.

United States, Department of Agriculture. *The Agricultural Estimating and Reporting Services of the United States Department of Agriculture*. Misc. Pub. 703. Washington, 1949.

———. *Cotton Prices and Markets*. Bulletin 1444. Washington, 1926.

———. *The Crop and Livestock Reporting Services of the United States*. Misc. Pub. 171. Washington, 1933.

———. *Factors Affecting the Price of Cotton*. Technical Bulletin 50. Washington, 1928.

———. *A History of Agricultural Experimentation and Research in the United States, 1607–1925*. Misc. Pub. 251. Washington, 1937.

———. *Perquisites and Wages of Hired Farm Laborers*. Technical Bulletin 213. Washington, 1931.

———. *Relation of Land Tenure to Plantation Organization*. Bulletin 1269. Washington, 1924.

———. *A Study of the Tenant Systems of Farming in the Yazoo-Mississippi Delta*. Bulletin 337. Washington, 1916.

———. *Yearbook of Agriculture*. Washington, 1905–32.

———. Department of Commerce. *Cotton Production and Distribution, 1925–1932*. Bulletins 160–69. Washington, 1926–32.

———. *Fifteenth Census of the United States: 1930, Agriculture*. Washington, 1932.

———. Senate. 71st Congress, 1st Session. *Hearings: Confirmation of Members of Federal Farm Board*. Washington, 1929.

———. Senate. 72nd Congress, 2nd Session. *Hearings, on s. 5121: Relief For Unemployed Transients*. Washington, 1933.

Newspapers

Arkansas Gazette. Little Rock, Arkansas.

Atlanta Constitution. Atlanta, Georgia.
Austin American-Statesman. Austin, Texas.
Baton Rouge State-Times. Baton Rouge, Louisiana.
Birmingham News. Birmingham, Alabama.
Chicago Tribune. Chicago, Illinois.
Daily Clarion-Ledger. Jackson, Mississippi.
Dallas Morning News. Dallas, Texas.
Houston Chronicle. Houston, Texas.
Houston Post-Dispatch. Houston, Texas.
Jackson Daily News. Jackson, Mississippi.
Manchester Guardian Weekly. London, England.
Memphis Commercial Appeal. Memphis, Tennessee.
Memphis Press-Scimitar. Memphis, Tennessee.
Montgomery Advertiser. Montgomery, Alabama.
New Orleans Item. New Orleans, Louisiana.
New Orleans Times-Picayune. New Orleans, Louisiana.
New York Times. New York, New York.
Shreveport Times. Shreveport, Louisiana.
The State. Columbia, South Carolina.
Wall Street Journal. New York, New York.
Washington Post. Washington, D. C.

Books

Anderson, William. *The Wild Man from Sugar Creek.* Baton Rouge: Louisiana State University Press, 1975.

Barger, Harold, and Landsberg, Hans H. *American Agriculture, 1899–1939.* New York: National Bureau of Economic Research, 1942.

Beals, Carleton. *The Story of Huey P. Long.* Philadelphia: Lippincott, 1935.

Benedict, Murray R. *Farm Policies of the United States, 1790–1950.* New York: Twentieth Century Fund, 1953.

———, and Stine, Oscar C. *The Agricultural Commodity Programs.* New York: Twentieth Century Fund, 1956.

Bernstein, Irving. *The Lean Years.* Boston: Houghton Mifflin, 1966.

Billington, Monroe Lee. *The American South.* New York: Scribner, 1971.

Brinkley, Alan. *Voices of Protest.* New York: Alfred A. Knopf, 1982.

Daniel, Pete. *The Shadow of Slavery: Peonage in the South, 1901–1969.* New York: Oxford University Press, 1973.

Ezell, John S. *The South since 1865.* London: Macmillan, 1963.

Fite, Gilbert C. *American Farmers.* Bloomington: Indiana University Press, 1981.

———. *George N. Peek and the Fight for Farm Parity.* Norman: University of Oklahoma Press, 1954.

Gantt, Fred, Jr. *The Chief Executive in Texas.* Austin: University of Texas, 1964.

Goldenweiser, E. A., and Truesdell, Leon F. *Farm Tenancy in the United States.* Washington: Government Printing Office, 1924.

Green, A. Wigfall. *The Man Bilbo.* Baton Rouge: Louisiana State University Press, 1963.

Hair, William Ivy. *Bourbonism and Agrarian Protest: Louisiana, 1877–1900.* Baton Rouge: Louisiana State University Press, 1969.

Haystead, Ladd, and Fite, Gilbert C. *The Agricultural Regions of the United States.* Norman: University of Oklahoma Press, 1955.

Hicks, John D. *Republican Ascendancy, 1921–1933.* New York: Harper & Row, 1963.

Holley, William C., and Arnold, Lloyd E. *Changes in Technology and Labor Requirements in Crop Production: Cotton.* Philadelphia: Works Progress Administration, 1938.

Hoover, Herbert. *The Memoirs of Herbert Hoover.* Vols. 2–3. New York: Macmillan, 1952.

———. *The New Day: Campaign Speeches of Herbert Hoover.* Stanford: Stanford University Press, 1928.

Hopkins, Harry L. *Spending to Save.* New York: Norton, 1936.

Hopkins, John A. *Changing Technology and Employment in Agriculture.* Washington: Government Printing Office, 1941.

Howard, Perry. *Political Tendencies in Louisiana.* Baton Rouge: Louisiana State University Press, 1971.

Hubbard, W. Hustace. *Cotton and the Cotton Market.* New York: Appleton, 1924.

Johnson, Charles S., Embree, Edwin S., and Alexander, W. W. *The Collapse of Cotton Tenancy.* Chapel Hill: University of North Carolina Press, 1935.

Kemp, John R., ed. *Martin Behrman of New Orleans: Memoirs of a City Boss.* Baton Rouge: Louisiana State University Press, 1977.

Key, V. O., Jr. *Southern Politics.* New York: Vintage Books, 1949.

Kirwan, Albert D. *Revolt of the Rednecks: Mississippi Politics, 1876–1925.* New York: Harper & Row, 1965.

Lander, Ernest McPherson, Jr. *A History of South Carolina, 1865–1960.* Columbia: University of South Carolina Press, 1970.

Long, Huey P. *Every Man a King.* New Orleans: National Book Company, 1933.

———. *My First Days in the White House.* Harrisburg: Telegraph Press, 1935.

McKay, Seth S. *Texas Politics, 1906–1944.* Lubbock: Texas Tech Press, 1944.

Martin, Thomas. *Dynasty: The Longs of Louisiana.* New York: G. P. Putnam's Sons, 1960.

Maverick, Maury. *A Maverick American.* New York: Covici, 1937.

Mertz, Paul E. *New Deal Policy and Southern Rural Poverty.* Baton Rouge: Louisiana State University Press, 1978.

Mitchell, Harry L. *Mean Things Happening in This Land.* Montclair: Allanheld, Osmun & Co., 1979.

Molyneaux, Peter. *The Cotton South and American Trade Policy.* New York: National Peace Conference, 1936.

Myers, William S., and Newton, Walter H. *The Hoover Administration: A Documented Narrative.* New York: Scribner, 1936.

Myres, S. D., Jr., ed. *The Cotton Crisis.* Dallas: Arnold Foundation, 1935.

Percy, William A. *Lanterns on the Levee.* Baton Rouge: Louisiana State University Press, 1973.

Raper, Arthur. *Preface to Peasantry.* New York: Atheneum, 1974.

Reed, Ellery F. *Federal Transient Program: An Evaluative Survey.* New York: Committee on Care of Transients and Homeless, 1934.

Reynolds, George M. *Machine Politics in New Orleans, 1897–1926.* New York: Columbia University Press, 1936.

Romasco, Albert U. *The Poverty of Abundance.* New York: Oxford University Press, 1965.

Saloutos, Theodore. *Farmer Movements in the South, 1865–1933.* Los Angeles: University of California Press, 1960.

Sindler, Allan P. *Huey Long's Louisiana: State Politics, 1920–1952.* Baltimore: Johns Hopkins University Press, 1956.
Stokdyk, Ellis A., and West, Charles H. *The Farm Board.* New York: Macmillan, 1930.
Street, James H. *The New Revolution in the Cotton Economy.* Chapel Hill: University of North Carolina Press, 1957.
Taylor, Henry C. *Agricultural Economics.* New York: Macmillan, 1922.
Tindall, George B. *The Emergence of the New South, 1913–1945.* Baton Rouge: Louisiana State University Press, 1967.
Vance, Rupert B. *Human Factors in Cotton Culture.* Chapel Hill: University of North Carolina Press, 1929.
————, Ivey, John E., Jr., and Bond, Marjorie N. *Exploring the South.* Chapel Hill: University of North Carolina Press, 1949.
Wallace, David D. *South Carolina: A Short History, 1520–1948.* Chapel Hill: University of North Carolina Press, 1951.
Watkins, James L. *King Cotton.* New York: Negro Universities Press, 1969.
Webb, John F. *The Transient Unemployed.* Washington: Works Progress Administration, 1935.
Wilbur, Ray L., and Hyde, Arthur M. *The Hoover Policies.* New York: Scribner, 1937.
Wilds, John. *Afternoon Story.* Baton Rouge: Louisiana State University Press, 1976.
Williams, T. Harry. *Huey Long.* New York: Alfred A. Knopf, 1969.
Wilson, Joan Hoff. *Herbert Hoover: Forgotten Progressive.* Boston: Little, Brown, 1975.
Wilson, Walter. *Forced Labor in the United States.* New York: International Publishers, 1933.
Woodman, Harold D. *King Cotton and His Retainers.* Lexington: University of Kentucky Press, 1968.
Woodward, C. Vann. *Origins of the New South 1877–1913.* Baton Rouge: Louisiana State University Press, 1951.

Unpublished Materials

Balsamo, Larry T. "Theodore G. Bilbo and Mississippi Politics, 1877–1932." Ph.D., University of Missouri, 1967.
Bissett, James H. "The Public Life of Ross Shaw Sterling." M.A., Trinity University, 1963.
Ginzl, David J. "Herbert Hoover and Republican Patronage Politics in the South, 1928–1932." Ph.D., Syracuse University, 1977.
Hall, Lillian J. "A Historical Study of Programming Techniques and Practices of Radio Station KWKH, Shreveport, Louisiana, 1922–1950." Ph.D., Louisiana State University, 1959.
Helms, John D. "Just Lookin' for a Home: The Cotton Boll Weevil and the South." Ph.D., Florida State University, 1977.
Lemmon, Sarah McCulloh. "The Public Career of Eugene Talmadge: 1926–1936." Ph.D., University of North Carolina, 1952.
Miller, David B. "Origins and Functions of the Federal Farm Board." Ph.D., University of Kansas, 1973.
Mills, Warner E., Jr. "The Public Career of a Texas Conservative: A Biography of Ross Shaw Sterling." Ph.D., Johns Hopkins University, 1956.
Moe, Orville O. "The Federal Farm Board." M.A., University of Washington, 1932.
Norman, Theodore. "The Federal Farm Board." Ph.D., Harvard University, 1939.

Paul, Carl L. "Ross Shaw Sterling." M.A., University of Houston, 1952.
Pope, Robert D. "Senatorial Baron: The Long Political Career of Kenneth D. McKellar." Ph.D., Yale University, 1976.
Saucier, Bobby W. "The Public Career of Theodore G. Bilbo." Ph.D., Tulane University, 1971.
Smith, Seldon K. "Ellison Durant Smith: A Southern Progressive, 1909–1929." Ph.D., University of South Carolina, 1970.

Articles

Adams, Hancock. "Helping Out 'King Cotton,' " *National Republic* 17 (April 1930): 8–9, 44.
Ashburn, Karl E. "The Texas Cotton Acreage Control Law of 1931–1932," *Southwestern Historical Quarterly* 61 (July 1957): 116–24.
Bader, Louis. "British Colonial Competition for the American Cotton Belt," *Economic Geography* 3 (April 1927): 210–31.
"Bankers, Not Legislators, Will Cut Cotton Acreage," *Business Week*, 9 December 1931, 26.
Bean, Louis H. "Changing Trends in Cotton Production and Consumption," *Southern Economic Journal* 5 (April 1939): 442–59.
Becker, Joseph A. "Regional Shifts Large in Major Crop Acreage During Decade 1919–1929," *Yearbook of Agriculture, 1932* (Washington: Government Printing Office, 1932), 485–86.
Borman, Ernest G. "This Is Huey P. Long Talking," *Journal of Broadcasting* 2 (Spring 1958): 111–22.
Brucher, Herbert. "A Cure for Too Much Sugar," *Review of Reviews* 84 (July 1931): 49–51.
"The Brussels Sugar Convention of 1931," *International Sugar Journal* 33 (August 1931): 391–401.
Chadbourne, Thomas L. "The International Stabilization of the Sugar Industry," *American Labor Legislation Review* 21 (December 1931): 383–85.
Chambliss, Leopold A. "Cotton Growing in the West," *World's Work* 34 (March 1920): 507–10.
"Cotton and Wheat Lead Commodities to New Lows," *Business Week*, 19 August 1931, 8.
"Cotton Crisis," *Time*, 24 August 1931, 10–11.
"Cotton Paper," *Time*, 3 August 1931, 13.
"Cotton Prohibition," *Outlook*, 9 September 1931, 37.
"Cotton's Week," *Time*, 14 September 1931, 17.
Cox, Alonzo. "New Cotton Areas for Old," *Southwestern Political and Social Science Quarterly* 8 (June 1927): 49–60.
Crowther, Samuel. "The Cotton Crisis," *Country Gentleman* 92 (January 1927): 4–5.
Daniel, Pete. "The Transformation of the Rural South, 1930 to the Present," *Agricultural History* 55 (July 1981): 231–48.
"Destroy and Prosper," *Nation* 133 (26 August 1931): 198.
"The Development of Cotton Growing in the British Empire," *Nation* 112 (24 November 1923): 749–51.
"Drop-A-Crop," *Time*, 21 September 1931, 11–13.
"Drop-Half-A-Crop," *Time*, 28 September 1931, 18.

"East Texas Prorated," *Time*, 14 September 1931, 16.

Fausold, Martin L. "President Hoover's Farm Policies, 1929–1933," *Agricultural History* 51 (April 1977): 362–77.

Fite, Gilbert C. "Southern Agriculture since the Civil War: An Overview," *Agricultural History* 53 (January 1979): 3–21.

———. "Voluntary Attempts to Reduce Cotton Acreage in the South, 1914–1933," *Journal of Southern History* 14 (November 1948): 481–99.

"Governor Long's Drop-A-Crop Cotton Plan," *Literary Digest* 110 (19 September 1931): 8–9.

Grant, Philip A., Jr. "Southern Congressmen and Agriculture, 1921–1932," *Agricultural History* 53 (January 1979): 338–51.

Gray, George W. "Embattled Cotton," *World's Work* 60 (September 1931): 30–35.

"Gum for Cotton," *Time*, 13 April 1931, 18.

Hard, William. "Hoover Picks His Men," *Review of Reviews* 80 (August 1929): 46–51.

Higgs, Robert. "The Boll Weevil, the Cotton Economy, and Black Migration, 1910–1930," *Agricultural History* 50 (April 1976): 335–50.

"The International Sugar Accord," *Current History* 34 (June 1931): 422–23.

"King Cotton's Throne Moves Westward," *Literary Digest*, 105 (21 June 1930): 45–46.

Koerselman, Gary H. "Secretary Hoover and National Farm Policy: Problems of Leadership," *Agricultural History* 51 (April 1977): 378–95.

Leeming, Joseph. "Dixie Versus the British Empire," *Review of Reviews* 74 (July 1926): 66–69.

Lemmon, Sarah M. "The Agricultural Policies of Eugene Talmadge," *Agricultural History* 28 (January 1954): 21–30.

———. "The Ideology of Eugene Talmadge," *Georgia Historical Quarterly* 38 (September 1954): 226–48.

Link, Arthur M. "The Cotton Crisis, the South, and Anglo-American Diplomacy, 1914–1915," in J. Carlyle Sitterson (ed.), *Studies in Southern History* (Chapel Hill: University of North Carolina Press, 1957), 122–38.

McBride, George M. "Cotton Growing in South America," *Geographical Review* 9 (January 1920): 35–50.

McCorkle, James L., Jr. "Louisiana and the Cotton Crisis, 1914," *Louisiana History* 18 (Summer 1977): 303–21.

———. "The Louisiana 'Buy-A-Bale' of Cotton Movement, 1914," *Louisiana History* 15 (Spring 1974): 133–52.

McCormick, Thomas C. "Cotton Acreage Laws and the Agrarian Movement," *Southwestern Social Science Quarterly* 12 (March 1932): 296–304.

McWhiney, Grady. "Louisiana Socialists in the Early Twentieth Century: A Case Study of Rustic Radicalism," *Journal of Southern History* 20 (August 1954): 315–36.

"The Men Who Will Tackle the Big Farm Relief Task," *Literary Digest* 102 (27 July 1929), 8–9.

Murphy, William C., Jr. "Dramatic Secrecy of the Crop Report," *Literary Digest* 116 (23 September 1933), 8.

———. "President Hoover's Cabinet," *Current History* 30 (May 1929): 269–75.

"New Jobs for King Cotton," *Business Week*, 23 September 1931, 24.

"New Roles for Cotton," *Literary Digest* 110 (26 September 1931): 42.

"New Uses for Cotton," *Literary Digest* 109 (2 May 1931): 50–51.

"No More Cotton?" *Time*, 31 August 1931, 11.

O'Brien, Patrick G. "A Reexamination of the Senate Farm Bloc, 1921–1933," *Agricultural History* 47 (July 1973): 248–63.

Owen, Eugene D. "The Sabbatical Year," *Agricultural History* 12 (January 1938): 32–45.
"Police and Planters Hunt for Pickers to Save an Early Crop in Mississippi and Arkansas," *Newsweek*, 19 September 1936, 10.
Pusateri, C. Joseph. "The Stormy Career of a Radio Maverick, W. K. Henderson of KWKH," *Louisiana Studies* 15 (Winter 1976): 389–407.
Reed, William G. "Competing Cottons and United States Production," *Economic Geography* 8 (July 1932): 282–98.
"Representative Black Plans Legislation to Abolish Cotton Forecast of Department of Agriculture," *Commercial and Financial Chronicle* 123 (9 October 1926): 1826–27.
"Salvation by Suicide," *Business Week*, 2 September 1931, 48.
Shideler, James H. "Herbert Hoover and the Federal Farm Board Project, 1921–1925," *Mississippi Valley Historical Review* 42 (March 1956): 710–29.
Shofner, Jearell H. "The Legacy of Racial Slavery: Free Enterprise and Forced Labor in Florida in the 1940's," *Journal of Southern History* 47 (August 1981): 411–26.
Smith, Alfred G. "The Statisticians' Error Cost Cotton Growers $100,000,000," *Country Gentleman* 84 (23 February 1924), 15, 36.
Snyder, Robert E. "The Cotton Holiday Movement in Mississippi, 1931," *Journal of Mississippi History* 40 (February 1978): 1–32.
———. "Huey Long and the Presidential Election of 1936," *Louisiana History* 16 (Spring 1975): 117–43.
Spillman, W. J. "Changes in Type of Farming, 1919–1924," *Yearbook of Agriculture: 1926* (Washington: Government Printing Office, 1926), 203–7.
Stern, Max. "Cotton Goes West," *Nation* 123 (14 July 1926): 29–30.
"Suspension of Cotton Planting for One Year Proposed by Senator Smith," *Commercial and Financial Chronicle* 115 (9 September 1922): 1160–61.
"Texas Tries," *Time*, 24 August 1931, 14.
"Wheat and Cotton Are Steadier but Not by Farm Board Aid," *Business Week*, 26 August 1931, 15–16.
Whisenhunt, Donald W. "Huey Long and the Texas Cotton Acreage Control Law of 1931," *Louisiana Studies* 13 (Summer 1974): 142–53.
———. "The Transient in the Depression," *Red River Valley Historical Review* 1 (Spring 1974): 7–20.
White, Melvin Johnson. "Populism in Louisiana During the Nineties," *Mississippi Valley Historical Review* 5 (June 1918): 3–19.
"Who's Huey Now," *Time*, 26 October 1931, 13.
Williams, T. Harry. "The Politics of the Longs," *Georgia Review* 15 (Spring 1961): 20–33.
Wilson, Joan Hoff. "Hoover's Agricultural Policies, 1921–1928," *Agricultural History* 51 (April 1977): 335–61.

Index